TABLE OF CONTENTS

How's it Feel, Tough Guy?

From Prisoner of Pride to Prisoner of Hope

Leah,
I hope you enjoy this
story as much as I enjoy
hearing your voice! Use your
gift to honor Him!
Mike Palombi
Romans 15:13

By Mike Palombi

DEDICATION

To Dr. Richard Sheridan, my mentor, and friend,

Thank you for investing in my life. Your burden to improve the lives of at-risk youth and the example you set as a man will most definitely impact the legacy I leave for generations to come. *"Iron sharpens iron, and one man sharpens another."* (Proverbs 27:17)

...and to Heidi, my "Excellent wife,"

whose steadfast love and respect for me is a constant source of encouragement each and every day of my life. *"Every good gift and every perfect gift is from above..."* (James 1:17)

...and above all things, to you, Lord,

for the good times in my life, but even more, I thank you for the difficult times that led me to you. In all of your ways you are good Father, and your love is everlasting. It is true, you are a faithful God who does make all things new, and I pray this book honors you the way I intend it to.

"Blessed is the man who walks not in the counsel of the wicked, nor stands in the way of sinners, nor sits in the seat of scoffers; but his delight is in the law of the Lord, and on his law he meditates day and night. He is like a tree planted by streams of water that yields its fruit in its season, and its leaf does not wither. In all that he does, he prospers." (Psalm 1:1-3)

FOREWORD

Moving from the dark side of life requires change. One characteristic of man that continues to be passed on is his inability to base behavioral decisions on choosing the difficult right over the easy wrong. My friend Mike Palombi provides all of us who desire change a raw, honest, and uncompromising look at the ingredients required to alter the course of life that will surely end in disaster.

How's It Feel, Tough Guy?, the story of Mike Palombi's amazing life, will take you deep inside the heart, soul, and mind of one of the most intriguing, colorful, and dynamic personalities I have ever encountered.

I first met Mike over twenty years ago when I was the director of a school for learning-disabled, emotionally disturbed adolescents. Mike was seeking an opportunity that would allow him to share his building trade skills and the consequences of poor decision-making choices with our youngsters. He successfully accomplished both goals. Moreover, his life and example truly encouraged many seemingly hopeless teenagers to take responsibility for their own lives.

You are about to read a fascinating and gripping tale of one American's fight to alter self-destruction. And you will find yourself right in the middle of so much more than just one man's life. Palombi's story is both courageous and inspirational. It just may rekindle your faith in the human spirit and prompt you to reevaluate your own life.

Semper Fidelis

Richard A. Sheridan

PREFACE

The truth is, I believed a lot of lies. How else can I explain how I wound up in prison? The simple answer (as if there really is a simple answer to something so complicated) is that one of the many consequences attached to believing lies is serving prison time. But I don't give simple answers to questions that require me to explain my incarceration and my subsequent commitment to overhauling my life.

Boiling down my sins to the "terroristic threats" and "extortion" that I was sentenced for only partially explains how I ended up in prison. That criminal act was altogether the result of a much larger deep-rooted problem having to do with the condition of my heart.

After hearing my story of redemption and restoration through decades of getting smacked upside my head – both literary and figuratively, most people decide, "You should write a book, Mike!" But all I've ever done about writing a book is stand in defense against why I couldn't write a book. At the top of my record of excuses was the advice my college English professor gave me on the first day of class my freshman year, *"I've reviewed your SAT scores and there's no other way to say this: You're gonna fail this class if you don't drop it!"*

For decades, I yielded to her disapproving counsel, and to that of others like her, believing I didn't have the capacity, or the "smarts," to write a book. But now I can just add her skeptical remarks and the hopeless comments of others to the list of lies I once believed. And there have been many of them.

One judge who heard my appeal decided about me, *"It's a shame that people like him even exist. I only wish I could give him more time!"* For me, the cumulative effect of those words proved to be ruinous when it came to my attempt to live a fruitful and abundant life.

If I haven't learned anything else on my journey of change, I've learned that the greatest enemy of accomplishment is the fear of failure. Remarkably, my fear of failure was challenged while driving in my car and listening to a song called "*The Voice of Truth*" by the Casting Crowns:

"But the giant's calling out my name and he laughs at me

Reminding me of all the times I tried before and failed"

Writing this book has become a challenge to set aside my fears and do what I believe God wants me to do despite the fact that I am not anxious to do it. Today, I have chosen to listen to the voices of the people whom I believe God appointed to encourage me to author such a book. Therefore, this story is my testimony of God's unmerited favor despite the fact I did nothing to deserve it.

The reader should know that apart from God, I have no story, there is no miracle, no redemption, no restoration, and there is no salvation. Apart from God, my story is like that of any number of people in whose hands I hope this book lands—people who believe the same lies I once believed and whose deceptive beliefs robbed them of the very life God intended them to live.

I have said that going to prison was a condition of the heart. Repentance, too, is a condition of the heart. We can will ourselves to do many things, but true human reform exists only where there has been a sincere change of heart. Surrender is the posture from which hearts are changed, and only from a place of surrender can we humble ourselves in order that we may begin to hear a new voice... a voice of truth!

"And they have conquered him by the blood of the Lamb, and by the word of their testimony."(Revelation 12:11)

PART ONE

Bad Company

CHAPTER ONE

†

A Companion of Fools

"Whoever walks with the wise becomes wise,
but the companion of fools will suffer harm."
(Proverbs 13:20)

My biggest regret in life is that there are people who are worse off for knowing me. First on that list of casualties was my girlfriend Lucy. She wasn't supposed to be there that day, the day that detectives from the Essex County Organized Crime Strike Force gave me the beating of my life.

Lucy had seen the entire thing take place and probably thought that the two of us were gonna die. Beaten and bloodied, I could vaguely make out the image of Lucy still sitting in the passenger seat of my 1976 yellow Mustang and crying hysterically at the two detectives pointing handguns at her, while they yelled, "Keep your hands on the windshield!"

Lucy's father J.D., my partner quite literally in crime, had given me strict orders, "Don't bring Lucy with you when you go to Newark to see Vinny. I don't want her knowing about our business." Our business that day included copping a couple ounces of cocaine and then goin' to shakedown this guy Vinny who owed us money.

When I left J.D.'s home that morning, a big two-story colonial with a built-in pool on a nice piece of property in Lakewood, New Jersey, I did exactly the opposite of what he had told me to do. I don't know. Maybe it's just me, but it didn't seem to make a lot of sense to drive around the state of New Jersey with a couple of ounces of blow in my car. It was about as much as sixty packets of sugar, which in the scheme of things, isn't a lot of blow for a dealer. But if I got caught with it, I was looking at five to ten in the slammer. Since I was gonna bring the coke back to J.D.'s house anyway, I just decided to pick it up on my way home from Newark. That turned out to be nothing short of an outstanding decision.

What wasn't outstanding, however, was my next decision. Though I'd promised J.D. that I wouldn't bring Lucy with me to Newark, I stopped by the waterfront home we were renting in Bricktown, and picked her up anyhow. At the time, Lucy was eighteen and I was twenty-two. We had been going together for about a year, but I had known Lucy since she was thirteen or fourteen and running around the neighborhood with some of my friends' younger brothers and sisters.

Shortly before we began dating, Lucy had gone through a very difficult time in her life. She had become pregnant, and the father, who was much older than Lucy, wasn't much interested in fathering a baby with her. And even if he was interested, J.D. wasn't. During the days leading up to the birth of her baby, Lucy and I spent a lot of time talking about her troubled young life, especially about her mom, an alcoholic and a cocaine addict living in Las Vegas. Lucy rarely saw her.

What's more, she had lived through her dad serving a six-month stint in the county jail for possession of stolen property and then again for distribution of drugs. The bottom line was, J.D. was making Lucy give her baby up for adoption. She tried to act all tough about it, but I learned through our conversations that deep down, Lucy's tough girl image was just that, an image to hide her anticipation and fear of having a baby so young. It turns out that Lucy wasn't as tough as her mouth made her out to be. When she allowed me to see behind the walls she put up, I encountered a young girl who was kindhearted but bruised from a difficult childhood. That's when I had become attracted to her.

When I got back to our house, I asked Lucy to take a ride with me to Newark. I told her that I had to pick up some money from a couple of people that had bought jewelry from me. What I didn't tell her was the truth. I figured she'd stay in the car while I hit up Vinny for the money he owed J.D. and me, and she wouldn't be the wiser.

Vinny was a blue collar guy from Long Island in his mid-fifties with graying hair. He was a few inches shorter than me, but stocky. He was married with a couple of kids, but apart from that, I couldn't tell you anything about the guy.

Vinny had stiffed me with a couple of bad checks for some jewelry I'd sold him. In addition to that, he wasn't paying "the vig," a weekly interest on an outstanding loan he had taken from J.D. The way the loan worked was you made the weekly vig until all of the money borrowed could be repaid in one lump sum. I'm not sure how Vinny came up with the paper to make the weekly payments, but that's pretty much true about all of the people we did business with. They had their pay from their day job, and then they had their other sources of income.

Vinny had been popped with stolen property and later caught a third degree conviction on that charge. I guess those were some of the lengths he went to in order to make his payments to us and to have what he wanted.

The gold chains I sold to Vinny were legit, but the loan, well, that was a different story. Vinny was repaying the loan at a rate of interest that exceeded the rates approved by law. In simpler terms, the loan was illegal, but that's what Vinny had agreed to.

Anyway, after disappearing for a couple of weeks, Vinny called J.D. and told him that he was having a hard time coming up with the moolah. J.D. was pretty angry and began making threats.

"You're gonna get a beatin' and a couple of broken arms!" J.D. threatened Vinny.

"How much do I gotta come up with?" Vinny asked.

"Enough to save your life!" J.D. spouted.

But this was nothing new. I'd met Vinny earlier in June of 1982 when I had to smack him in the head for not making his payments on the same loan. J.D. took me to Newark to "have a conversation" with Vinny, figuring that my physical size – I was 6'-1", and 225 pounds of solid muscle – might intimidate him. I didn't think anything of it. I figured it was just a friendly loan between two guys, and so like any young kid who wants to get on the good side of his girlfriend's father, I agreed to take a ride.

On the way to Newark, J.D. reached into the glove box of his 1982 red Honda Civic, and pulled out a bag of blow.

"You do coke?" he asked.

"When I can afford to, I do," I answered.

"Here, try this stuff. This will make your socks go up and down."

I took the bag of blow from J.D., stuck the straw in the bag, and started sniffing. When he saw how much I snorted, J.D. almost drove off the road.

"Oh, gorilla nose, what a ya doin'? You tryin' to put me out of business? I gotta pay for this stuff you know? You just snorted, like, two grams of coke in that big gorilla nose of yours."

That's when I decided that my girlfriend's old man was pretty cool. Until then, we'd only exchanged small talk. But now, we were bonding over blow.

When we got to Newark, we went to the air freight company where Vinny worked. I waited in the car while J.D. went inside to get Vinny. When they came out of the building, I could tell by the teed-off look on J.D.'s face that he was upset. I couldn't hear what he was saying to Vinny because of the planes flying overhead, but finally, J.D. came walking back to the car.

"Go have a conversation with this mammalucco!" That's Italian for idiot, and J.D. had no patience for idiots.

While J.D. stayed near the car, I walked up to Vinny, got in real close, and shoved my finger at him. He grabbed my hand and warned, "Don't put your finger in my face."

Smack! I slapped Vinny hard in the head. "I didn't come up here to hear you tell me what to do," I told him. "I'm here to tell you what to do and you'd better do it. If I have to come back because you're not payin', it ain't gonna be no party," I warned him. In that moment, I fulfilled what I'd been taught all my life to do: Hit people.

***

"Can we go to the parade?" I asked my mother. It was Memorial Day 1963 and my parents had just had a big fight. Their confrontations usually ended with my father punching holes in the walls or breaking something.

"Go ask your father," my mom dismissed me.

"I'm afraid to," I said. I was four years-old, and a happy-go lucky-kid with a crew cut and a smile on my face most all of the time. In the summer months, I had stains on my knees from crawling around in the dirt with my toy trucks. But even at that tender age, I knew to be careful around my dad when he was angry.

"Dad's not mad at you," she assured me. "He's mad at me." She shooed me into the new bathroom where my father was busy spackling sheet-rock. It was part of his ongoing effort to renovate our house in North Brunswick, New Jersey, an older two-story colonial with a barn-like, or Gambrel, roof. The house was kind of run-down, both inside and out, and little by little my dad was doing a good job fixing it up.

I stood silently behind him, working up the nerve to speak to him. My dad wasn't a big man, but to a four year-old, he sure seemed big. I watched as he worked from a step ladder, a trowel in one hand, the metal hawk that held the spackle in the other, his Pall Mall cigarette hanging from his lips. The sounds of his trowel were rhythmical as he swept it across the sheetrock and then back to the hawk. He squinted as smoke from his cigarette drifted into his eyes, and then he loaded up his trowel with more fresh spackle. I swallowed hard and eked out, "Daddy, can I go to the parade?"

Without a word, my father turned and smacked me in the face with the trowel full of spackle. I felt the warm plaster shoot up my nose, splatter into my eyes, and ooze into my mouth, and I began to cry.

Then he just turned away from me, and with no remorse went back to the business of spackling the walls. In the same way after I hit Vinny, I turned and without remorse, I walked back to the car with J.D.

***

When I arrived in Newark that day, this time with Lucy in tow, I went to the air freight company where Vinny worked once again. It was a huge warehouse across from Newark Airport.

"I'll be right back," I told Lucy as I headed inside the warehouse, leaving her in my car. I asked around for Vinny, but a few people said he wasn't there. Just as I was about to leave, a guy I'd never seen before opened a door and yelled my name.

"Mike? Are you looking for Vinny?"

"Yeah," I said.

"Vinny's on the phone and wants to talk to you."

Right away, I became suspicious, wondering how this guy knew I was there looking for Vinny. Further, how would he know my name? Cautiously, I walked back toward the door from where the guy called my name. He was now sitting behind the glass partition of the receiving area. He handed me a phone's receiver through an opening in the glass.

"Who are you?" I asked as I reached to take the phone from him.

"I work with Vinny," he answered.

"Hello?"

"I just spoke to J.D.," Vinny explained on the phone. "I'm out for lunch, trying to get the money I owe. I got about eight hundred bucks, but I don't want you to hang around my job waiting for me."

"Okay," I said. "Where do ya want to meet?"

"Meet me in the Holiday Inn parking lot, where we met last time, in a half-hour."

"Fine."

When I got to the Holiday Inn, I cleaned the parking lot for cops, and then I backed into a space in the front of the hotel, away from any other cars. From this position, the entrance to the hotel lobby was to my right, and the entrance to the parking lot was to my left. I could pretty much see everything coming and going.

I noticed a tall guy who appeared to be homeless hanging out in the front of the hotel. He was wearing a long, dark-colored trench coat like the kind Colombo used to wear, and wandering around the parking lot, picking up aluminum cans, and stuffing them into a large plastic garbage bag. I also noticed a yellow taxi parked at the front door of the hotel lobby. The driver of the cab was reading a newspaper.

I started to feel very uneasy about the situation, particularly because Vinny was taking longer than he had said he would. It wasn't like I could just pick up my cell phone and ask him where he was — it was 1982.

As time passed, I was getting angrier at the way Vinny was disrespecting me by making me wait. I was also getting more paranoid. That guy in the long overcoat was still looking for cans, and that taxi near the front door of the hotel never moved.

"Ya know, I think they're cops," I told Lucy, keeping my eye on the guy with the bag of cans.

"What do you mean?" She looked up from the cassette player, where she had been picking out a Springsteen song. She thought I was there just to pick up the money Vinny owed me for the jewelry. But she didn't know the entire truth about why we were there.

"Nothin'. I just think they look like cops." But something didn't feel right about the whole situation.

Just then, a white passenger van filled with men pulled into the parking lot. As it drove by, I noticed that everyone in that van was looking at me like I owed them money or something. I started going over the events of the day in my head: *"How did Vinny know to call me at his job and tell me to meet him here? Wouldn't he have had to been watching me to know the exact time I was there? Ah, I'm probably watching too much TV."*

Finally, Vinny came rolling in in a white late-model, four-door sedan, and parked about seventy-five to a hundred feet away from me. I told Lucy to stay put, got out of the car, and walked over to meet him, aggravated that he had made me wait, number one, and number two, he was making me walk over to him.

"Been waiting long?" Vinny asked.

My nature was to punch him in the face for asking me a stupid question but I just wanted to get the money and get out of there. "No, I ain't been waitin' too long."

"I couldn't get the money, man."

"You said you had eight hundred bucks," I reminded him.

"I may have to wait until Monday to pay up," he explained.

"No!" I raised my voice. "Get the money today, or I'm gonna level you right here!"

"I don't want to get hurt," he said.

"That's what's gonna happen! You're gonna get hurt!"

Vinny seemed to want to get into the specifics of the loan that he was paying off to J.D., but I didn't want to hear it.

"Whatever you're talking about has nothing to do with me," I cut him off. "You told me you're gonna have eight hundred dollars and if you don't, I'm gonna hurt ya right here." He just grinned and said, "I ain't givin' ya nothin'."

That's when I lost it.

Without another word, I punched the grin off Vinny's face, and then ripped his watch right off of his wrist. Then I looked to my right, and in that instant I thought, *"I'm dead."*

Several guys with guns, perhaps six or seven of them, were running toward me from all directions, but none of them were wearing anything identifying them as cops. And that guy in the long overcoat picking up aluminum cans? Yeah, he was one of the guys running at me with a gun.

I started to run and made it about two steps before I took the butt of a gun to my head, stopping me dead in my tracks.

"I'll blow your brains out! Police officers. You're under arrest!"

Honestly, I was a little relieved. I mean, these guys were cops, and so I wasn't getting whacked.

The cops quickly cuffed my hands behind my back and said, "Now we're gonna see how bad you are!" And that's when they proceeded to give me the beating of my life. As one cop repeatedly lifted my head by my hair and smashed my face into the hood of Vinny's car, his fellow officers were simultaneously pistol whipping me and delivering severe blows to my body by way of kicks and punches. In the midst of the beating I couldn't ignore the insolent smile on Vinny's face as he stood there watching his detective pals paint the front of his white car red with the blood pouring out of my head.

At the very end of the beating, the cop who had been smashing my face into the hood of the car pulled my head back and held it out as if to offer it to anyone else who might want to take another punch. A detective to whom I refer as "Nicky Newark" ran toward me and threw a punch to my face without breaking stride.

To this day, I can still see Nicky smiling, rubbing his punching hand with the other hand, and gloating, "I still got the knockout punch."

Yeah, he was pleased with himself alright, as if punching someone in the face who had their hands tied behind their back was some kind of an accomplishment or something. The fact is, I wasn't impressed with Nicky, and even though my hands were cuffed behind my back, he didn't knock me out.

I wanted to be the tough guy. I wanted so badly to scream, "You hit like a woman!" But I knew that would only encourage Nicky and his pals to continue to beat me, and quite frankly, I didn't know how much more I could take.

This was police brutality at its finest, but it wasn't the first time cops had beaten me up with my hands cuffed behind my back. In fact, the last time it had happened, it came down to something as stupid as snowballs.

***

My friends and I had been out all night at one of our college keg parties. In February of 1979, I was a sophisticated moron, (sophomore) at Southern Connecticut State College in New Haven, where I majored in phys. ed., but I spent all my time and energy playing football and partying. We spent that evening drinking Budweiser, playing quarters, and chatting it up with some of the college co-eds.

The party ended around two a.m., and we began to head home on foot. There was three feet of snow on the ground, and the temperature was hovering in the teens. We lived no more than a mile off campus at the

Austin House, a men-only residence filled with football players and wres-tlers from the college. At the time, it was the craziest place I'd ever lived.

Before we called it a night, some of my knucklehead friends and I decided to throw snowballs at unsuspecting cars passing by our house. We were greatly amused when one of the targets we hit put on the brakes and slid to a stop on the hard-packed snow covering the roads. From across the street, we hammered the immobile target with snowballs, and the frustrated driver revved his engine, only to spin his tires faster and faster without moving. That just made the situation funnier to a bunch of drunken college kids, so naturally, we continued to pummel the car with snowballs. All of a sudden, the two front doors opened and it became apparent that the men emerging from the car were cops.

Everyone high-tailed it into the house except for me and my friend Dean. Standing our ground, we watched as the cops trudged through the snow and onto the sidewalk where we had been wailing their car with snowballs.

"It's a little cold for a T-shirt, isn't it?" one of the cops asked me. He was right. It was February and probably about twelve degrees outside, but I wasn't feeling a thing. I don't remember much else of what he said until he got to the part where he concluded, "You're under arrest."

"For what, throwing snowballs?" I snickered.

"That's right. Now place your hands behind your back!"

"I ain't goin' to jail for no snowballs," was all I said, and I began walk-ing away. The cop grabbed my shoulder and pulled on me, and that's when I turned around and knocked him out with one punch. I was a strong kid, a middle linebacker who thought nothing of hitting anyone who put their hands on me, not even a cop. I punched the cop dead in his face and sent him flying through a row of hedges eight feet tall that were covered in snow. Then, in all of our drunkenness, me and Dean busted out laughing when the cop disappeared from sight in an avalanche of snow that fell from the tall bushes above. It reminded me of one of Wile E. Coyote's foiled ACME schemes while trying to apprehend Roadrunner.

Unfortunately, his partner didn't find it so funny. He came charging after me, stupidly leading with his face, so I did the same thing to him: I punched him in the face as well. Regrettably, their back-up showed up at the same time, and that's when the party really ended. After getting me into handcuffs, four cops lifted me off the ground and carried me about fifty feet to a paddy wagon. On the count of three they threw me inside the wagon like a sack of potatoes, and slammed the doors shut behind me.

They drove the paddy wagon into an empty parking lot across the street, and turned off the engine. When the doors opened, they yanked me out and, while I was still in handcuffs, gave me a proper and thorough butt-whoopin' for assaulting two of their fellow officers.

***

But the beating I took in New Haven for resisting arrest paled in comparison to what Nicky and his boys did to me in Newark when I surrendered without resistance. Nicky and his crime-fighting pals behaved like street thugs with badges, and their behavior made them no better than the tough guy that they arrested that day: me.

As Nicky put me in the taxi – yeah, the taxi that had been parked in front of the hotel – one cop said sarcastically, "We oughta tie him to the roof of the car like a deer." I was bloody. So bloody in fact that Nicky said to his partner, "We can't let anybody see him like this or we'll all go down."

Just before Nicky got in the taxi with me, I could hear him tell Vinny that he could go home, explaining to him, "You'll hear from us soon." It was obvious that Vinny had sung like a canary, but even at this point, I didn't know just how bad things really were for me. During the ride to the prosecutor's office, I sat in the back of the cab, thinking, *"It's a good thing I didn't stop to pick up that package of blow!"*

I have heard it said, "If you show me who your friends are, I'll tell you where you're going to be in five years." I was twenty-two years-old, handcuffed and riding in the back of a cab. Where I was heading – Essex County Jail – had everything to do with who my friends were.

The taxi cab came to a stop outside a parking garage across the street from the jail. One of the detectives pulled me out of the taxi and walked me inside to the bathroom.

"Clean yourself up!" he ordered. I turned to show him my hands were cuffed behind my back, and looked at him as if to say, "Duuhhh! Are you kidding me? How am I supposed to clean my face with my hands cuffed behind my back?"

"I'm going to take the cuffs off," he conceded, "but if you try to run, I swear to God, I'll shoot you."

He unhooked the cuffs from the back and re-locked them in the front. He turned on the water, and pointed to the sink.

"Hurry up," he said, his eye on the door.

I had, among other things, a nasty gash in my head that would not stop bleeding. And more than likely, that cut resulted from being pistol-whipped by one of my "heroes" among the detectives. This detective didn't even give me a paper towel to clean up with. So I just used my hands with water and did the best I could.

Finally, we left the bathroom, and he brought me out to the taxi where the other cops where waiting.

"We can't let anyone see him like that," said one of the detectives. Though I'd cleaned up my wounds, I still looked like I'd just received a beat-down. One of the cops threw his coat over my head while the rest surrounded me, and Nicky said, "It's time to meet my boss."

CHAPTER 2

✝

Deep Waters

"The words of a man's mouth are deep waters..."
(Proverbs 18:4)

"Right now, you're facing six indictments, totaling sixty years in prison," the prosecutor threatened, waving the indictments in my still bloodied face.

As far as I was concerned, Vinny had provoked me to do what I did. I mean, really. What I did shouldn't even be a crime. Sixty years? Huh. The truth is, I was more anxious about what J.D. might to do to me when he found out I had taken Lucy to Newark with me.

"I'm with the Organized Crime Strike Force, and those are my detectives who arrested you today. Do you know what a prosecutor does?"

I'm thinking, *"What is this, a pop quiz?"*

Ya know, I just met this Sherlock, and his annoying grasp for the obvious was already getting on my nerves. I could tell by his small stature and arrogant demeanor that he must have gotten picked on in school. A real Napoleon Complex, this one.

"He puts criminals in jail, and I'm gonna see to it that you get there," he continued his Law 101 lecture. "You had better start thinking about making a deal." In other words, he was saying, "Tell me what I want to know and it will go better for you."

There I sat with my hands and feet cuffed to a chair that was bolted to the floor in the middle of a room at the prosecutor's office. According to him, I was in big trouble, but the truth is, I couldn't figure out what I had done that warranted sixty years in prison. Then I heard the doorknob turn, and in walked Nicky Newark, along with Lucy.

"Take a good look at your boyfriend," Nicky told her. "He's gonna be an old man by the time he gets out of prison."

Then he barked at me, "Is that what you want? Because that's what you're gonna get if you don't start talking!"

Lucy started crying. "Tell them what they want to know, Mike," she pleaded.

It wasn't that simple though. Telling the detectives what they wanted to know would be entering into deep waters, because the words they wanted to hear could send her father to prison for a long time. Besides, the life expectancy of a snitch is not very long. Giving people up never entered my mind, but I did consider the possibility that someone would think I might rat on them. And that could be hazardous to my health.

"I don't know what they want me to tell them, Lucy."

"Say goodbye to your boyfriend," Nicky snapped. "The next time you see him, he's gonna have gray hair." Nicky grabbed Lucy by the arm, and they left the room with the prosecutor, leaving me alone. In the silence, I was left to consider the consequences of both honor and betrayal. Neither one of the choices was very appealing, but certainly, breathing was better than not breathing.

On the way to the College Hospital to tend to my wounds, Nicky informed me that he'd had a detective take Lucy to Port Authority so she could catch a bus back home to Bricktown. He let her go, and that was the best thing that happened all day. At the hospital though, the X-rays of my head showed that I had a fractured skull.

Actually there had been two fractures – the one on my head and the one on Nicky's hand. That's right: Nicky had broken his thumb while punching me in the face, and I couldn't have felt more satisfaction when I saw him with his hand in a cast. Having a hard head paid off.

On the doctor's report produced at trial a year later, under the section where it asks you to explain how you were injured, Nicky wrote that he was "hit in the fist by a head."

"Are you asking us to believe," my lawyer smirked, "that my client was head-butting your hand with his head and that's how you broke your hand?"

Although the doctor was adamant about making me stay in the hospital, Nicky wasn't hearing it. He told the doctor that I had just been taken into custody, and that he needed to interrogate me. So they stitched me up, and we were on our way.

Once we got back to the prosecutor's office, we got down to the business of the interrogation. But first, Nicky informed me that J.D. had been taken into custody, and was being held in the Ocean County Jail on a $200,000 bond.

"You better start talking, because you know he's gonna try and talk first," Nicky told me, staring at his brand new cast. "That's how this game works, and he's got a lot more to lose than you do. The first one to talk gets the deal."

I may have been new to interrogation, but I knew without a doubt that J.D. would never talk. It was during the interrogation that I learned that Vinny had been wearing a wire when I got pinched. Every word I had said to him in the parking lot was on tape.

The day before, Vinny had gone to the prosecutor and complained he was the victim of a usurious loan. In other words, he was in deep with a loan shark. So he agreed with Nicky to have his conversations with J.D. recorded, the first one at ten the night before my arrest. Nicky played them for me.

"Hello?" J.D. answered the phone.

"How you doin', J.D.? It's Vinny."

Vinny started making excuses. "My car broke down, and I had to lay out a couple of hundred bucks there. So I'm broke. I'm tryin' to scrape together some money."

"Vinny, you got more stories than Carter got pills. You're just lookin' to get yourself hurt, that's all. All's you do is run and hide, so now we're gonna play the game my way."

"I don't wanna get hurt, J.D. but you know how long I been payin' you?"

"I don't care if you have to pay me until you're a hundred and ninety."

Vinny told J.D. he needed the weekend to come up with the paper, but J.D. wasn't trying to hear it. J.D. shouted, "You ain't got ten minutes, because I'm gonna find you and you're gonna get hurt!"

"All this time, you don't take nothin' off the top," Vinny complained. "It's just the vig, ya know what I mean?"

"This is fine," J.D. responded. "You do what you gotta do, and I'll do what I gotta do. I told you. It's that simple with this life. That's all. This kid is so mad right now, he's lookin' to go to your wife. Just be lookin' for me. Even better, be lookin' for my friend."

"How much do I gotta come up with?" Vinny asked.

"If I was you, I would come up with the most you could come up with, to save your life."

Vinny swore, "If I don't come up with the money Friday, J.D., you do anything you want to me."

J.D. conceded, "I'm gonna hold you to your word Vinny. I'm gonna hold you to your word."

Without any words, Nicky removed the tape and inserted the next tape, recorded that afternoon, when Nicky had Vinny call J.D. at the nursing home that his father owned and operated. This was J.D.'s day job, sometimes.

"J.D., it's Vinny. I got about eight hundred bucks. Can you meet me at the Holiday Inn at about two o'clock?"

J.D. let Vinny know, "The kid's on the way up. Where are you? You're in the joint, right? He should be there by now. Make sure you give him the eight hundred because otherwise, it's good luck, Frank Buck, today. Tell him to call me before he does anything to you."

I didn't know who to be angrier at, J.D. for running his mouth on the phone or Vinny for setting us up. As I listened to the tapes, I realized that even lying couldn't get me out of this one. I was in deep trouble. I've never been asked so many versions of the same questions over and over and over again. They must have had to pass a test on how many ways you can ask the same question using different words. It felt like the questions were never going to end as they tried to get to the truth. This, I was used to.

***

We were playing a game called Time Bomb, my brothers, my uncle and me, in our basement during a family gathering with my mother's side of the family. We'd wind up the game's round black plastic ball that looked like a bomb until it started ticking, and then continue to pass the bomb to the next player in the circle, until the bomb went BOOM! If the bomb was in your hands when it stopped ticking, you were out of the game.

But when the bomb stopped ticking and "exploded" in my uncle's hands, he fell back onto a chair, acting as though he had been killed. We all began laughing hysterically, when his chair broke, and he fell to the floor. This was hilarious stuff to a six year-old.

The next night at dinner, however, no one was laughing.

"Who broke the chair in the basement?" my father interrogated us kids.

"Uncle Jimmy broke the chair by accident," I told him. "We were playing Time Bomb."

But Dad didn't believe us.

"I won't tolerate lying!" he began to raise his voice. "You kids have to take responsibility for your actions, even if it means suffering the consequences," he warned us.

"Stop eating!" he shouted, banging his hand down on the kitchen table. I watched the water skip from my glass onto my scalloped potatoes.

Nobody said a word. We just stared at our plates, hoping his tirade wouldn't end with a belt on our butts. "No one is leaving this table until I find out who broke the chair!" Then, just like the Time Bomb game, I waited for him to explode. Tick, tick, tick, tick… suddenly, my father took his arm, and with one swipe, cleared the table of all of the food and dishes onto the floor with a loud crash.

"I want to know who broke the chair! One of you broke that chair, I know it! The longer you wait, the worse it's gonna be!"

He was scaring everyone, including my mother. It seemed his rant would never end.

"I did it," I blurted.

My father stopped shouting and stared at me in icy silence and disgust.

"Go up to your room and wait for me," he ordered. I knew what that meant. I knew what was coming, but all I wanted to do was stop my father's yelling and screaming, and offering, "I did it" made it stop. What I learned at six years-old was that it wasn't important to tell my father the truth. It was important to tell my father what I knew he would want to hear.

***

By now, the side effects of my head injury were beginning to show. The detectives asked me questions, but my head had a hard time staying upright on my shoulders. I nodded in and out of consciousness, only to awaken to even more questions. I wanted the interrogation to end, so I did exactly the same thing I had done with my father: I told the cops what I knew they wanted to hear. After all, they had me dead to rights, threatening and assaulting Vinny on tape. What was I gonna do, say I didn't do it? I didn't deny that I came up to Newark ready to give Vinny a beating if he didn't pay, but I denied that J.D. had sent me up there to do it. I pointed to the part in the tape where I said, "It has nothing to do with me," that is, Vinny's loan with J.D. "I came up here to get the money Vinny owes me for the jewelry I sold him," I told the cops.

Nearly twelve hours after my arrest, the questioning finally ended.

From there, I was taken over to the "Newark Taj Mahal," otherwise known as the Essex County Jail. I knew this was the place I would call home for a while. I also knew it was considered at the time to be the most violent county jail in the nation; I'd seen it in a documentary that I'd watched on TV shortly before I was locked up. According to the show, there had been lawsuits filed against the city of Newark for extreme over-crowding and deplorable living conditions inside the jail.

Once inside the jail, Nicky talked privately to one of the officers there. I am pretty sure the conversation centered on the skull fracture he'd given me, because I was not put into general population, but instead I went straight to the infirmary.

The next day, I was able to make a collect call home, and the first call I made was to my mother. I didn't even know if she knew I was locked up. After thinking about how I was going to break the news to her, I figured I'd just wing it. I placed the collect call home through the operator, and I could hear the phone ringing on the other end.

"Hello?" she answered.

"You have a collect call from Mike Palombi. Will you accept the charges?" the operator asked.

"Yes, yes, yes," my mother cut her off. She could hardly wait to chew me out.

"Where are you?" she demanded.

"I'm in the Essex County Jail, Mom."

"What the heck is wrong with you?"

"It's not what you think, Mom."

"What do you mean it's not what I think? The story's all over the newspapers, it's on the radio. Everyone's gonna know I'm your mother. Who is this guy J.D.?" she demanded from me.

"Why do you want to know?"

"Because I'm going to go see him! He got you into this mess. Now he better get you out of it."

I explained to her that J.D. was Lucy's father, and that he was locked up, too.

"When you come home, I'm gonna wring your neck. Everybody's going to know I'm your mother!" she repeated. "Just keep your mouth shut in there and don't talk to anyone about why you are there. I can't believe you can be so stupid!"

I was thankful she couldn't get her hands on me. Make no mistake about it: My mother was among the very toughest of women that I had ever known. At just three years-old, she lost her mother, then endured years of torturous physical and emotional abuse from a mentally ill step-mother. And she'd throw fists with the neighborhood bullies who tried to pick on her six younger brothers and sisters. Her family was so poor that in the winter of 1947, her family lived in a tent on the property of a friend in Wall Township.

I felt safer in jail than facing her out in the streets.

A couple of days later, I was called from my cell for a visit. The only visits allowed in the county jail were phone visits, where you talk on a phone receiver to the visitor on the other side of the glass. The jail was so overcrowded, prisoners were allowed to visit for just three minutes at a time.

I don't know who I expected to see sitting there, but I didn't expect it to be my father. And yet, there he was. Even after I was nearly killed in a head-on collision back in college, he never even came to see me in the hospital.

As I picked up the phone, his chilling and hostile stare cut right through me. I could tell he was disgusted by the sight of me. Dad spoke first.

"So tough guy, how's the fast money?" he asked. I felt my body tighten right away as I absorbed the blows of his verbal reprimand. I may have started crying if I didn't distract myself from the pain of his words by reaching into my jumpsuit pocket and pulling out a bag of Bugler tobacco and rolling papers. As I rolled a cigarette, my father continued.

"I'm embarrassed by you. I didn't raise you to do these things."

I didn't say anything as I put the cigarette to my mouth and lit it.

"What's that, pot?" he asked.

"No Dad, it's a cigarette."

He finally got around to noticing the stitches over my eye and the bruises on my face from the beat-down I had taken.

"What happened to your face?"

"That happened during the arrest, Dad."

Then there was a pause filled with a loud silence.

"You know somethin', you're an idiot," he decided. "I'd like to punch you right in the face myself!"

"Inmate Palombi, times up." Finally, there was a cop around when I needed one.

Thank God we only had three minutes to visit, and yet it was three minutes too long. I returned to my cell feeling discouraged, wishing he had never come to visit me.

Within a week of my arraignment, one of J.D.'s associates came up from south Jersey to bail him out. It wasn't good enough that the prosecutor got the bail money, but now he wanted to know how J.D. had come up with the $200,000 in cash. When I asked him what he told the prosecutor, J.D. replied, "I told him I got two hundred friends that gave me a thousand bucks!"

Unfortunately it was going to take a little more time to get me out of jail. J.D. needed to get additional money together to get me released, but he assured me it would not take long.

Right about the time J.D. went home, I was moved into a cell right outside of the infirmary. I questioned the move, wondering why they didn't just keep me in the infirmary. I will admit though, if you had to be locked up in the Essex County Jail, this was the place to be. It was away from the noise and most importantly the violence, including beat-downs by gangbangers and a shiv to the stomach for looking at someone the wrong way. Still, I wondered why I was put there.

I met a couple of guys in that area outside of the infirmary, but it was Derrick, a big dude, low key, and in his thirties, who helped me get the lay of the land. He gave me advice regarding the do's and don'ts of jailhouse life. I needed all of the advice I could get because, other than a night in jail for my drunken snowball incident in New Haven, I had never been locked up before. Jail life was all new to me.

Derrick's advice read like a Miss Manners' Book for Convicts:

- Be respectful and don't act like you're better than anybody else.

- Whatever's going on apart from you has nothing to do with you, so don't stick your nose in it.
- Don't touch anything that don't belong to you.
- Don't get friendly with the cops. That'll put a target on your back quick.
- Go about your business quietly and unnoticed.
- Most important, don't appear weak!

We spent the next three days smoking weed and yukking it up. But I made sure that the one thing I didn't talk about was the reason I was in jail. I was suspicious of the move outside the infirmary, and while Derrick seemed genuine enough, he could have been an informant. I told him what I was arrested for, but I didn't get into any details.

"Oh, you're the guy I read about in the paper," Derrick said.

"Yeah, that's about the extent of it," I replied.

But with Derrick's friend, Anthony, it was a different story. Derrick asked him over to my cell to smoke a joint with us. You know, kinda like a meet-and-greet with your new neighbor. But Anthony refused to smoke weed with a white boy like me, taking offense at Derrick's invitation.

"Why you askin' me if I wanna smoke weed wit the devil?" he asked Derrick." I ain't smokin' no weed wit a white man." Anthony was eighteen or nineteen and wild. The older guys in the joint referred to young guys like him as jitterbugs, many of which were in gangs.

"You oughta treat people right," Derrick replied. "You never know when you might need his help."

"I'll never need the help of a white boy!" Anthony decided.

Hey, that just meant there was more weed for me.

A couple of days later, I was moved to lockup, where you go for punishment for violating institutional policies. The thing is, I'd done nothing wrong to warrant the move. In a way, I didn't care too much. All the kicks and punches to the back and body from the beating I had endured in the parking lot had taken their toll on me and by now, I could hardly move due to the pain in my back.

Lockup was probably safer than being sent to general population where I might have had to defend myself. While it may have been the safer place, it wasn't the most pleasant. My cell was small with a solid steel door that blocked out the light. My steel bed had no blanket, mattress, or pillow, and the overhead light didn't work, so I was in total darkness most of the time. The frigid October air blew in through the broken windows on that tier of the jail. My body throbbed in pain, and I couldn't stay warm. Worse, there was nothing to distract me from experiencing every miserable minute I was in there.

I could be wrong, but I believed the move to lockup to be an attempt by the prosecutor's office to get information out of me, particularly after what happened next: A cop came down the tier to take names for anyone who wanted to use the phone. I was suspicious of the invitation, because lockup is a place of punishment and so, phone privileges aren't allowed there. Perhaps the prosecutor hoped that I would call J.D. and say something damaging on the phone. Who knows?

Of course, I took advantage of the rare phone privilege, and called home to explain to my mother that I was in lockup, and that was why she hadn't heard from me in days. I told her what I thought was going on with the move and suggested that she run it by the attorney J.D. had retained for me.

The next day, I was sitting on the cold, concrete floor of my cell, holding my knees into my chest to help ease the pain in my back. I was using the corner of my cell to prop myself up, because my back injury didn't allow me to lie flat. I could hear footsteps walking toward me. They stopped outside of my cell door.

"Open it up," an officer said.

I heard the key slide into my cell door's lock and turn. The door opened, and I squinted as the daylight from the windows across the tier flooded my cell.

"Let's go. Outta here," bellowed the "white shirt," a high-ranking guard.

I tried to get up, but pain shot up my back. I couldn't move.

"Let's go! You wanted outta here. You're outta here." I knew that my attorney had something to do with it.

"What, you need help getting up?" he continued, and then he yanked me off the floor by my head and dragged me across the cell. As he slammed my head into the bars out on the tier, he yelled, "I said get outta here!"

This cop made Nicky's treatment of me seem tenderhearted and compassionate in comparison.

The officers walked me off the tier to a room near the infirmary. It didn't take long for me to realize that this room was predominantly filled with the mentally ill or people trying to be classified as mentally ill in order to beat a murder rap. It also didn't take long to realize that with sixteen beds in a room housing thirty-four people, it was gonna be awhile before I had a bed. I hoped I wasn't going to need one though, because I learned that my bail reduction hearing was coming up.

In the meantime, I had to stick it out. I confined myself to a spot on the floor, and began to observe the insanity around me. One guy was taking a shower with his jailhouse jumpsuit on, while another guy was crawling around the floor, barking like a dog. Other men walked around twitching and moving their limbs uncontrollably, while still others behaved like zombies from the side effects of the medication they were taking. The rest were doing the Thorazine Shuffle, constantly shuffling their feet as they went nowhere.

I wondered if this "One Flew Over the Cuckoo's Nest" scene was for real. And yet, this is where I would spend my next week at the Essex County Jail. The bed shortage meant that every night at eleven, I was given a cot to sleep on, and every morning at six, the cot was taken away. During the seventeen hours in between, I sat on the floor, or I stood to stretch my legs.

On the bright side, this room was heated, unlike the wing over at lockup. But, in a room filled with mostly young men who had no exercise and didn't play well with others, there were a lot of fights. Everybody knew the rules: Lose the fight, go to lockup. The cops didn't care if you were being bullied, if someone was trying to rip you off, or trying to take your manhood. They didn't care who started it or who may have just been defending themselves against attackers. If you lost the fight, you left the room.

You always had to watch your back in there, because anything could happen at any time, and you knew the cops weren't going to help. You were most vulnerable when you were asleep, because there was nothing stopping another inmate from robbing what little stuff you had or from hurting you if that was what he wanted to do.

As fate would have it, a familiar face came walking into the psycho ward. It was Derrick's buddy Anthony, who had declared me the devil, the guy who said he would never need the help of a white boy.

I watched with a grin on my face as he carefully worked his way around the room full of nut jobs. He seemed to have lost that hip and cool swagger he'd had when I first met him outside the infirmary. As a matter of fact, he looked pretty darn nervous.

I stared at him until we finally made eye contact. When he recognized me, he could hardly contain himself. I swear he wanted to hug me.

"Yo, what's up?" he sounded relieved. He came walking over, grabbed my hand to shake it, leaned over, and said, "These brothers up in here is crazy!"

After what I imagine was an exceptionally long night for him, Anthony sat on the floor next to me, and said real quietly, "You know I was thinkin'? Maybe we should sleep with our backs to each other from now on. You know, like you watch my back and I'll watch yours?"

"I'm okay with that if you're okay with the devil watching your back," I replied. That got a chuckle out of him.

So, each night, we would sleep with our cots close together, our belongings between us and our backs to each other, so we only had to worry about being ripped off or attacked from one direction. But even that wasn't a safe bet.

One night, we woke up choking from smoke to the screams of an inmate near us who had been lit on fire while he was asleep for what he may or may not have done to another inmate during the day. The fact is, in that room, you didn't have to do anything to anyone for something like that to happen; you just had to be there. That poor sap never saw it coming, and you normally don't in jail. One second, he was sleeping on his cot, and the next, he was on fire, screaming, and beating himself with his hands. The men around him threw a blanket over him, and took him to the floor to smother the flames.

After going back to bed, I laid awake the rest of the night, wondering when it was going to be my turn.

CHAPTER 3

✝

The Way of Greed

"Such are the ways of everyone who is greedy for unjust gain;
it takes away the life of its possessors."
(Proverbs 1:19)

A few days later, my bail was reduced to $50,000, and J.D. was able to pay it. Who knows, maybe he found fifty more friends with a thousand bucks!

After fifteen days in one of the toughest county jails in the country, I was going home. My mother and brother came to pick me up, but it wasn't the joyous and carefree reunion one might expect. After all, I knew my days of freedom were numbered and that, more than likely, I would be returning to the nightmare I'd just left, but for a much longer period of time.

On my first day home, I was more than happy to return to my job filling potholes and cleaning up road kill for the Ocean County Road Department. Only, I had been suspended from my job pending a hearing because of my criminal indictments. What happened to innocent until proven guilty?

Ultimately, the county made me an offer that, at the age of twenty-two, I just couldn't refuse. They paid me to leave! I couldn't believe it. They paid me twenty-five hundred bucks to quit my job. I thought, for $2,500, I'd find a new job, and that's exactly what I did.

My mother reached out to a relative who helped me get a job as a security guard at an indoor flea market in Wall Township. Who in their right mind would hire a kid who allegedly worked as a strong-arm for a loan shark to guard their store?

In any event, they did hire me, and it was like owning my own strip mall. Whatever I needed was there, and best of all, everything I wanted was free! I started my overnight shifts by hitting the deli for some fresh Italian food. I usually went for the pasta and sausage and peppers. The owner of the deli was a first-generation Italian lady, and man, she could cook!

After I loaded up on dinner, I stopped by the bakery for some dessert. Never could get enough sweets. Then, I'd take my food and head back to the office where the security cameras were, and turn on a pot of coffee and the TV. I usually watched back-to-back rerun episodes of "The Honeymooners." I could watch that stuff a hundred times, and it was always funny to me.

After dinner, I had my coffee and a smoke. With my belly full and the store secure, I'd do a few lines, and finally get on with the most difficult part of my night: becoming a master at the original Pac-Man game in the arcade. I would spend about six hours of my shift with Blinky, Inky, Pinky, and Clyde all night long for a quarter. It was as simple as drilling a hole through the top of a quarter, putting a small string through the hole, and then tying the string around the quarter. I'd slowly lower it into the machine's coin slot until I heard the game register. Then I moved the quarter up and down racking up about a hundred games before I'd break the string, allowing the quarter to fall into the change box. All night long I could hear "waca, waca, waca, waca," as I ran up the points with Blinky and his crew chasing me.

Around 6:30 the next morning, I would start winding down with Pac-Man and go shopping. I started a little side business selling clothes to friends, and friends of friends, with some of the merchandise that I would take out of there.

I can't even believe I got paid for this job.

One night, J.D. came by to see where I worked. We did a few lines, and then I showed him around the place. As we began the tour, his eyes lit up like he was a kid in a candy store.

"You never told me there were jewelry stores in here," J.D. said.

"Don't even think about it," I warned him.

"What are you kidding me? Do you have any idea how much money we could make?"

"Do you have any idea how much time we could do?" I reminded him. But that didn't stop him. He started asking me about the place: questions about camera locations, entrances and exits, and most importantly, whether I was there when the store owner moved the jewelry in and out. J.D. was dead serious about robbing the place, and honestly, he had a pretty good plan – right up until I asked, "What are you going to do about me?"

"What do you mean what am I going to do about you?"

"I mean, how am I going to explain to the cops that you, the jewelry thief, just happened to be here at the same exact time the jewelry store owner was bringing in his new stock? Isn't that going to send up a red flag, you know, with me being the security guard who's out on a $50,000 bond and awaiting trial on six indictments?"

He thought about it for a minute, hatching up his plan.

"We'll shoot you to make it look good," he replied with a straight face, as though he'd just suggested we should go out for a bite to eat or take in a movie. My mouth dropped open.

"Well, I won't shoot you anywhere serious," he offered.

"How thoughtful of you!" I answered. When one of the requirements to rob a place includes me getting shot, you better believe any place you hit me is too serious. Bottom line is, if I'm getting shot, it's not going to be because I agreed to it.

"Yeah, I guess not," he decided. And that's the last I heard of J.D.'s plan to rob the place where I worked. It wasn't long after that J.D. told me to quit the job at the flea market.

"What are you doin' over there anyway?" he asked. "At the end of the week, you don't have two nickels to rub together."

So I quit the job and began spending most of my time with him, learning the trade skills of the street. That was okay with me. I liked J.D. and his friends, and they liked me. At the tender age of twenty-three, I was impressed by all the wrong things. With no job, I began earning money illegally by selling cocaine and stolen merchandise. I'd also run some menial tasks for J.D., like filling up his tank with gas, or going to the store to get more cut for the coke, powder that looks like coke to add weight and pad our wallets. You know, little things just to save him time. Nothing was little to J.D. though. He always acknowledged the small stuff I did by throwing me a few grams of coke.

We used to earn some extra paper by booking bets with some of the local guys who liked to gamble on football games. But I almost got in serious trouble with J.D. in the winter of 1982, when I held back some of the bets from J.D. for myself.

That year, Miami was giving away two points against the Jets in the AFC Championship game. Even though the Jets had lost to the Dolphins twice that season, the first time big and the second time by a point, I believed that the Jets would beat the Dolphins outright in the big game. For that reason, I held back from J.D. every bet that picked Miami to beat the Jets by more than two points, and I turned in all of the bets that picked the Jets to beat Miami.

That backfired big-time! That game between the Dolphins and the Jets became known as the "Mud Bowl." For three days leading up to the AFC Championship game, it rained. Yet the Dolphins' head coach Don Shula ordered that the tarps protecting the turf be removed from the field, turning it into dirt soup. My guess is it was part of his plan to eliminate the running threat of the Jets NFL leading rusher, Freeman McNeil.

Not only did that cost the Jets the game, but it cost me several thousand dollars. That was a lot of cake and worse, how was I going to pay it? I was in a real jackpot. I had no choice but to go to J.D. and tell him what I had done.

"Oh, what are trying to do, get me killed?" he shouted. "Don't I look out for you? Don't I take care of you? I trust you with my wife, I trust you with my daughter, and this is what you do to me behind my back?"

"I didn't think I was gonna lose, J.D," I explained.

Tapping his finger on my head he said, "No, you didn't think, period! Now you want me to save your butt, right? How much you in for?"

"I'm in for $3,800."

"I'm gonna cover this note, but you're gonna pay back every dime. You understand me? I don't care if you have to sell your stinkin' car! It's the only way you're gonna learn."

Soon, I was really hard-up for cash, so I started installing ceramic tile again, a trade skill I'd learned from my dad. I put a small ad in the classifieds for tile repair and grouting. My first job was retiling J.D's master bathroom, and then I did some work in his father's nursing home. More often than not, however, I preferred the riskier methods of earning fast money. Like J.D. would say, "I do what I gotta do."

The thing is, I didn't have to do any of it.

I liked the arrogant confidence of J.D. and guys he hung out with, as well as their defiant attitudes and tough guy images. I can recall walking into a Gold's Gym with J.D's friend Sal, a wise guy with a sense of humor.

"Hey, moron!" he shouted into the crowded weight room, and every muscle-head in the place turned to look at us. Personally, I thought we were in big trouble, but not Sal. He just turned to me and with a big smile declared, "There's a lot of morons in here, Mikey."

Amazingly, no one in the gym said or tried to do a thing. We walked through the weight room like we owned the place. And oh, how I wanted to be just like Sal and the guys. I believed that others were jealous of them and would be jealous of me, too, if I imitated their ways. They were respected, and I wanted that same respect. I quickly became a person who snubbed his nose at authority and saw law enforcement as my enemy. I even began to imitate my idols.

I chose to do what I did, and I enjoyed doing it. It was fun and exciting to me to skirt the law, but more importantly, I saw this lifestyle as a way to have things I never thought I would have and do things I never thought I would do.

All my life, I had believed, "I'll never own a home like that, or drive a car like that, or have a woman like that." Yet this lifestyle could provide all of those things for me, and it didn't require long hours of hard physical labor or a four-year education. All I needed was the nerve to do what the law said I couldn't do and the ability to convince myself that regardless of how I obtained something, the method I used to obtain it was inconsequential.

Yet, while I may have been enjoying what I was doing, Lucy wasn't. She was upset with me and her father, because I was spending all of my time with J.D. and no time with her. I couldn't even tell her why I was spending so much time with him, but I remember we had some big fights over it. She knew I was up to no good, because she knew her dad. Somehow though, we managed to stay together.

As time was passing and the trial was drawing near, my attorney convinced me that I would serve little or no time for the crimes of which I was accused due to my lack of criminal history. So much for sixty years, Mr. Prosecutor! I wasn't even worried about the upcoming trial or the outside chance that I may have to serve time. In fact, I kind of liked all the attention it was bringing me.

After I had gotten out on bail, I noticed that J.D. and Sal treated me more like an equal, and I loved it. They were including me in on conversations where before they had excluded me. They were introducing me to more people, and the people they introduced me to respected me simply because I was with J.D. and Sal. I felt like a big shot. I think I had the kind of relationship with them that I'd always wanted to have with my father. It seemed nothing I ever did was good enough for my dad, but I never had a problem being good enough for J.D. and Sal.

What's more, they were funny, liked to have a good time, gave me compliments, and looked out for me. If I didn't have money, they would throw me a few bucks, and if I needed a ride, they would let me borrow their cars.

Sal had a Delorean, like the one from "Back to the Future" with the gull-wing doors that opened over your head. At a cost of twenty-five grand, it was an expensive toy to own in 1982, and when Sal let me drive it, my head swelled.

Strangely enough, the car's developer, John Delorean, was arrested at about the same exact time I was, and charged with conspiring to sell cocaine. He beat the rap because it was later determined that the FBI had entrapped him.

Anyway, there were times when I would be sitting at a red light in the Delorean, knowing full well that people on the sidewalk and in other cars were staring at me. So I would nonchalantly pull out a bag of coke and feel a weird sense of affirmation from their gaze as I dipped my straw into the bag and took a hit for everyone to see.

Once I even turned to the guy staring from the car next to me and said, "It comes with the car!"

Five days before the trial was to begin, J.D. and I went to the local diner, as we often did. Along the way, J.D. told me, "Word has it, Vinny's been whacked."

"What do you mean Vinny's been whacked?" I asked, shocked at the news.

"He's dead. He was into a lot of people for money," he explained. "It could have been any number of people who did it." I was suspicious of the timing of the whole situation, and I soon found out that I was not the only one. One thing was certain at this point: The concerns I had earlier about someone thinking I may give them up quickly resurfaced.

Later that day, I called my mother from J.D.'s house just to touch base with her.

"Michael, where are you? What have you done?" she asked, frantic.

"What are you talking about?" I asked.

"The apartment is surrounded by cops," she said. "That jerk that arrested you came with a warrant, and they are searching the apartment." They'd told my mother that I was their primary suspect in Vinny's murder.

"Please tell me you didn't kill that man," she begged.

"No, Ma. I didn't do it," I assured her. But Nicky wanted to see me right away, I could hear him over the phone sweating my mother, and so I told her, "Send Badge Nose over to J.D.'s house. That's where I'm at."

I wasn't worried about seeing the cops, because I had nothing to hide, at least as it related to Vinny's murder. What I did have to hide was all the cocaine I had stashed at the house. I didn't know if they had a warrant to search J.D.'s house as well. Of course, I didn't want to flush the coke down the toilet, so I began snorting as much of it as I could. And I kept on snorting the coke right up until Nicky and his boys pulled up to J.D.'s house, got out of their cars, walked up to the front door, and rang the doorbell. It killed me, but I had to flush about a half-an-ounce of coke down the toilet and answer the door.

I opened the door to several officers, weapons drawn on me, with Nicky leading the way.

"Nice and slow," he ordered. "Put your hands on your head and come outside of the house. Do you have any weapons on you? Any hand grenades? I have a warrant to search you and your vehicle."

As the cops began searching me, Nicky asked, "You think you're going to get away with killing my witness?"

"I didn't kill your witness," I replied.

"That's not what I heard," Nicky barked. He said an anonymous tip came in telling them I had committed the murder.

"Either you're lying or you got a bad tip," I answered.

When the cops were finished searching me, they went to search my car. As they began taking the seats out, I yelled "Hey, what are you doing? Someone is coming in a few minutes to buy the car!"

Selling the car was important for a couple of reasons, not just for paying J.D. back the money he'd laid out for the football bets that backfired on me, but also because I was suspicious that the cops had put a listening device in my car.

"Hopefully, we'll be done by the time the buyers get here," Nicky said, and no sooner did he get the words out of his mouth a young kid pulled up with his parents to check out my car.

"What am I going to tell him now?" I asked Nicky. "He's here to look at the car."

"What should we tell them?" Nicky asked one of the other detectives.

"Uh, tell 'em we made a mistake," he made up on the spot. "Just say we thought you were selling drugs out of your car, but we got the wrong guy."

I went over to the potential buyers' and asked calmly, "Are you here to look at the car?"

"Yes we are. Is everything okay?"

"The cops made a mistake and they'll be out of here in just a few minutes, if you didn't mind coming back." I looked over at the cop next to me as if to say, "Isn't that right, detective?" and he smiled and nodded at them in agreement. When the buyers came back later and bought the car, they said, "Well, at least we know there are no drugs in the car!"

Before the cops left, they reminded me that I was the only one left alive who could talk about the crime, and that I might want to very seriously consider my loyalty and what the consequences of such loyalty could mean.

"Look detective, my attorney says I ain't doin' more than six months," I boasted. "That's no reason to kill a man."

"Oh, is that what he told you?" Nicky replied. "Well, you tell your lawyer and your partner when you see them that there will be a trial and you will go to prison."

As Nicky began walking away, he turned and asked me, "By the way, what are you doin' tonight?"

"I'm goin' to a nightclub in Seaside with some friends, why?"

"I don't know. I'm just thinkin' you should be careful. You never know what someone might drop in your drink." And he turned and walked away.

When they left, I considered what he'd said. How could I not? It was hard for me to imagine that J.D., my girlfriend's father, would be involved in anyone's murder let alone kill me. Then again, if convicted, he would be a three-time loser, and there was a lot more at stake for him than there was for me. His two prior convictions would significantly impact how much time he'd receive if found guilty at our trial.

It didn't help my paranoia that I was addicted to cocaine, pills, crystal meth, and booze. *"Why wouldn't he kill me?"* I asked myself. And I couldn't think of many good reasons why he wouldn't. If in fact J.D. did play a role in Vinny's murder, then more than likely a conversation had already taken place surrounding a decision to murder me.

So, I moved in with him.

I had two reasons for doing that. At the time, I did believe there was a good chance that I would be killed and when it happened, I didn't want my mother to see it, or even worse, get killed herself. Also, moving in with J.D. would demonstrate my loyalty to him and could possibly prevent a decision to kill me if that's what he or others connected to him intended to do. I would stay with J.D. until the trial – or until he had me killed.

"There's someone who wants to see you," J.D. called to tell me the next day.

"Who wants to see me?" I asked.

"This guy Johnny."

"Who is he?"

"He's a guy I go to for different things."

"I don't even know him. Why does he want to see me?"

When I told J.D. I was busy, he said, "I'm not *asking* you to go, I'm *telling* you to go."

So J.D. and I took a ride up to a restaurant in Newark. On the way, he explained that we were going to a sit-down with someone who had concerns about things I may or may not have known about him and whether or not I had revealed any information about him to the cops the previous day.

"This is ridiculous," I replied. "How can I reveal information about somebody I don't know?" I didn't like this at all. It smelled rotten to me, and J.D.'s silence about the specifics of this guy wanting to meet me wasn't making me feel any better.

When we got there, I noticed a group of men I had never seen before just hanging around out in front of the restaurant. As we walked up, J.D. exchanged pleasantries with the men and told them who we were there to see.

The apparent leader of the group asked J.D., "Who's the kid?"

J.D. said, "He's with me."

"He's with you? Okay, let's go."

Once inside, I met Johnny, a tall, good-looking Italian guy, mid-thirties, with a full head of dark hair, wearing a suit and tie. When he saw us coming, he got up from his table to greet me like he'd known me my entire life.

"Hey, get over here. You want somethin' to drink. Drinks are on the house." He was loud and drawing a lot of attention from people in the restaurant. I watched as J.D. gave Johnny a hug and then kissed him on the cheek. I followed J.D.'s lead and did the same. Then Johnny pointed at the menu and offered loudly, "Come on, sit down, get somethin' to eat."

When we sat down at the table, a waiter came over to take drink orders. Johnny leaned forward and pointing with his finger, told the waiter, "Now you see that broad over there? Send her a drink on me."

"Uh, Johnny, that's her husband with her," the waiter warned.

A menacing look of anger quickly replaced the smile on Johnny's face.

Grabbing the waiter by the shirt and pulling him close, he spat, "I don't care if that's the Pope himself sittin' wit her. Send it over now!"

After some small talk around the table, Johnny leaned over to the guy who had brought us in, and making sure I saw him, pulled a handgun from behind his jacket where it had been tucked into his belt.

"Hold onto this," he said. "I'm going to have a conversation with the kid in the bathroom." I couldn't tell you what kind of gun it was other than it was the kind of gun that could kill me.

"Come on kid, let's go have a talk," He told me, motioning toward the bathroom.

When we got there, Johnny locked the door behind us, and pulled a bag of coke out of his suit jacket pocket. He was looking in the mirror with his back to me, checking himself out. He stuck a straw into the bag of coke, raised it to his nose, and he asked me matter-of-factly, "So kid, what did you tell the cops about me?"

He stared hard at me in the mirror, waiting to hear my response.

"I don't even know who you are!" I blurted.

Johnny turned around, and using the straw to point at me as he smiled, he said, "That's good kid. That's a real good answer."

He came closer and patted me gently on the cheeks a couple of times before he continued: "Cuz ya know, if you do ever say somethin', you're gonna be next week's sausages, if ya know what I mean."

I was crystal clear about what he meant. While we did a couple of lines together, Johnny explained that the cops were jealous of people like him and now, people like me.

"We're the good guys, you see," he reasoned. "The cops just use their badges and position of authority to do the same things we do." Waving his hand he added, "Forget about it. "Don't let 'em' scare you. They can be bought and sold. I do it all the time."

I remember how sincere he was when he explained those things to me, like he was an uncle filling me in on the facts of life. I have no doubt that he believed every word he was saying.

He unlocked the bathroom door, and we went back to the table and finished our drinks. Then J.D. and I left the restaurant.

On the ride home, I was pretty quiet and so was J.D. I still didn't understand the purpose of this meeting. Why would a man I don't know, and who doesn't know me, want to find out what I said about him to cops who were investigating me about a murder?

The next day, J.D. called to ask me to drive him north to a meeting near the Meadowlands. On the ride up, we did a lot of coke. The thing about the coke was it made me feel good, more upbeat and confident than when I wasn't using.

"Who are you meeting?" I asked J.D.

"Johnny."

"How do you know him, anyway? You never told me."

"I told you, Johnny's a guy I go to for different things." I understood that to mean stop asking questions, because if he wanted to tell me who Johnny was, he would have told me already. I'd only met Johnny once, but I was able to gather that he was somebody that J.D. answered to. When Johnny said jump, J.D. jumped.

When I dropped J.D. off that evening for his meeting, he told me to go hang out at the bar inside the Sheraton Hotel across from Giants Stadium.

"I'll come and get you when I'm done."

But hours went by, and I had been drinking heavy and doing a lot of blow. I couldn't even feel my face anymore when I put the glass to my mouth to take a drink. Whatever booze didn't make it into my mouth spilled down the front of me.

While I sat there dribbling on myself, the L. A. Rams came walking into the lounge area. Their larger-than-life images were distorted by how stinkin' high I was. Others in the lounge were star-struck autograph-seekers, but for me, the superstars' presence made me feel a deep sense of regret for what could have been.

***

As usual, I was partying. It was the summer of 1979, and I was home for college break. Me and some of my pals were meeting friends of mine from school at a seaside club called the Osprey in Manasquan. I especially liked the Osprey, because I had friends there who were bouncers and bartenders, so not only could I get in for free, I could drink for free, too.

We went to the bar to see the Backstreets, a band that played only Springsteen covers. We were drinking Long Island iced teas and flaming shots of Sambuca, and singing along with the band all night long. We were juiced long before we ever got to the Osprey, but when we came out of the joint, we were *wasted*. Staggering, slurring our words, can't-find-our-car wasted.

My buddy Scott finally spotted the car on Main Street, and called shot-gun, which meant that me and my pal, the aptly nicknamed, Kegger, would have to squeeze into the back seats of Bobby's yellow 1969 Mustang Mach 1.

"You okay to drive?" Scott asked Bobby. Placing one hand over his left eye, Bobby reported, "I can see perfectly!"

He fired up the engine, and we began to head home for the night. I couldn't sit up straight in the rear seat of the fast-back without my head hitting the roof of the car, so I laid my head back on the seat, and gazed up through the rear window.

"Hey Kegger, this is a great view of the stars," I said.

That's all I remember before the collision sent me head-first through that very same window. We had made it only a couple of hundred yards from the Osprey before Bobby passed out at the wheel, drove into the oncoming lane, and hit another car head-on. My body never totally exited the car before falling back into my seat, unconscious. The engine of the car was now in the front seat where the Bobby used to be, and Bobby's seat was shoved back and on top of Kegger's legs. Both Bobby and Kegger were trapped, but alive, miraculously suffering only minor injuries. Scotty on the other hand, reportedly opened his door, got out of the vehicle, and, after making sure the other driver was okay, instructed Bobby to "crank it up before the cops get here!" as if that were an option.

When I woke up, I was lying in the road being attended to by EMT workers. I could hear the sirens of multiple emergency vehicles on the scene, as well as the unmistakable compressor and extraction sounds of the Jaws of Life removing my friends from what remained of the car. The rear window's glass had left a V-shaped laceration nearly twenty inches-long on my head; I'd been scalped.

In the emergency room of the Point Pleasant Hospital, I went in and out of consciousness. At times, I could hear my drunken friends acting out in the emergency room, while the nurses and security guards tried to calm them down. Eventually, I met the neurosurgeon, a small man who spoke with a strong Indian accent. As the surgeon described my injuries to me, he took hold of my hand and in a serious voice said, "Michael, I need you to be very brave. You have a significant laceration on your head that needs stitches, and because you have a severe head injury, I cannot give you any medication for pain." His parting words were, "We will get through this together."

Before the doctor left to prepare for the procedure, he informed me that my mother and brother had arrived at the hospital. I began to call out for my brother Steve, and the doctor allowed him to come into the room, while my mom stayed in the waiting room.

Next, the doctor began to remove the blood-soaked bandage covering the enormous wound on my head. Then, like flipping a flap-jack, the doctor nonchalantly lifted my scalp completely from my head, and exposed a large portion of my skull. And that's when Steve passed out onto the floor. The doctor didn't even glance over his way.

While a nurse tended to Steve, the doctor shaved my head along the outer edges of the wound where he intended to complete the process of suturing it up. Finally, picking up a small scrub brush, the kind we used in our home to clean our fingernails, the doctor looked me in the eye and said, "Are you ready? Okay, here we go."

He began by scrubbing my exposed skull with a cleansing solution to remove hair, chips of glass, dirt and other debris. By now, Steve was awake again, and sitting next to me in a chair, holding my hand, all the while staring at the floor. A nurse who seemed to be a motherly type of woman, probably in her late thirties, was holding my other hand, playing the cheerleader, constantly encouraging me and telling me what a great job I was doing contending with the tortuous procedure. A priest had been called in to give last rites, and was positioned behind the doctor near the wall, looking down and most probably deep in prayer.

Turns out, I'd need that prayer. One afternoon, days after the procedure, the neurosurgeon came into my hospital room to check on me. The swelling in my head was giving me terrible headaches, so the doctor inserted a tube in my head to allow the build-up of fluid to drain.

"So, you go to college," he said, looking over my files.

"Yes."

"And I see here that you play football."

"Yeah. But I'm going to miss next season because of bad grades," I explained. "Still, I expect to be eligible by the spring."

He shifted in his chair.

"Mike, we have a problem," he said. "You can't go back to school. Your head injury has affected your short-term memory, and I don't even want you to try to remember anything."

I took a deep breath as he continued.

"Furthermore, you're demonstrating signs of epilepsy. You were treated for it with medication as a child and, up until now, you've been very fortunate that none of the concussions from football have made it reoccur. However, as a result of your head trauma, we are seeing signs of it again."

"So what does that mean, doctor?"

"It means that in no uncertain terms, your gridiron days are over."

I said nothing. Tears welled up in my eyes.

"You know, Mike, most people wouldn't have survived that accident. You're lucky to be alive."

Maybe in his eyes I was lucky, but from where I was lying, alive was a very unpleasant place to be.

***

It hadn't even been three years since I was chasing down quarterbacks and stuffing fullbacks at the line of scrimmage at college. Now, like my head, my dream to play in the NFL had been scalped and laid dead like road kill on the backstreets of Manasquan. Watching the Rams saunter through the bar, I couldn't help but wonder if I could have ever been a professional athlete.

When I was a sophomore linebacker at Southern Connecticut State College, we played a game in Boston against Northeastern University.

That day, the Huskies' tight end, Dan Ross, who wound up playing for the Cincinnati Bengals, was being scouted in the torrential rain. A local newspaper reported my efforts on the field, which included a blocked punt for a twenty-four yard return that my team converted to a touchdown. Plus, I had ten unassisted tackles. My efforts would earn me a spot on the All Eastern College Athletic Conference defensive team.

As I walked off of the field after the game, I crossed paths with the scout who was wearing a Washington Redskins jacket.

"Good game, Forty-seven," he told me.

"Thanks," I answered, rain pelting on my helmet.

"You're a sophomore, right? You should have a great career ahead of you. I'll be watching."

It was maybe a five or ten-second interaction, tops, but I was thrilled about it. I mean, I'd caught the eye of a professional scout! That was enough to prove to myself that maybe someday, I could play pro. Yet three years later, here I sat, a has-been, strung out on drugs and facing prison time. All of my glory day memories were nothing but a bunch of what-ifs. In the year leading up to the trial, I had lost nearly forty pounds, thanks to all the cocaine, meth, and hard liquor I had pumped into my body. Instead of preparing to battle the Los Angeles Rams, I was bracing for a legal fight with the State of New Jersey in just two more days.

I lit a cigarette and stared into the drink in front of me, wondering whether or not J.D. was ever coming back from his meeting with Johnny. It was about eleven p.m. by now, and I was nearly out of coke. And I never liked being without it. I'd start jonesing for the drug before it was even gone.

Me and coke were like Linus and his security blanket from "Peanuts." I had an emotional attachment to the drug. Without it, my behavior would become unpredictable (as opposed to how wonderfully predictable it was while I was using), and something as simple as disagreeing with me could turn violent quickly. Also, I didn't like the feeling of fatigue that came when the high from the drug wore off.

All of a sudden, I was startled by someone tapping me on my back. It was the guy who'd met us out in front of the restaurant the night before, the guy who asked, "Who's the kid?" I like to call him Tiny. There was no mistaking him. He was grossly obese, he had gold on every finger, gold around his neck. Everywhere I looked on him was gold. I think gold did for Tiny what spinach does for Popeye. He caught his breath and passed along a message:

"Mikey, J.D. wants you to meet him under the bridge," he said, as if he thought I knew what he was talking about.

"What bridge?"

He referred to a bridge down the street.

"J.D. told me to meet him *here*," I countered.

"Well, there's been a change in plans, and now you're gonna meet him down the street under the bridge. Now let's go."

Vinny's murder, the comments the cops made to me about my loyalties, the coke, it all made me so paranoid, I was frozen in my seat. I tried to stall.

"I don't know no bridge," I said.

"Come with me. I'll show you outside."

But I stayed on my bar stool, terrified. There was no way I wanted to go outside with him. I mean, why would J.D. want to meet me under a dark bridge in the middle of a swamp when he told me he would come get me when he was done meeting with Johnny? Maybe something happened to J.D.? Soon, I was certain J.D. got whacked. This was the first time something like this had ever happened to me. I was beginning to think this was it. This was the night I was going to die.

"Come on, let's go," Tiny demanded, and he waved his hand in a gesture for me to move out of the seat.

I downed what was left of my drink, threw some singles down onto the bar, and headed out of the hotel lounge. Watching the big man's every move, I kept my distance as I walked to my car. Even in the condition I was in, Tiny would have had to shoot me, because there was no way he could catch me on foot.

"Are you okay? You don't look so good." He pointed to the bridge and said, "You see the bridge over there? That's where you're gonna meet J.D."

I got into my car, and as I started it up, I looked back to see where Tiny was. He was standing outside of his car, watching me. When he saw me look back, he began gesturing with his hand as if shooing a fly.

"Go! Get outta here."

As I drove toward the bridge, I tried to sort out the desperate thoughts racing through my mind. *"Was I about to get whacked?"* Then again, if I didn't go to the bridge and there was no intention of killing me, I was going to give someone a reason to want to kill me.

I thought about the bonds I had made with J.D., his family, and his friends, and how we were like family. And yet, I also thought how many times I had laughed and joked with J.D. since our arrest and simultaneously wondered, *"Would this man have me killed?"* Now I was worried that he may be dead.

"You're the only one left alive who can talk," Nicky Newark had reminded me. After Vinny's murder, I was suspect of anyone and everyone who came near me.

On the outside, I'd always played the tough guy. My attitude said, "I can do time standin' on my head." But on the inside, I was terrified. I tried to drown my fear of being murdered with near-lethal amounts of drugs and alcohol. No matter how many ways I considered the question,

"Why would they want to murder me?" I always came back to the same conclusion: *"Why* wouldn't *they want to murder me?"*

As I drove to the bridge that night, I felt like a lamb on the way to the slaughterhouse. The dirt road leading to the underside of the bridge was so dark that if anything were to happen to me, I thought, *"Even the rats won't find me back here."* The tall reed grass that grows in the marshlands of the Meadowlands now eclipsed from sight my view of the hotel and Giant Stadium. When I got there, no one was under the bridge, so I stopped my car and sat in darkness, waiting for J.D. to arrive, the car in drive, with one foot on the gas and one foot on the brake.

"I can't believe I am even sitting here," I thought. *"What the heck is wrong with me?"*

Then, off in the distance, car lights appeared in my rear-view mirror. I toyed with the idea of just driving away, but what excuse could I give for doing that?

The car – a black limousine, its tinted windows up – pulled up next to me, and I thought, *"This is it."* I could feel my heart pounding out of my chest and a lump in my throat. I broke out in cold sweats, and the hair on my neck stood up. I waited for what I was certain would be the sound of gunshots and glass breaking.

After what felt like an eternity, the windows on the limo began to open. I watched for any sign of a weapon, ready to hit the gas hard. As the windows lowered, I heard loud screams calling out my name.

"Hey Mikey!" The limo was full of people, and everybody in it was partying.

I pounded the steering wheel several times and started yelling, "Are you kidding me? Unbelievable!"

Of course, J.D. didn't know I'd thought I was getting whacked, so he didn't know what I was so uptight about. He cautioned, "Oh, show a little more respect! What's wrong with you anyway? Next time we'll bring you with us."

With that, the limo pulled away.

All this time I was thinking I was going to die, and that J.D. was already dead, and it turns out he was out partying like an eighteen year-old after his prom.

CHAPTER 4

†

Eating the Fruit of My Ways

*"Because they hated knowledge and did not choose the fear
of the Lord, would have none of my counsel and despised all my
reproof, therefore they shall eat the fruit of their way, and have
their fill of their own devices." (Proverbs 1:29-31)*

The newspapers that the jurors were carrying into court for our trial didn't have anything nice to say about me and J.D. The *New York Post's* article, "Key Witness Slain in Loanshark Case," speculated about Vinny's murder being a contract hit. It said that Vinny was going to be a key witness in the case of two men who had shaken him down over a usurious loan, and named J.D. and me as those two men.

Two days before our trial began, the prosecutor told reporters for the *Newark Star Ledger*, the most widely read paper in New Jersey, "All the circumstances are such that it would be the most remote coincidence if there were not a relation between the upcoming trial and this murder." What juror is not going to be swayed into thinking J.D. and I had whacked Vinny after reading that?

When we appeared before the judge, our attorneys filed a motion to dismiss the case, because the State was absent their key witness. To the best of my recollection, there had never been a precedent set for such a case, because this trial would be the first of its kind – that is, a trial that had tape-recorded conversations of an unavailable witness as its exclusive State's evidence. If the judge allowed the tapes in as evidence, we believed that any jury picked would have no alternative other than to find us guilty.

We also knew, if the judge dismissed the tapes as evidence, there could be no trial because there would be no evidence.

Our attorneys argued that the admission of "the recorded tapes were the sum and substance of the State's evidence, and without the ability to confront and challenge the testimony of the State's sole witness, Vinny, we would not receive a fair trial." Everything the State presented in the form of testimony would be hearsay.

Plus, all of this publicity wasn't helping matters. It seemed like every time we turned around, there was another article in the paper linking us to Vinny's murder. Our attorneys pointed to the headline in the *Post* as evidence that we couldn't receive a fair trial in Newark.

When the trial started in October, we were hopeful that the judge would come to his senses and dismiss the incriminating tapes. Not a chance. The judge allowed the tapes in as evidence, but our lawyers believed the judge's decision was not made within the context of the law, so we could use it on appeal.

Once the jury was selected, the prosecutor and our attorneys gave their opening statements, and then the judge asked, "Is the State ready to proceed?"

"Yes we are."

"Then you may call your first witness." And the games began.

For me, the trial was uneventful until about the third witness was called. I didn't know him by name, but I recognized him as the guy who had handed me the phone through the glass to talk to Vinny the day I got arrested. It turned out that this guy had identified me to Nicky Newark and the prosecutor during discovery. But he wouldn't go there now.

When the prosecutor asked him to point me out in court, he refused.

"When you handed the phone out the window, what happened to the phone, Mr. Vitale?"

"The person took the phone," he replied.

"Was that person who took the phone male or female?"

But the witness didn't fall for the trick question, "Judging by the voice, I would have to say a male."

"At some point and time, did you get the phone back?" the prosecutor probed.

"Yes, sir."

"How did you get the phone back, Mr. Vitale?"

"I heard it drop on the counter."

It seemed that Vinny's murder had caused this witness to rethink what he had or hadn't seen that day.

"I'll go to jail before I testify in this case and point him out," he said.

When it was my lawyer's turn to examine the witness, he pointed at me and asked, "Have you ever seen my client before?"

"No, sir."

"No further questions," my lawyer said.

I had caused another man to fear for his life, and in some twisted way, it confirmed that I was, in fact, a tough guy.

The day ended with the next witness doing the same thing – refusing to point me out. Yeah, you heard me. A tough guy.

The following morning I noticed a couple of jurors heading into the jury room with newspapers under their arms. J.D. talked to his lawyer about it right away.

When we went into the courtroom that morning, J.D.'s attorney approached the judge before the jurors came back in, and pointed out that there was an article in the *Star Ledger* that said our trial had been postponed when the main witness was shot and killed.

He explained that some of the jurors had been seen walking into the jury room with newspapers. But the judge decided that it didn't matter, because in his experience, jurors are committed to reaching a verdict based on what they see and hear in the courtroom. And with that, he dismissed what felt to us like a potentially big problem.

The State called their next witness, and as it turned out, I knew this witness very well. They called my girlfriend, Lucy, to take the stand and testify against me and her father. The State had served her with a subpoena just days before the trial, and there was no way around it. She had to take the stand. It was going to be a long, long, day for Lucy.

At times she didn't cooperate with the prosecutor.

"What did you see Michael doing to the man he was talking with?" asked the prosecutor.

"I don't know. I was looking down." Lucy answered.

The prosecutor handed her a document.

"Now I show you what has been marked S-20 for identification. I'll ask you to take a look at it and tell me if you've ever seen it before."

"Yes," Lucy answered,

"And tell me what it is?"

"It's my statement," Lucy answered in a soft voice.

"I couldn't hear you. Can you keep your voice up? What is that document?"

Gently clearing her throat, Lucy answered, "It's my statement."

"That's the statement you signed on October 29, 1982. Is that correct?"

"Yes."

"And in your statement, you said that you observed your boyfriend Michael Palombi do something to the man he was speaking to. Is that correct?"

"Yes."

"And so I'm going to ask again, what is it that you saw Mr. Palombi do to the man he was speaking with?"

"He hit him."

"I couldn't hear you. Could you say that louder so the jury can hear you please?"

"I saw Michael hit him."

Any time that Lucy didn't answer a question, the prosecutor kept making her read the statement that she had signed under duress and threats of being locked up. The statement, by the way, that made no mention at all of how brutally the cops had beaten me while Lucy watched. Had I listened to J.D.'s instructions, Lucy would not be on the stand.

Next to take the stand was my hero, Nicky Newark. I'm not saying I didn't commit a crime, but from the minute he took the stand, Nicky lied like a criminal. I'm sure it was all in the spirit of getting a conviction on two men he felt deserved to go to prison.

It's funny that as a criminal I had an expectation for the cops to tell the truth. But as I sat there listening to Nicky testify, I couldn't help but think back to what Johnny had said that day in the bathroom: *"The cops just use their badges and position of authority to do the same things we do."*

"When the doctor went to treat you," my lawyer asked Nicky, "I take it he asked you what happened. Is that correct?"

"Yes. There was more than one doctor looking at me," replied Nicky.

"Do you recall telling the doctor that you were a thirty-six year-old white police officer struck in the right hand by a head? Do you recall making that statement to a doctor at the College Hospital on October 29, 1982, that you were struck in the right hand by a head?"

"I didn't say that."

"Sir?"

"I don't recall saying something like that."

Nicky was about to learn how it felt to be in Lucy's seat.

"Maybe I can refresh your recollection," added my lawyer. "I am referring you to the fourth page of the document under consultation and recommendations and ask you whether that refreshes your recollection as to how you described your injury."

"I've read it."

"Does that refresh your recollection?" Reading from the document my attorney continued, "Did you tell them that you injured your hand when your hand was hit by a head?"

"I don't think I said that."

"Okay. In fact, it wasn't his head hitting your hand. It was your hand hitting his head?"

"It's on what side you're on when you're getting it (hit)."

At one point the judge turned to Nicky and warned, "Detective, there are laws as to how much force is needed when affecting an arrest."

My attorney had accomplished what he set out to do with Nicky. He made him look like a fool on the stand and the bonus was, the judge's spontaneous reprimand of Nicky seemed to help my cause.

"I have no further questions for this witness."

Next to take the stand was J.D., and trust me, the prosecutor could hardly wait to get his turn with him but he was going to have to wait while J.D. spent the day answering questions asked by his own attorney. We knew the prosecutor was going to mount his assault against J.D. by using the self-incriminating recorded conversations. The strategy of J.D.'s attorney was to diminish the impact the tapes would have on the jury by talking about the content of those conversations before the prosecutor did.

"What did you mean when you told Vinny he was going to get a couple of broken arms?" J.D.'s attorney asked.

"That's just an expression I use. I didn't really mean anything by it."

"What about when you told Vinny he was gonna get a beating?"

"Again," J.D. responded, "it's just an expression. An idle threat."

After spending a day and a half trying to neutralize what would be the prosecution's attack, the prosecutor was called to cross examine J.D. He started off slow, pointing out for the jury J.D.'s two prior and separate criminal convictions for distribution of cocaine and for possession of stolen property. Then Sherlock began his real assault.

"You testified yesterday and today that you use a lot of expressions. Do you remember saying that?"

"Yes," J.D. answered.

"Do you use those expressions on your wife?"

"I object, your honor!" his lawyer said.

"Do you use those expressions on anyone else?"

"Friends, my son. My daughter," J.D. remarked.

"How many times have you told your friends and your daughter, 'You're going to get a couple of broken arms?'"

Without hesitation J.D. answered, "A number of times."

"How many times do you tell your friends, 'You got to get a beating? That's what it's all about?'"

"Used it on my son."

"Yeah, and, 'Enough to save your life?' How many times you tell your friends, 'Enough to save your life?'"

"Well, maybe not in the same context."

Line, by line, by line, the prosecutor went through every threat J.D. had made to Vinny on the phone. Then the prosecutor began his mission to link me and J.D. together for the conspiracy charge.

"When you said, 'Be looking for my friend,' you meant Michael Palombi, didn't you?"

"Yeah."

"Isn't it a fact you were sending Michael Palombi up there to administer a beating because you didn't get your money?"

"No, sir."

"Isn't it a fact the way the game was going to be played now, he had to get a beating first before he would continue paying the money?"

"Not necessarily."

"But you knew Michael Palombi was going to hurt Vinny?"

"I don't know anything. I can't say what Michael Palombi was gonna do."

"When you tell Vinny to 'Give him the eight hundred and tell him to call me, okay? Tell him to call me before he does anything to you,' did you make that statement?"

"Yes, sir."

"And you made that statement because you didn't want Michael Palombi to do anything to Vinny because you were going to get your money, right?"

"Michael Palombi had nothing to do with me on this matter," J.D. responded.

After hours of relentless interrogation, the prosecutor indicated that he had no further questions. As for me, I never took the stand during the trial. I was a young kid and probably no match for a seasoned prosecutor who could have easily had me contradict J.D.'s testimony. We determined that we would take our chances without me taking the stand.

On the morning of October 20, 1983, our attorneys and the prosecutor gave their summations to the jury. Before the jury began deliberating, the judge instructed the jury as to the principles of law and how those principles applied to our case. Upon completing his instructions to the jury, the judge sent them to lunch escorted by an officer of the court.

When the jurors returned from lunch, one of them asked the officer who'd escorted them there, "How long do we have to deliberate before there's a mistrial?"

Apparently, even the jury was afraid of me. But I couldn't care less. If that's what it takes to get a mistrial, then so be it.

While the jury deliberated, if I wasn't in the hallway, I was in the bathroom doing blow or sneaking a cigarette. Interestingly enough, the sign in the men's room said I couldn't smoke, but it didn't say a word about doing coke.

The longer it took the jury to make a decision, the better it was for us, so I didn't mind all the sitting and waiting. After what that cop had said about the juror's question, I was getting hopeful for a mistrial.

At 6:30 that evening, six hours after the jury had begun deliberating, they had not reached a verdict. The judge gave them the option to keep going or to return in the morning, and the jury decided to return in the morning.

That evening I spent at home with Lucy.

"Listen Lucy," I said. "There's a good chance I'm gonna get convicted tomorrow. The lawyer says I ain't gonna do no time, but with Vinny getting murdered and all, your dad thinks we're in big trouble. Nobody's gonna believe we didn't do it. He thinks we'll get the max."

"That's not gonna happen because you're a good person and you've never been in trouble before," Lucy cried. "I know my dad isn't innocent. But you did nothing wrong."

"Lucy, I did do something wrong, and you better prepare yourself for the worse."

"I don't want to hear this. You did nothing wrong. I love you and I'm never gonna leave."

I told Lucy that if I went to prison, she should leave me, because it would be too difficult to carry on our relationship while I was in prison. Looking back, I'm not so sure what she ever saw in me, but she refused to leave. She promised me that she would never leave me while I was in jail, and I think more than anything that night, hearing Lucy say those words meant my life mattered to someone.

The next day, it took the jury three more hours to arrive at their decision. When they activated the jury room light, I knew they'd made a decision about where I'd be spending the next few years, maybe decades, of my life. Talk about your socks goin' up and down.

"Hey Mikey," J.D. called after seeing the light go on.

When I looked his way, he tilted his head as if to say to me, "Come here." I followed him into the bathroom, which we checked for people, like we always did, and then we each lit a smoke.

I leaned against the door so no one could walk in.

"So, what do you think is gonna happen, J.D.?"

He pulled out his bag of blow.

"I think if the prosecutor has his way, they're gonna put us *under* the jail. I'm tellin' ya. That's what I think."

"If we get convicted, do you think they'll revoke our bail?"

"In a New York minute."

Sniff. Sniff.

"C'mon. Let's go get our butts handed to us."

Back in the courtroom, the judge instructed the court officer to escort the jury back in. Additional officers were summoned into the courtroom, and two stood behind J.D., and two stood behind me. The judge asked J.D. to rise, and the business of learning our fate was underway. I'd never felt so nervous in my life.

The foreman rattled off the charges and the verdicts:

Conspiracy to commit theft by extortion and criminal usury:

Guilty.

Extortion:

Guilty.

Criminal usury:

Guilty.

Terroristic threats:

Guilty.

Four charges. Four guilty verdicts.

My life was now in the hands of the jury. I had six charges, including two that J.D. wasn't even charged with. I stood numb and staring down at the table in front of me.

"Mr. Foreman, as to the defendant, Michael Palombi, Count One, charging conspiracy to commit the crimes of theft by extortion and criminal usury, how do you find?"

"Guilty," he replied. As the word "Guilty," was spoken, I noticed white flakes of cocaine falling from my nose onto the defense table in front of me.

The public announcement of my poor choices continued.

"As to Count Two charging theft by extortion, how do you find?"

"Guilty."

"As to Count Three charging criminal usury, how do you find?"

"Not Guilty."

I couldn't believe it. I was found not guilty of something!

"As to Count Four charging robbery, how do you find?"

"Not guilty."

Again, a not guilty. At this point I was two for four. "*Maybe there's still hope*," I thought.

"As to Count Five charging terroristic threats, how do you find?"

"Guilty."

So much for hope.

"As to Count Six charging aggravated assault on a law enforcement officer?"

"Not guilty."

King Solomon could not have expressed it any better, the proverb that speaks to the kind of choices that had put me in that lowest of low moments in my life: *"There is a way that seems right to a man, but its end is the way to death."* (Proverbs 16:25)

The judge thanked and dismissed the jurors. Then the attorneys and the prosecutor argued about the revocation of our bail. Having been found guilty, we were no longer presumed innocent, and in the State's eyes, there was a greater propensity for us to flee. It was at this point, the judge decided to revoke our bail pending sentencing, and the officers who had been standing behind us immediately took us into custody.

As the officers cuffed me and began to escort me out of the courtroom, my sister Colleen walked up to an officer and asked if she could give me a very small version of the New Testament. The officer allowed it, and Colleen put it in my hands. She had tried on many occasions to talk to me about God and giving my life to the Lord, whatever the heck that meant.

The fact of the matter was, I just didn't believe in God. I didn't buy any of that God stuff. Back in the day, I would get stoned in front of the TV, and while clicking around the channels, I'd sometimes come across evangelists talking about how God could change my life. After the preaching and all of the biblical encouragement, they would turn on the tears and the next thing you know, they were asking for money.

"Are you kidding me? These people must have lost their minds!" I thought. I just couldn't believe that so many people could be scammed into sending money to these television preachers. The truth is, I wanted nothing to do with preachers, religion, or God, and I certainly wasn't giving them my money. Say what you want about me, but I never scammed anyone. I made agreements with no hidden agendas. If you didn't keep your end of the deal, then there was a problem. It's that simple.

With the New Testament in my hand, I was escorted into a holding cell outside of the courtroom with J.D.

"If you got anything on you, you can give it to me now," the officer said.

J.D. and I told him that we had nothing on us, and so, the officer placed us side by side in individual holding cells. The judge allowed our families to come and say goodbye. I can still see my mother standing there looking at me, sad, like I was an animal in a cage.

"Take it one day at a time," she said. I just sat there on the hard steel chair looking down at the floor.

Big shot.

Cool kid.

Tough guy.

That quality of achievement I was feeling earlier, well, it was diminishing real quick. Who's the tough guy now?

"I'm sorry it has to be this way, Michael," my mother continued.

"Mrs. Palombi," J.D. interrupted. "I just want to say, I'm sorry."

"I know you are, J.D. I'm sorry too," my mother told him.

After that, the doors closed and our families were gone. My mother was not fond of J.D., but his apology acknowledged to her that he was aware he was the reason I was sitting in the cell next to him. We were silent for a while, when J.D. had a thought.

"For my money, I shoulda wore jeans."

"What did you say?" I asked.

"For my money, I shoulda wore jeans."

I'm thinking, *"Are you kidding me?"*

"That's great, J.D. We just got sent to jail for who knows how long and your great epiphany is you shoulda wore jeans?"

"I knew wearing a suit wouldn't make a difference today."

I didn't even respond. Soon, I heard a loud sniffing sound coming from J.D.'s cell. Snniifff! Snniff!

"What are you doing, J.D.?"

"What do you think I'm doin'?"

"I thought you flushed it down the toilet."

"What are you, crazy? Do you know how much this stuff costs?"

That was the thing about J.D., nothing fazed him. So, together we continued to snort the remainder of the coke while waiting to go to Intake.

An elevator door opened in our holding area, and officers removed us from our cells, placed us on the elevator, and took us down to a tunnel connecting the courthouse to the jail. As we approached the other end of the tunnel, I could feel reality setting in. The first thing I noticed was the smell. Prison has a smell about it and when it doesn't smell like human waste, it smells like industrial strength cleaning chemicals.

Next, I could hear the sound of inmate voices echoing off the concrete walls, and the sounds of buzzers buzzing and steel doors opening and closing.

It was at Intake that J.D. and I said goodbye. We knew we would be going our separate ways when we left that room, and we didn't know if or when we would see each other again. But we knew there was no way that the jail would allow us to lock in together.

In the midst of all that had happened, and despite whatever I might have thought at the time, I cared a lot about J.D. Yeah, I know I had worried whether or not he would whack me. But the fact is, at the end of the day he didn't whack me, and I was going to miss him.

J.D. affectionately patted me on the cheek and said, "You've been like a son to me." It took every bit of strength I had not to cry as we parted. His words meant a lot to me, because really, I didn't feel like a son to my own father. Even though I was going to prison, and even though J.D. was the cause, I felt loved by J.D. As tough as he was, he had a way about him that let me know he cared about me. And while my father said he cared about me a thousand times in words, he said he *didn't* care a thousand times by his actions. And the action that spoke louder than words was his discipline.

***

There were times that my father would hit me with whatever was in his hand. A carpenter's level, a concertina he played, a trowel full of spackle. Then there were the times when he would say, "Go to your room. I'll be up in a minute."

I could hear him move out of his chair and begin his ascent up the stairs. Stair by stair, I became more and more frightened as I listened for the unmistakable sound of his belt being removed. There was no other sound like that. By the time he opened the door to my room, the belt was positioned in his right hand, ready to deliver the beating he intended to give me. There I'd sit with my crew cut, wearing short pants and a T-shirt. I was just a little boy, perhaps five or six years-old.

"Pull your pants down and bend over the bed!" he would order. As I bent over the bed and braced myself for the beating, my father gave his final instructions: "I don't want to hear a sound, and if I do, you're gonna get it worse!"

I don't understand how my father thought such a discipline could be in the best interest of his child, but he should have been careful what he wished for. After the age of eight, I never cried for him again. As much as he said he didn't want to hear a sound from me, I figured out that it really bothered him that I didn't respond to his physical discipline. After that, it didn't matter what he did to me. I refused to give him the satisfaction of making a sound or shedding a tear.

Just a couple of years before my father passed away, he told me that he had been really concerned about me as a child. When I asked him why, he said, "Because you never showed any emotion."

I can still recall those beatings as if they happened yesterday. The sounds of my father's belt hitting my flesh while he simultaneously yelled at me for whatever silly thing it was that I had done wrong, like arguing with my brothers or sister, or a bad report from my mother when he came home from work at the end of the day. I got hit for nothing more than being a child.

After those beatings, I'd go into the bathroom to assess the damage. I would stand there with my back to the mirror and my pants dropped low beholding the images of huge welts on my body left by my father's leather belt. I was amazed at how many different colors my skin could turn from being hit.

He was supposed to love me, but the bruises and welts on my body spoke a much different message. The welts said betrayal. They said breach of trust. In the privacy of the bathroom, I would cry into a towel so he couldn't hear me, though not from the pain from the beating. I cried because the beatings he gave made me feel painfully unloved by him.

***

"Strip down out of your street clothes," ordered the officer. "Put these on." He handed me two pairs of white boxer shorts, a gold-colored jumpsuit, some plastic shower shoes, and bedding. Anything else I required, I would need to barter with cigarettes or wait until commissary the following Tuesday.

When the buzzer sounded, the steel gate to an elevator opened, and an officer escorted me up to my tier with my personal belongings. Along the way, I could hear the muffled sounds of inmates yelling through the steel elevator compartment.

Looking down at the floor, I said in a low voice, "Good times."

The officer offered, sarcastically, "Yeah, good times alright."

When the elevator stopped at my tier and the door opened, the noise coming from the day room was as loud as at any night club I had ever been in. The cop swung open the steel mesh gate separating me from him and allowed me access to the cell block.

The officer belted out to his fellow officers, "Fresh meat!"

As the elevator door closed behind me, an officer signaled me over with his hand.

"You're in cell number seven hundred-thirty. Go wait by the gate." As I waited for it to open, I could see down the long dimly lit tier. The gate opened and instantly, the inmates hanging around turned to look.

It was apparent as I began to head down the tier that there wasn't going to be a warm and fuzzy reception. From the looks of it, I was the only ray of sunshine up there and the way these guys were looking at me, I felt like an intruder.

"Can I get by?" I asked, drawing hard stares from the men I had asked to move. Most of the guys, if not *all* of them, were missing at least some of their teeth and more than likely, it wasn't because they didn't brush them regularly.

No, judging by the hostile tone of this place, I just knew it. "*There's no way I am leaving here with all of my teeth.*"

As I made my way to my cell, I could smell the aroma of jailhouse incense, made from dried orange peels to cover the smell of pot and other odors. But it wasn't enough to mask the smell of human waste coming from a nearby cell.

When I got to cell seven-thirty, I walked in and laid my belongings on the steel bunk. It didn't take long to survey my new home, as I could stretch my hands out and touch the steel walls to either side of me. Thankfully, I didn't have to share my cell with anyone.

On the wall opposite my bunk was the most amazing drawing of Diana Ross and the Supremes I had ever seen. The life-like portrait was in black and shades of black, and took up nearly the entire side wall of the cell, which was about eight-feet long by six-and-a-half, seven-feet high. It looked like it had just been completed, and I kind of liked it. I thought, "*How does a guy with that much talent wind up in a place like this?*" Other than that, the Essex County Jail was just the way I'd left it. Ah, home, sweet home.

I set up my bed by unrolling a musty mattress that was approximately two-and-a-half inches thick. I added a pillow, a sheet, and a wool blanket, and I'd finished making my bed. Apart from going to chow, I pretty much just hung out in my cell. The one other white guy on the tier stopped by to meet me, like the welcoming committee for the jail's smallest club. He gave me the low-down about the cliques on the tier, and strongly suggested that I carry a shank, a jailhouse knife. He said he could make me one for a carton of cigarettes, but I declined his offer. Why take the chance of getting caught with a weapon and catching another charge?

It was getting late, and the lights went out. Each cell, however, had a light that could be turned on or off. I couldn't sleep, so I thought maybe I would read a little of that New Testament that my sister had given me.

I flicked on the light and suddenly, I saw hundreds, if not thousands, of cockroaches scamper into the smallest crevices of the steel walls. It happened so fast, I paused to think, "*Did I just see what I think I saw?*"

I turned the light off and waited for about a minute before turning it back on. When I did, there were roaches racing around my cell. On the one hand, I was amazed at how fast they disappeared into the walls, but on the other hand, I wasn't fond of sharing my cell with thousands of roaches. Funny though, you get used to a lot of things in jail that you're not fond of. In the meantime, it gave me something to do when I got lonely and bored: Lights on. Lights off.

Having experienced a plague of sorts, I thought this would be an excellent time to read the New Testament. I didn't see anything in it that really jumped out at me, but I figured I would give it a shot. From that point on, I made it my business to read a little from the New Testament every day. What did I have to lose?

I usually followed up my reading with a short prayer that was intended to test the existence of God in a deal where I'd swear to Him, "I'll never do it again" if He could just get me out of this one. Amen! I didn't really believe anyone was listening anyhow.

A month after I was convicted, I'd find out how long I would have to share a cell with a thousand cockroaches. I was heading over to the courthouse to stand before the judge for sentencing.

I figured that at the very least, I would get to see Lucy and our families in court. It's what we call in prison "an outing." I was nervous, but my lawyer was still confident that I would not get a lot of time, if any at all. Like he'd said, I had no prior criminal history. Certainly, he believed the judge would be hard-pressed to justify serving me with any kind of significant time.

The sentencing was going to be done the way everything else had been done. J.D. and I would be together in the courtroom, and he would receive his sentence first.

J.D. had a lot to be concerned about. He was now forty-two years-old and a three-time offender with all of his convictions happening within a ten-year time frame. That combination provided a legal basis for the prosecutor to make an application to the court to request that the sentencing judge impose upon J.D. an extended term of imprisonment.

J.D. was prepared for the fact that he may receive a ten-year prison sentence and would have to serve five of the ten years behind bars. However, if the judge found in favor of the prosecutor's application to impose an extended term, then J.D. would automatically receive double the amount of time he was sentenced to.

All of the detectives who were part of the sting came into the courtroom for the sentencing. However, there was no one there from Vinny's family that I was aware of.

The judge cited J.D.'s prior conviction, the tapes and his failure to deny allegations made by Vinny and decided he was at risk to commit another crime. The judge concluded, "There appears to be no rehabilitation possible."

"Will the defendant please rise."

Sitting there was nothing short of frightening. I remained seated in handcuffs while J.D. stood. As officers of the court surrounded J.D., the judge imposed sentencing:

"It is therefore, ordered and adjudged that the defendant be and is sentenced for Count Two, committed to the custody of the Commissioner of the Department of Corrections for the term of fifteen years and until released in accordance with law, serve seven-and-one-half years before parole eligibility.

"Count Three, committed to the custody of the Commissioner of the Department of Corrections for the term of seven years and until released in accordance with law, serve two-and-one-half years before parole eligibility. This term to be run consecutive to the sentence imposed on Count Two."

The two other counts were either merged or run concurrent with time he had already been sentenced to.

In all, J.D. was sentenced to twenty-two years in prison, and had to serve a minimum of ten years of hard time before he would become eligible for parole. His wife, his sister, and Lucy sat crying behind us.

By the time he'd come home from prison, his young children would be young men and women, and who knows the toll this would take on his marriage? After his sentencing was completed, an officer quickly removed J.D. from the court. There were no hugs and no goodbyes. That's the difference between the movies and real life. The family had no closure. They watched in tears as their husband and father was led away in shackles. I could see the look of satisfaction on the faces of the cops and the prosecutor assigned to our case. From where they were standing, this was closure for Vinny's family.

The detectives didn't even stay in the courtroom to see me sentenced, and their departure spoke volumes to me. It was never about me. It was only about J.D., but since I was there, they might as well take it. Now it was my turn.

"Will the defendant please rise?" the judge said. Officers of the court stood behind me. "Mr. Palombi, do you have anything you would like to say to the court before I impose my sentence?"

"I just want to say that I am sorry for my behavior and I know that this is not how I want to spend my life. I would ask that your honor give me another chance."

After my statement to the court, my attorney requested that the judge consider sending me to a youth correctional facility rather than to prison, since at the age of twenty-three, I was still an eligible offender.

But the judge said that prison was in order for a person convicted of a first or second-degree crime. He added that the nature of my offenses likely meant I was involved in organized crime. What's more, he felt I would be a bad influence on youthful offenders, and so a more appropriate placement would be in a state prison.

"It is therefore ordered and adjudged that the defendant be and is sentenced," the judge said. "Count Number Two, Second Degree Theft by Extortion, I commit you to the custody of the Commissioner of the Department of Corrections for the term of seven years and until released in accordance with law…serve three years before parole eligibility. For Count Number Five, Third Degree Terroristic Threats, I commit you to the custody of the Commissioner of the Department of Corrections for the term of four years and until released in accordance with law … serve two years before parole eligibility, concurrent with sentence imposed on Count Number Two."

I noticed that no one was crying for me.

I couldn't believe what had just happened. "*There must be some kind of mistake,*" I thought. Tugging on my lawyer's suit jacket like a kid trying to get his father's attention. I asked, "How much of this time do I have to do?"

"Right now you have to serve at least three years," he explained, and my heart sank.

"What? You said that I wouldn't serve more than six months!"

"I know, I know. We're going to have to appeal it."

Until then, I'd have to appeal to my mother. I turned to her in court, and asked her to visit me before she left the jail.

They took me from the court and brought me back to a holding cell, where I waited for my mother's phone visit. When she arrived, I tried to convince her, "We could post bail pending the appeal, and I could get out while we fight this thing. This is *wrong.*"

My mother looked me right in the eye through the glass partition and without hesitation said, "I don't have that kind of money, Michael. Now go serve your time!"

As I stared at her through the visiting booth glass, I thought, *"Did she just tell me to go serve my time?"* Her words didn't register right away, but when they did, it felt like a punch in the face, but that wasn't anything new.

***

I was swimming in our above-ground pool with my brother the summer I was five. My older brother thought it would be fun to take one of those hard plastic floating devices called a sea sled and stand on it, balancing on it to keep it at the bottom of the pool. When he stepped off of the sled, it shot up out of the water like a rocket, hitting me right above my right eye. I reached for my forehead, and when I pulled my hands down, they were covered in blood. Soon, the water started turning red as the blood poured from the cut above my eye. I climbed out of the pool and ran to my mother, crying. When I got to her, blood dripping down my face, she grabbed me by both shoulders and began shaking me hard.

"Stop crying like a baby! Now stop it! Boys don't cry!" To my mother, crying and being weak went hand-in-hand.

***

Apparently, asking for bail was no different from crying. She wanted me to stop it, and stop it now! I stood up in the visiting booth with the phone down by my side and screamed at her through the glass.

"What do you mean, 'Go serve your time?' You act like he just sent me to my room for the weekend!"

My mother gave me a look that said, *"Is this really how you're gonna act?"* which, of course, served to make me even more angry. I used every combination of profanities imaginable, and smashed the phone down on the receiver before I stormed out of the visiting booth, passing an inmate who was handing out lunch, which was, essentially, a slice of American cheese between two slices of stale bread. I tried to ignore him, but he kept asking me if I wanted a cheese sandwich. Finally I turned around and yelled, "WHAAAAT?"

"Do you want a cheese sandwich?"

I snatched the sandwich out of his hands, smooshed it up in a ball, and whipped it onto the floor.

It was clear to me that I had been sentenced for a crime I had nothing to do with. The judge thought I was involved in Vinny's murder, and he was going to make me do the time without proof of the crime.

When I got back to my cell, I saw the New Testament on the sink, and I became even more fired up. I picked up the Bible and slammed it right into the toilet. As I continually flushed the toilet, I confessed out loud:

"This Bible stuff is bull!" Flush.

"This doesn't work!" Flush.

"I read this book and prayed for four weeks, and for what? So I could end up with seven years instead of six months?" Flush, flush.

"I knew there was no such thing as God!" Flush.

"And if there is a God and that's His idea of abundantly more, I don't want it!" Flush, flush, flush.

Nobody dared to come near me. In the midst of all of that flushing and cussing, the New Testament clogged up my toilet, its pages soaked with stale toilet water and the leather cover ruined. In fact, the toilet stayed clogged up clear until the day I left the Essex County Jail. God sure has a righteous sense of humor.

Sentencing day had been a bad day all around, but the fun wasn't over yet – there was one more surprise. One of the Correction Officers (CO's) called my name.

"Palombi!"

"What's up?" I asked.

"You got a legal visit," he said.

I wasn't expecting anyone because my sentencing had been completed, and my attorney had told me he would talk to me in a few days. Let's face it. My mother wasn't coming to visit any time soon. Who could it be?

The cops took me to a room downstairs, and when the door opened, I saw the prosecutor, standing there with a victory smile on his face.

"Ya know, you don't have to spend a day in jail," he told me. "You can go home right now. All you have to do is tell me what I want to know about J.D."

I wanted to knock his bright shiny white Chiclet teeth right out of his mouth. To him, my life was like a game piece he was moving around the Monopoly board. But he wasn't looking to trade properties; he was looking to trade a life for a life. His offer was like trying to give me Baltic Avenue in return for Boardwalk. I stared at him like I was trying to burn holes into him with my eyes. What did he think, I came in yesterday's mail? Then, in the spirit of J.D., I told him, "You can pound salt! I have nothing to say to you."

I turned and told the C.O. to get me out of there and bring me back to my cell.

"Well, you can go back to jail then!" the prosecutor decided.

That evening, I was lying in my cell, considering all that had happened that day.

"*If I live, what am I gonna do with the next three years?*" I wondered. The answer was easy.

"*I'm gonna do what I always do. I'm gonna stay high and, if I have my way, I'm never even gonna remember I was here.*"

*Happy-go-lucky
Mike at 5 years old*

*By nine, all that is
missing is the
prison number*

*Me and my father
my first year of
football, 1969*

*Middle linebacker
at Southern
Connecticut State
College, 1979*

*At 20, my focus was
that of an athlete*

*Christmas 1983 with Mom
At 23, a life of addiction
destroyed the athlete
and devoured 20% of my
body weight*

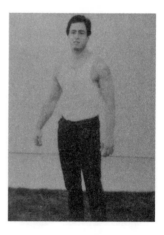

*By 25, my focus was
now on the Lord and
the beginnings of
restoration is evident*

PART TWO

Salvation is Calling

CHAPTER 5

†

Pride vs. Surrender

"I was ready to be sought by those who did not ask for me;
I was ready to be found by those who did not seek me."
(Isaiah 65:1)

I was down about thirty cigarettes when the bell rang for "count," otherwise known as the inmate roll call.

I reached into my jumpsuit pocket and tried to hand Lenny the thirty cigarettes I owed him from the card game, but before I could give them to him, he pushed them back with his hand and said, "You owe me thirty *packs*, cracker, not thirty cigarettes."

I laid the cigarettes on his bunk, and as I left his cell I said, "Don't even try it, Lenny. I owe you thirty *cigarettes*."

As I made my way back to my cell, Len shouted, "You're gonna pay me, cracker!"

"You're paid all you're gettin' paid!" I told him.

Lenny had a reputation for ripping people off and trust me, he didn't care if it was your personal possessions or your manhood. About a week earlier, he and his crew had ripped off some young kid for a sweatsuit he'd received during a visit. When the kid refused to give it to them, Lenny went in and took it by force, knocking him unconscious and leaving him in his cell beaten and stabbed, with the shank sticking out of his face.

But stealing sweatsuits was nothing compared to Lenny's other jailhouse offenses. On Thanksgiving Day 1983, Lenny draped a bed sheet from the steel bars at the end of the tier nearest the officer's station to obstruct their view of the inmates they should have been overseeing. Then, while most of America was enjoying family, football, and a Thanksgiving feast, Len and his boys proceeded to take a mop handle and do unspeakable things to several men on the tier. This went on for much of the day.

I could hear men begging Lenny for mercy from what appeared to be a ritualistic form of prison hazing. Unfortunately, there's no mercy in hell, and each of the men were overcome by the group of men attacking them. Despite the victims' screams and perpetrators' cheers, the cops, like accomplices to the crimes committed that day, allowed it to happen.

There was no mistaking what I was dealing with and no reason to believe that Len and his boys wouldn't do the same exact thing to me that I had seen them do to others. But it took me a full day's labor to earn a pack of cigarettes in prison. If he thought I was gonna give him the equivalent of thirty days of wages, he had another thing coming.

After lights out, Lenny and his friends began taunting me. As I laid there in the darkness of my cell, he told me that I had until the following Tuesday to pay him. I knew for sure he meant business, because I had seen him in action, but I also knew for sure I meant business as well. I wasn't payin'!

The next morning at breakfast, I sat next to Tommy, the guy who had come into my cell the first night I was in jail and offered to make me a shank for a carton. I didn't need to explain to him what was going on because he and everybody else could hear our conversation from their cells the evening before.

"Did you reconsider my offer?" Tommy asked.

"Yeah, I did. When can you have it?" He told me he had just finished making one that he would sell to me, "but you've got to show me good faith."

I told him if I liked what I saw, I would pay him five packs now and pay the balance after the next commissary.

"What if you ain't here after the next commissary?" he asked.

"To tell you the truth, Tommy, I haven't thought that far ahead."

After breakfast, I went back to Tommy's cell to check out the shank. It was different than most of the shanks I had seen, but it would serve my purpose well. The handle was crafted from a toothbrush and the end had been melted into a very sharp point to penetrate the body. He had melted into the plastic razor blades that were positioned north, south, east, and west of the handle. Everything about this shank had bad intentions, but so did Lenny. It would be the perfect weapon. I spent the next several days mentally preparing to do what I knew I had to do.

Yet the night before the deadline was one of the worst nights of my life. In fact, throughout much of the night I was consumed with fear. I considered my options: If I didn't pay Lenny, I would be severely beaten or perhaps even killed. On the other hand, if I paid Lenny a debt I didn't owe him, I might as well send out a mass memo telling every inmate in the joint that I was a punk, and so they could abuse me at will. Finally, my last option – I could kill him. There was only one unattractive part to that choice and that was the part where I'd catch a murder rap and spend the next twenty-five years in prison. There were three options available, and every option had grave consequences.

After considering all of my choices, I determined that even dying would be better than giving in to Lenny's threats to pay. Bottom line, paying Lenny was not an option. Before I dozed off, I fantasized, *"We'll see how bad Lenny is when he's breathin' out of his stomach."*

When Tuesday morning arrived, I got out of bed and went to the day room for chow. Everyone knew what was going to take place after the movement from chow back to our cells, and as a result, the energy in the day room was tense and very quiet, like the place could blow at any moment. This wouldn't be the first or last time someone would be carried off this tier on a stretcher.

I got my breakfast and sat down to eat. Lenny and his crew sat together with their game faces on, staring hard at me from just one table away.

When I finished eating, I got up and walked right by them, answering their hard stares with a stare of my own. I wanted to demonstrate to them and everybody watching that I wasn't intimidated. Knowing what was about to unfold, however, was indeed intimidating.

After emptying my tray, I went straight back to my cell and got my shank. I had hidden it inside of a book by cutting away the middle of several pages to create a compartment where I could store the weapon. I took the shank out of the book, and placed it in my right hand as if I were holding an ice pick while chopping ice. That way, I could have a strong grip and simultaneously hide it in the sleeve of my jumpsuit.

Pretending to read, I sat on my bed waiting for Lenny and his men, and sure enough, within minutes they came into my cell. There were five of them in all: Lenny and right behind him, standing shoulder to shoulder and spanning the width of the cell, the other four men.

Clapping his hands hard and rubbing them together as he spoke, Lenny announced, "Today's pay day."

With my adrenaline pumping and my eyes wide like saucers, I stood up, holding the book in front of me to help hide the shank in my right hand.

"I told you, Lenny, I ain't givin' ya nothin'."

He started laughing at me, and then turned to his crew to say, "You hear that? He ain't givin' us nothin'!" I almost wanted to thank Lenny for turning his back and offering me up his jugular vein. There it was, right in front of me ready for the taking. I tightened my grip around the shank and thought, *"Take him out now."*

A millisecond before I was going to stab him, I heard the following words audibly spoken: *"How's it feel, tough guy?"* But none of the guys in my cell had said it. Not Lenny. Not his jamokes. Not me.

In the exact moment that I heard those words, every cell in my body was consumed by an overwhelming sense of shame.

"How's it feel, tough guy?"

Those words stopped me dead in my tracks. I studied every face in front of me, trying to figure out who was talking, but no one in front of me had spoken those words. And yet, I instantly understood their meaning:

How does it feel to be my victim?

How does it feel to be the target of the threats of others who want to hurt me?

How does it feel to experience a genuine fear of losing your life for not complying with a threat to pay money you do not owe?

Well... how's it feel, tough guy?

My eyes frantically searched beyond the men in front of me, out of the cell and onto the tier, to find who may have spoken those words. But there was no one there.

It hadn't occurred to me until that exact moment that I, the extortionist, was being extorted. The things I admired, the things I had bragged about, the very things I had given my life to, brought me to my end, and now, I found myself standing in what amounted to be a game of chess. The five of them confronting me made it clear that I was in check. It was my move, and I had better make a good one because it might be my last. It might be checkmate!

I had often times heard the saying, *"Pride comes before the fall,"* but heeding the warnings of that saying had always proved difficult for me.

The day I met Vinny in the parking lot is a perfect example of what

I'm talking about. There was nothing about sitting in that parking lot that felt right but my prideful belief that I was to be paid something I wasn't owed kept me from listening to the inner voice that was telling me to get out of Dodge. And we all know how that day turned out.

So it was with Lenny, Pride declared to me that, *"Even dying would be better than giving in to his demand to pay."* Pride assured me that if I didn't stand my ground and use force, I would become open game for other inmates as well. Pride would have even had me dismiss the words I'd heard that day, *"How's it feel, tough guy?"*

For my entire life, Pride had prevailed over how I thought, what I said and what I did. But there was one thing that Pride couldn't overcome that day in my cell: My ability to *feel*. I had felt shame, regret, and remorse for the very behaviors that just seconds before, I would have bragged about.

By then everything had unfolded just as I had imagined it would, only I didn't do a thing. I abandoned my plan to stab Lenny, leaving the shank tucked into my sleeve. Instead, I just stood there and fixed my gaze on Lenny and his crew. I knew that I was standing face-to-face with the evil I had become. In their eyes, I saw my anger. In their voices, I heard my contempt. With them, I was in harm's way, and I thought to myself, *"What have I become?"*

After a few moments of the five us staring at one another, I spoke calmly, "I'll pay you Tuesday." Without exchanging any words, Lenny and the others simply turned and left my cell. Surrender had overcome Pride. Yet it wasn't anything I'd ever been taught.

***

My parents had always taught me to stand my ground. To do anything else was considered weak. I learned that lesson through my own father's threats after my brother and I surrendered to a neighborhood bully.

I was eight in the summer of 1967 when my dad gave me and my six year-old brother Lou some loose change to go buy ice cream at the local convenience store. On the way home, a neighborhood bully threatened to beat us up if we didn't give him our ice cream. He was a chubby kid with rosy cheeks and a bad hairdo, but he was bigger and stronger than me and my little brother. We didn't want to endure a beat-down, so we gave it to him.

When we got home, my father asked us where our ice cream was, and I told him what had happened.

"You let that guy take your ice cream?" he shouted. I tried to explain that the kid was eleven years-old and much bigger.

"I don't care how old or how big he is. You're gonna go back there and you're gonna kick his butt. And if you don't, I am gonna kick yours! Now go!" he ordered, pointing his finger towards the door.

Considering the limited options before us, we returned to where the bully had taken our ice cream. He was still there, playing basketball with his friends, all kids I went to school with. I think they played with him out of fear, because he didn't have any friends his own age. As we approached him, he stopped playing basketball and began to taunt us about how good the ice cream had been.

"Are you bringing me more ice cream?" he said, laughing. "This time, bring me chocolate or I'll beat your butt."

I just kept walking toward him without saying anything.

He bounced the ball off of my stomach and, as it rolled away, he made a fist and threatened, "Now go get the ball!" I chased down the ball and carried it back to him just like he'd told me to do.

And then I bounced the ball hard right off of his nose.

Turns out, it's hard to throw punches when you're standing there holding your bloody nose. But it sure made it easier for my brother and me to take the opportunity to beat the bully up, just like our father had told us to.

When we got home, we confirmed that we had done what our father had told us to do. He rewarded us by taking us out for ice cream.

***

I may have had to pay Lenny thirty packs of cigarettes, but choosing Surrender saved my life that day. It wasn't the brawl that everyone had looked forward to, but there's nothing anticlimactic about saving your life. Not to mention the fact that while Lenny may have never been the wiser, choosing Surrender had surely saved his life as well.

In retrospect, Lenny and his crew were not my opponents at all that day. In fact, my conflict with them simply revealed that the real opponent I confronted was me. The power of Surrender had saved me from myself.

At the time, I didn't believe in God. In fact, I wasn't even looking for God, so I didn't know that the voice I'd heard in my prison cell was God. But what other explanation was there? Who else could have asked such a life-changing question?

"How's it feel, tough guy?"

Like the knife of a skillful surgeon, "How's it feel, tough guy?" cut me to the core and exposed me for just exactly who and what I had become. Pure and simple, I was now able to recognize myself as the man the jury determined I was – a criminal and a drug addict who had failed at everything he had ever set his hands to. I knew I deserved to be exactly where I was, but now I sat stunned on my bed, wondering how this had happened to me. How did I get here?

Those were great questions, but before I would find answers to them there was something I had to take care of: I committed to do something about the fact that word might get around that I was a punk. When recreation was called out, one of the two times it had been called during my first month at the Essex County Jail, I jumped at the opportunity.

When we got to the gym, I stopped to look around and take every-thing in. Most guys were playing basketball, others were lifting weights, and still others were boxing. There may have been fifty men in the gym, and of all the men I saw, I was the only white boy in there. It was the first time I had experienced anything like that – being the minority, that is.

There was a guy in the gym named Malik whom I had become friendly with, and we were both standing there watching a couple of guys boxing. I didn't know either one of the boxers because they locked in on the north side of the jail, and I locked in on the south side.

But one guy, a man I call Trenton after the writing on his T-shirt, looked to me like a veteran fighter. He'd been in prison for a couple of years, and it was obvious that he spent considerable time working out with weights. Trenton was probably in his late twenties, making him five or six years older than me, and he was a couple of inches taller too, and a bit more muscular. He was making quick work of his opponent.

"You're not thinking of boxing, are you?" Malik asked me.

I smiled and said, "That's exactly what I'm thinking."

"I don't know, Mike. He's pretty good."

"That's okay I'm going to go for it. How do I go next?"

He told me to just grab the gloves from whoever stops first. I'll be honest, it was my hope that Trenton would stop first, but as fate would have it, Trenton's opponent quit first.

"Who's next?" barked Trenton.

After I got the gloves from the guy that Trenton had just schooled, I called Malik over to help me put them on. The gloves were antiquated, and seemed as if they were filled with straw that, over the years, had either disappeared or had been forced into other parts of the glove. The only protection these gloves offered was the leather between your fist and the face you're hitting.

As I started putting the gloves on, the entire gym went silent.

"Don't do it, Mike," Malik warned. "You're going to get hurt – seriously hurt."

But my plan wasn't to win a fight. My plan was to prove I wasn't a punk.

Soon, inmates – including Lenny and his crew – crowded around, waiting to see what was about to unfold.

"He ain't gonna bust a grape," one inmate said.

"Look at ole John Boy. He thinks he can fight," another decided.

The moment the fight started, I punched Trenton in his face as hard as I could with an overhand right. When I connected with his face, Trenton stumbled backwards about three or four steps, and then fell to the floor. Just as he made contact with the gymnasium floor, the inmate crowd erupted in shouts and cheering.

"Oh my God! John Boy got his thing off!" someone shouted.

"Get up and fight!" another cheered Trenton on. And with that, he pulled himself off the mat, and we returned to battle, no timekeeper or ringing bell to tell us when the round had ended. We continued to exchange punches until I was so exhausted, I pushed off of Trenton to take a rest like other fighters I'd seen. I just needed to get a little air, but Trenton wasn't allowing it. As I stood there with my hands on my hips gasping for air, he kept moving forward, and suddenly unloaded a vicious punch to my face as if to say, *"You'll rest when I say you can rest."*

I managed not to hit the floor, and yet his blow was so hard, I couldn't chew solid food for days, leaving me on a diet of apple sauce and Kool-Aid. And yet, I loved every minute of beating the stuffing out of each other. When I decided to fight Trenton, I had made up my mind that I was going to stand toe-to-toe and exchange blow-for-blow, even if that meant getting knocked out. That strategy made for a great fight, and great entertainment for the other inmates. What's more, I accomplished what I had set out to do: Prove I was no punk. Besides, a couple of the guys were even fortunate enough to get the food I couldn't eat.

I went to bed that night feeling very good about how the day had turned out. Who wouldn't? After all, I had awakened to a day that appeared to offer no hope, and I went to bed with the promise of hope. Best of all, no one had to die.

CHAPTER 6

†

An Invitation to Change

"If you turn at my reproof, behold, I will pour out my spirit to you;
I will make my words known to you."
(Proverbs 1:23)

The next day started like all the rest: Loud bells waking me from sleep and then the officer's bellow, "Chow, out!" It didn't take long to realize, however, that I wouldn't be going to chow today, at least not to eat. The pain in my jaw was bangin' from the fight the day before. What I did do though, was something I had never done before: I read an entire book.

Even after fourteen years of education, I had never read a book cover to cover. Not because I didn't know how to read – I did. But because I didn't give a rip about anything. As I lay on my bunk that day, I could hear the squeaky wheels on the book cart coming closer to my cell.

I peered through the steel bars, and one book caught my eye, *"Holes in Time,"* written by Frank Constantino, a gangster who became a preacher while in prison. I wanted to know how he had turned his life around, so I reached through the bars, picked the book up off the cart, got comfortable on my bunk, and began to read.

Inside the pages were fifty words that spoke to me, and yet, the words weren't spoken by Frank Constantino, a counselor, or even a person of faith. The words were spoken by another inmate in prison with Constantino, who, along with Frank, had witnessed from a distance the rape of another inmate.

Angered by what he had seen, Frank snapped, "I'd like to see them try that with me."

"Why Frank? You're no different than them. You're a Taker. You take whatever you want and they're taking what they want. You're the same as them."

I knew that those must have been difficult words for Frank to swallow. The truth was, they were difficult words for *me* to swallow. I was no different than the guys who had extorted me. I, too, was a taker.

By the time I finished reading *"Holes in Time,"* I had no doubt as to who had asked, "How's it feel, tough guy?" I decided it was time to read another book: The Good Book. I got my hands on another Bible (since the one I had was still clogging my toilet). When I opened the Bible to a random page, my eyes fixed upon the following words, "Behold, I have refined you, but not as silver; I have tried you in the furnace of affliction." (Isaiah 48:10)

It seemed that God was speaking to me again, only this time He was speaking to me through His Word, and it felt to me like God was inviting me to change my life. The thing was, I was getting a really bad visual on the whole "furnace of affliction" thing. Prison was my furnace, and God wanted me to commit in a big way.

At the time, I struggled with what others would think if they saw me reading a Bible. I mean, how was I going to serve three years in prison reading about Jesus, Joseph, and Mary, when everyone else around me was reading porno or what amounted to jail house contraband. Maybe there was a compromise. I could be discrete about this whole Jesus thing and nobody will even be the wiser. After all, who is going to see me reading the Bible inside my cell?

One morning in November of 1983, a cop came by my cell and said, "Pack up, you're going to state prison!" I remember feeling a little anxious about the move, but then I remembered what Malik had told me:

"Trust me, Mike. Anywhere you go will be better than this. Just stay to yourself and you'll be fine." He explained, "You see how Lenny and his crew act up in here? In state prison somebody will kill them." That was the wise advice and hard-earned wisdom of a man who had spent many years in prison.

When I got down to the Intake/Discharge area, I was reunited with J.D. I didn't say a word about what had happened that day in my cell with Lou and his crew. How could I explain to J.D. that I had heard the voice of God speak to me? We had never talked about stuff like that, and besides, he was a Jew. The only time he used the name of Jesus Christ was when somebody cut him off on the road. I couldn't say, "Hey J.D. I'm reading the Bible!"

I didn't say anything about the Prosecutor calling me down after sentencing either. I didn't want J.D. to worry that the "Get out of jail free" offer might tempt me to turn on him. It hadn't been all that long ago that I needlessly worried he might whack me.

This was the first time I had seen J.D. since our sentencing. He seemed happy to see me.

"I heard the illustrious judge gave you seven years with a three stip?"

"Yeah, he's my hero alright."

"I knew I was gonna catch that extended term, and now I still gotta face the coke charges." J.D. got set up a couple of weeks before trial and got popped with two ounces of coke. I'm pretty sure my brother Lou had him set up. The two of them didn't get along that well because my brother had owed J.D. money for coke and didn't pay him back. Out of respect for me, J.D. didn't do anything to him but what he did do is he sold my brother's debt to someone who did collect it and it wasn't long after that that J.D. got popped.

The rest of the content of our conversation in the Intake/Discharge area surrounded the times we spent together on the street. "Remember when" was the beginning of many conversations in jail because there is nothing new in prison. Nothing comes around that you haven't seen before or you won't see again, many times over. Every day is full of the same exact sadness and despair that there was the day before, and the only day you look forward to, is the day you leave.

The day we shipped out was a beautiful fall day. When the door of the county jail opened, the cool fresh autumn air felt like a healing balm to my skin, which was cracked and peeled from the lye soap we washed ourselves and our clothes with. It had been nearly a month since I had taken a breath of fresh air.

As I stood at the exit of the county jail bound in prison irons, I closed my eyes, took in a deep breath, and soaked in the chilly fall air, thinking, *"This is a perfect day for football."*

I felt relieved as I left the Essex County Jail and stepped into the back of the prisoner transport vehicle. I was more than ready to leave behind the violence and deplorable living conditions the jail was known for, and to head to a relatively safer prison.

The transport vehicle was similar to the paddy wagon that had carried me to the county lockup in New Haven years earlier. There were bench seats on each side, and the back of the vehicle was separated from where the cops sat up front by a thick steel panel. There was a small door that guards could randomly open to observe the inmates they were transporting.

Once the vehicle was filled to capacity, we left the jail and headed to Prison Reception in Yardville. About halfway into the ride, an inmate sitting across from me asked if anyone wanted to smoke a joint. He hadn't been able to bring himself to dispose of it before we left the county, but he didn't want to still have it on him by the time we got to where we were going. Getting busted with drugs is not the way you want to start your bid. However, getting busted didn't stop us from smoking the joint. In fact, it seemed to be just the thing to take the edge off of how I was feeling.

After taking a long hit on the joint, I inhaled deeply and held my breath even longer than usual. I wanted to exhale as little smoke as possible in the event the Keystone Cops up front opened the small door that allowed them to observe us.

They never did.

How quickly I had forgotten about the audible voice in my cell. How quickly I had forgotten about God's invitation to refine me. I'd later find a passage in Proverbs that summed it up: *"Like a dog that returns to his vomit is a fool who repeats his folly."*

When I got to prison Reception, I went through the obligatory strip-search, personal information intake, and injections to protect me against any number of transmittable diseases, illnesses, and infections that are commonly found in prison. I was required to do it all naked, as were the dozens of men going through the process with me. Finally, each inmate was required to shower with a special shampoo for killing lice and crabs.

I was issued two sets of tan prison khakis, two T-shirts, two boxer shorts, two pairs of socks, work boots, sneakers, and a lightweight winter coat. Every piece of clothing had my state prison number on it. From that moment on, my state number would be my name. In the past, my name had always been a way to identify me. My personality and my personal accomplishments had given distinction to my name. There was no one else like me, but now I was simply inmate 74590, just one of thousands of criminals in the New Jersey State Penal System. From the way we dressed, to the food we ate, to the rules we followed, til the day we left, every inmate would be the same.

I knew I was being punished, and I knew I had treated others poorly, but even through eyes as deceived as mine, I could rationalize that such a process could only be intended to disempower and emasculate human beings. How could anything good ever be birthed from an institution whose purpose is punishment and whose method of operation is to demoralize its occupants as a means of controlling them?

After Intake, I was sent to the cell block where I would lock in for the next week. Compared to the Essex County Jail, Yardville was like going home. It was still concrete and steel, but the cell was cleaner, a bit bigger, had no obvious cockroaches, and best of all, my toilet worked.

Pleased by my new accommodations, I went to the day room to use the phone. I wanted to call Lucy and my family to let them know that I had been moved to a new location. I took my place in line behind twelve or so men who were probably waiting to make the same call home I was going to make.

When I was three people away from using the phone, a convict known by the nickname "Tiny" sauntered into the day room. As his stare canvassed the room, we made eye contact, and I knew immediately he was going to be a problem. He was probably in his early thirties, and by the way he carried himself, he appeared to be a veteran convict. Tiny started running his mouth about the long line for the phone, and how he wasn't gonna wait to make a call. He was a big dude, and not from lifting weights. His size was more likely the result of Big Macs on the street. As he moved his way up the line, I thought, *"Here we go."*

"Let me see now," Tiny said. He walked past each man on line like he was playing eeny, meeny, miney, moe, but Tiny already knew who was gonna be "it." When he had made his way to me, he stopped walking, turned to face me, looked me in the eye and said, "I think I'll get on line right here!"

"I don't think so," I warned him. Immediately, he got in my face.

"What? You got a problem with somethin' I said?" he spat. I got forty years, cracker. I'll kill you!"

I didn't say nothin'. I just stared back at him. Tiny continued, "Let's go. We'll settle this thing right now down the other end of the tier. No cops, just me and you, sister!"

At this point, I had been in the housing unit all of about thirty minutes. The day room was packed, and everyone in there was looking to see how I would respond. I knew there was no getting away from this because Tiny was talking real dirty to me. I had to face him.

"We'll see who does what when it's my turn to use the phone."

"You're darn right, we'll see!" he replied, and he stormed across the room, mumbling something to himself, took a seat in a chair, and began to stare at me. I wasn't going anywhere with him. I didn't know if he had a weapon or if other people would be down the other end of the tier waiting to do who-knows-what to the new guy. Tiny could have started this confrontation for any number of reasons, but one thing was for sure: Whatever was gonna happen between me and him, was gonna happen right there in that day room. I would see to it.

By this time, I was next on line for the phone. My staring back at Tiny seemed to aggravate him, and he began yelling again.

"Hey, cracker!"

I just kept staring at him with no response.

"Hey cracker, I'm talkin' to you!" he yelled even more loudly.

I answered with my own racial taunt – the one that white people aren't supposed to say. That got everybody's attention real quick. "My name ain't cracker! If you want to use the phone, you *ask* to use the phone! You're trying to chump me off in front of forty guys right here, and I'm telling ya right now, fat stuff, that ain't gonna happen. In about two minutes you're gonna see, win, lose, or draw, you ain't chumping me off in front of no one!"

Tiny just sat there with his arms folded. When I finished speaking, he began nodding his head as if he agreed with everything I had said.

"Bet. I respect that. I respect that," he said.

"Good. Now, if you want to use my turn to make a call, you can and I'll make my call later," I offered.

Tiny declined to use the phone, which proved to me that his antics were only for the purpose of testing my grit. But I was too worked up to make a phone call home.

The rest of my week at Yardville went by without incident. Soon I'd learn that I would be going to a medium security prison down in south Jersey. The first phase of construction on Southern State Correctional Facility had just been completed, and they were filling beds.

Prior to leaving Yardville, I told one of the C.O.'s that J.D. was my father-in-law, and that he was going down for at least ten years. I asked him if it would be possible for me to see him. The officer was good enough to walk me over to visit J.D. for about a half-an-hour. When I saw J.D., he told me that he was being sent to Trenton State Prison and had to stay there for at least five years before the classification panel would consider transferring him to another facility.

It was no secret that Trenton State Prison housed the most dangerous and notorious offenders in the state, and they also housed New Jersey's Death Row population. With that notoriety came a reputation for extreme violence in the prison. Yet despite the dire circumstances, we managed some smiles and enjoyed the time we had to visit.

In early December of 1983, I was en route to Southern State Correctional Facility. The ride was very quiet, and the atmosphere, very serious. I was full of anticipation, speculating about the place I would call home for the next three years. But it wasn't like any prison I had ever seen. From afar, it looked more like a concentration camp than it did a prison. It was a cloudless day, and the bright sun glistening off of the unnerving amount of razor wire woven into the towering chain-link fences seemed to emphasize its deadly intent.

The bus approached the front gate with caution. As a guard signaled for the gate to open, we rolled slowly into the receiving area where prison guards inspected the outside and underside of the bus. Next, a second gate opened and slowly closed behind the bus as it pulled in.

From here, I could see one more fence standing between us and the actual prison compound. At this time, all of the inmates were escorted off of the bus, and we were made to stand in a straight line while one of the C.O.s addressed us.

"You are not here to be rehabilitated. You are here to be punished! Rehabilitation is a thing of the past, and it is proven not to be an effective tool in dealing with criminal behavior," he informed us.

As we continued to stand there in prison irons, the C.O. spoke about the rules of the prison and the consequences for violating institutional policy. Next, we went into the strip room where they removed our irons and conducted a strip search. Finally, we walked to the front gate of the compound where a crowd of inmates had gathered to "welcome" us.

An officer spoke into his walkie-talkie, "Open the gate," and just like that we were inside the prison. Some of the guys already incarcerated knew some of the new inmates coming in, and called out to them. Others were there just to make inappropriate comments and size up the new guys coming in. It could be an intimidating experience for first-time offenders, but by now, I was getting used to it.

The next thing I had to get used to was that I had been sent to a prison with no cells. It had been built with a new concept in mind, and but for the cells in lockup, all of the living quarters in this prison were like that of a dormitory.

I hated it for many reasons. To begin with, I had safety concerns. After coming from Essex County, I didn't like the fact that if I had a beef with someone, they could easily get me when I went to sleep. While this was not considered a violent prison, all prisons experience violence, and on more than one occasion I had witnessed men being attacked in bed.

Perhaps the worst attack I had witnessed happened when an inmate took boiling water from the coffee and tea station and poured it on the face of a man sleeping in his bed and then proceeded to beat him as his skin melted off his face. On top of that, it took only one look around to know, that for the next three years, whether in sickness or in health or in good moods or bad, I was married to this situation. I would never experience a single moment of privacy!

After the first week, I was assigned to Unit Four, where I'd spend nearly all of my time at Southern State. When I went to chow for the first time, I was taken aback by the seating arrangements. After I got my food and went to get a seat, it was clear that men chose their seat according to their race. Finding a seat among my so-called own people was difficult. I saw an open seat at the "white" table and I took it, but it was clear that I was not welcome there. Maybe I was taking one of their buddies' seats, who knows?

Most of the looks and comments came from this one freckly faced guy who looked like he just stepped off the set of "Hee-Haw." I think he was trying to impress his friends at my expense.

"You got somethin' on your mind?" I asked. He looked at me with a confused look on his face as if to ask, *"Are you talking to me?"* He was acting like I had the wrong guy, but I knew better. I had the right guy, and right away, he let me know that he was a punk.

"You got somethin' on your mind?" I repeated.

"No," he said.

"Good, then shut your mouth!" He shut up, and I went back to eating my meal.

At the same time I was assigned to Unit Four, I was assigned to work on the rock pile, otherwise known as Detail Eight. If you came to this jail, you came there to work. My job at the time was really that of performing hard physical labor that consisted of digging huge holes by hand for French drains and then filling them with stone.

In some prisons, you have the option to work or not to work. Some guys choose not to work and just stay in their cells – "cell potatoes," not to be confused with couch potatoes, but in essence, the same thing. At Southern State, opting out of work wasn't an option. You either worked or went to lockup. If you still refused, and many men did, you were sent to another prison and your sentence was extended. All that to say, there were no cell potatoes at Southern State.

I was paid all of one dollar per day for my efforts on Detail Eight, but that was enough to buy cigarettes. Here I was, performing long hours of hard physical labor, because I made a personal choice to commit crimes so I wouldn't have to perform long hours of hard physical labor! What a humbling lesson and what a way to learn it. But that was nothing compared to what I was about to learn.

CHAPTER 7

†

All Things Are Possible

"But Jesus looked at them and said,
'With man this is impossible, but with God all things are possible.'"
(Matthew 19:26)

I just knew my mother had sent me the Walkman she'd promised to get me. I practically skipped the entire way to the prison mailroom. The Walkman meant a whole lot more to me than just listening to music. Sure, it was going to be good to listen to my favorite music by Springsteen, Bob Seger, and Aerosmith. But more than that, having a Walkman meant having a way to tune out the insanity around me.

The constant noise in the prison was enough to make you lose your mind. There was no way to escape the loud conversations of inmates competing to be heard over each other, the never-ending institutional announcements, televisions playing, toilets flushing, chairs and tables being set up and broken down, machines waxing the floors...the noise just never ended.

I stepped up to the mailroom window and signed the receipt for my package. That's when the officer unexpectedly handed me a Bible – in front of about a dozen guys in line behind me.

I had forgotten all about the fact that I had asked my sister for a Bible when I was in the County. The fact of the matter is, when I had seen men reading the Bible or the Koran in prison, I judged them. I questioned their sincerity about faith, and more than that, I perceived people of faith as being weak. I didn't want to subject myself to the same sort of judgment in prison, and I sure didn't want to appear weak. I hadn't forgotten what Derrick had said about weak appearances. I had rationalized earlier that I could just be discrete about the whole Jesus thing, since no one could see me read the Bible in my cell. Well, I wasn't in a cell anymore, so being discrete about reading the Bible was no longer an option.

Unrivaled by all of my excuses was this: I was embarrassed to be seen with a Bible in my hands. Who was I fooling anyway? You know, it hadn't been all that long before that I was out committing crimes, getting stoned, and laughing at all those Jesus freaks on T.V. Now what? I'm supposed to put on a happy face in prison and tell people, "Jesus loves me!"

I knew my life needed to change, and I wanted to take steps to make that happen, but I lacked the inner strength to do what would have been best for reclaiming my life. For now, I put the Bible in the bottom of a locker at the foot of my bed.

In the meantime, I stayed busy working the rock pile and getting back into shape. I lifted weights every chance I could, and I ran every day after work. It wasn't long before I began to restore to my body the size and muscle I had forfeited to drugs.

Yet I was still smoking weed and, occasionally, I would indulge in some hooch. As for cocaine, I stopped using it. Not because I couldn't get it – I could. Still, the changes in my body were the first real indication that I was beginning to change my life for the better.

One day while I was lying on my bed, I received a visit from Father Al, a Catholic priest at the prison. Even though he was in his sixties, it wasn't unusual to see him on the basketball court running around with the guys in his red Bargain City sneakers. He seemed to genuinely enjoy his relationship with the inmates and likewise, the inmates enjoyed him.

"Do you attend any services here at the prison?" he asked after introducing himself.

I'm thinking *"Here we go. I'm about to get a lecture."*

"No, I don't."

"Are you a Christian?"

"I'm Catholic by birth, but until recently, I didn't believe that God existed."

"Oh no? What changed your mind?" he asked.

"I got in a beef with some guys at the county jail over a gambling debt before I came here. I was about to stab one of them in the throat, and then I heard an audible voice ask me, *'How's it feel, tough guy?'"* I told Father Al.

"I don't know how to explain it other than the words I heard stopped me from stabbing the guy. Somehow, those words revealed truth to me. It was like I was living under a cloud of deception, and all of a sudden, I heard those words and something clicked. I knew everything I believed was a lie."

"Wow, that's a remarkable testimony," Father Al said. "You should come to my service on Sunday morning. We begin at eight a.m."

"Eight a.m.? I don't think so. Besides, I'm not going to church with tree jumpers!" Tree jumpers were convicted child molesters, many of whom went to church. I certainly didn't want others thinking I was aligning myself with the most hated group of inmates in prison.

"God loves all sinners," Father Al insisted, "even child molesters, if they truly repent."

"Well I'm not God, and I'm not going to church with them!"

He was silent for a moment, and then he asked, "Do you need a Bible?"

"I have one."

"Well, do you read it?" he asked.

"A little bit," I said.

"Well, I see you lifting weights all of the time," he said. "Building faith is just like building muscle. It takes intention, it takes repetition, and it takes endurance. You want to be careful. If all you do is work out your physical muscles, at the end of your life, you'll be nothing more than a good-looking corpse!" he said. "Speaking of corpses, are you saved?"

"What exactly does the question, 'Are you saved,' mean?"

"Have you accepted Jesus Christ as your Lord and Savior?"

If I hadn't heard God speaking to me in my cell, this conversation would have never happened.

"No," I told him.

Father Al took that opportunity to school me on the "concept" of being saved.

"It's very simple," he explained. "Sin separates man from the love of God in the same way this prison separates you guys from freedom. There's one big difference, though."

"What's that?" I asked.

"In order for you to experience freedom," Father Al continued, "you have to pay the State of New Jersey in full for the crimes you committed. In order to be saved however, Jesus had to pay in full for the price of your sin."

"For God so loved the world, that He gave His one and only Son, that whoever believes in him should not perish but have eternal life." (John 3:16)

Father Al had painted a simple, but effective picture for me that contrasted the punishment and payback of prison to the mercy and grace of a loving God.

"For by grace you have been saved, through faith. And this is not your own doing; it is the gift of God, not a result of works, so that no one may boast."(Eph.2:8-9)

Father Al called salvation (being saved) a gift from God to anyone who would receive it, even someone as messed up and sinful as me.

"Salvation isn't something you can earn," Father Al made clear. "I don't care how nice you are, how rich or famous you are, how much weight you can lift, or how many good deeds you can do. Nothing can bridge the gap of sin that separates you from God but the cross of Jesus Christ."

"I am the way, and the truth, and the life. No one comes to the Father except through me." (John 14:6)

When he finished talking he looked at me as though he were waiting for me to say something.

"Well?"

"Well what?" I said.

"Well, what are you going to do?"

"What am I going to do about what?"

"What are you going to do about accepting Jesus Christ as your Lord and Savior?" he asked.

"You just said there was nothing I could do."

"No, I said there was nothing you could do to *earn* salvation but there is something you must do to *receive* salvation. The Bible says, *'If you confess with your mouth that Jesus is Lord and believe in your heart that God raised him from the dead, you will be saved.'"(Rom. 10:9)*

But my life never mirrored a godly lifestyle. After thinking about it, I decided, "I don't think God can save me."

He looked so angry, I thought he was going to hit me.

"Who are you to say what God can do and can't do?" Father Al wasn't like those television preachers or even the priests I had seen in church as a kid. He was in my face and acting like my very life depended on every word he was saying.

I was becoming anxious because of the men beginning to linger around on the wing. I felt extremely self-conscious and uncomfortable talking about God with them around. They had that, "I'm getting annoyed and I wish you would leave" look on their faces. I quietly turned to Father Al and said, "Take a look around me. Don't you see what I am up against here? I gotta get through this time, and I don't think I can do that walking around with a Bible in my hand."

"Mike, this little three-year sentence is a cake-walk compared to what eternity has in store for you if you don't start making some changes in your life," Father Al wrapped it up. "This decision for Christ, Mike, is a matter of the heart!"

When he left, I humbly pulled out my Bible and, despite the men around me who could see its cover, I began to read. I soon decided that Father Al was right. If God truly existed, who was I to say what God could or couldn't do? I began by reading the entire Gospel of Matthew. I had never read the Bible before, that is, apart from a few lines here, and a couple of verses there. I was reading it now with the intention of set-tling the matter once and for all: Does God exist or doesn't He? It wasn't long after I began reading the good book that I became immersed in the account of Jesus's life. What I once considered a fairy tale turned out to be a true eyewitness account of an innocent man having been executed.

To me, this was organized crime at the highest level. The Jewish high priests (actually, gangsters) were determined to get rid of Jesus, because they felt like He was a threat to their power. The only problem was that the Jews weren't allowed to carry out capital punishment, so they came up with a scheme to bring Jesus before Pontius Pilate, the Governor of Roman Judea, where the death penalty could be enforced.

Jesus's alleged crime was blasphemy, based upon His claim to be the Son of God. But when the Jewish leaders brought Jesus before Pilate, they changed the charges against him, claiming that He was a king who did not advocate paying taxes to the Romans. I likened that to Nicky Newark charging me with assault when I'd never assaulted him. Pilate however, could find no fault with Jesus.

Unlike me, Jesus was never convicted of a crime, and yet Pontius Pilate bowed to the pressure of an unruly mob and delivered Jesus over to them to be flogged and then executed alongside two criminals. And here, I'd thought Nicky did *me* dirty with the trumped-up charges for assaulting him. What a miscarriage of justice.

The author of the Gospel of Matthew who gave us this account was not some ghostwriter from the distant future; he was a disciple of Jesus, and he had walked with Jesus in real time. He had witnessed first-hand the miracles that Jesus performed. He saw the lame walk, the blind see, and the dead raised. He was an eyewitness to the crucifixion, death, and resurrection of Jesus Christ, and in the end, Matthew died at the end of a sword as a martyr for Jesus.

From where I was sitting, Jesus was the original tough guy. He was mocked, spit on, and given a crown of thorns that ranged from an inch to two inches-long that soldiers continually beat into his scalp. He was flogged repeatedly until the whip containing bone fragments and pieces of metal turned his flesh into hamburger and left him in an unrecognizable state. After surviving a flogging that most men, if not all men, would have died from, Jesus was sent to suffer the excruciating slow death of suffocation by means of crucifixion.

I had spent my life rejecting God and the notion that His Son, Jesus, had died for my sins. As it turned out, I might as well have been right there with the guys who had nailed Jesus to the cross. It's easy to say the Jews killed Him to maintain their power, but the truth is, Jesus was killed for no other reason than to settle the debt for my sin. And for the first time in my life, I believed it.

"But to all who did receive him, who believed in his name, he gave the right to become children of God." (John 1:12)

That Sunday morning at eight, Father Al did a double-take when I showed up for church. The last time I had gone to church was Christmas Eve 1979 or 1980 when a group of us knuckleheads were tripping on acid and thought it would be fun to go to midnight mass. Even though one of my friends attempted to receive communion twice, we made it through the service without being kicked out. Before that, I couldn't tell you the last time I had gone to church.

In prison, church was different, and I liked it. Trust me, the prison chapel, a gray concrete block room with hard metal chairs, was absent the beautiful stain glass windows, the aroma of candles burning, and even the sounds of the magnificent pipe organs you may find in a church on the street, but the message was empowering to say the least. I was beginning to believe that my life had a purpose that was bigger than drugs, bigger than committing crime, bigger than being a tough guy.

It was like Father Al's sermons had been written just for me, to poke holes in my distorted world view.

"What I did or didn't do in my life did not depend upon rules, integrity or a belief in some God I couldn't see. It depended upon nothing other than my personal preference to do it or not to do it."

Father Al preached messages that convicted me personally and challenged me to grow as a man spiritually.

"There is an epidemic in this prison – in this world for that matter. Many of you live day to day within these prison walls feeling sorry for yourself. You have somehow become the victim."

Father Al was right, at least with regards to me. I felt like a victim because I believed in my heart that I was in prison for a crime I didn't commit – the crime of murder.

"What about the people you robbed? Did they deserve to be robbed? Did they deserve to be beaten…or raped…or extorted…or murdered?"

Ouch! Talk about being uncomfortable!

Now, this is the point where most congregants in America take an offense with the preacher and get up and walk out. I'm not going to say I didn't want to leave, but it wasn't like I could get in my car and go to the beach. I stuck around and continued to listen.

"But every day before you came to prison," Father continued, "you woke up and thought about how can I satisfy myself today? How can I quench my craving to have all of the things my heart desires? Each of you had a different response to that very same question, but each of you is experiencing the same result: Punishment!

"Men, the time you serve will not make you righteous with God. Obeying the law when you go home will not make you righteous with God. Only that which comes through faith in Jesus Christ will make a man righteous with God," Father Al preached.

His compassion for the men to whom he preached was evident, but at the same time, Father Al didn't mince words when it came to telling us what we needed to hear.

That was the first Christian service I attended in prison. I left feeling pretty bad about the person I'd become, but at the same time, I felt compelled to make some changes for the better.

***

"Who's that guy over there?" I asked my chess opponent. He's here every week but I don't see anybody talk to him." He was a young guy in his early twenties, and he looked to me to be out of place.

"Oh him? He's a Jesus freak," he answered. "You know, one of those religious guys or somethin.'"

After my game of chess ended, I went over and introduced myself. I extended my hand to shake his and said, "How are you? My name is Mike."

"I'm Bill," he said.

"I see you here every week, but I'm not sure why you're here."

"Me and my mother lead Wings of Eagles Prison Ministry. We come into the prison as volunteers to share the gospel of Jesus Christ with men here at the prison."

Bill was a Baptist Reverend and talked about God and Jesus Christ much the same way Father Al did. I'm sure that there were a lot of other things he could have been doing besides hanging out in prison, but every week he came to this place to volunteer his time with men that most of society runs from. It's not often that something – or someone – inspiring comes along in prison.

From that day forward, I would go to church on Sunday with Father Al, and I went to Bible studies with Bill or his mother Lynn on Tuesday evenings. They all impacted my life in extraordinary ways. In particular, I witnessed in their lives examples that I had never seen before. If you could imagine, Christian volunteers are not always the most well received visitors at a prison. There is skepticism by many who run the prison (referred to as "Custody") about the true intentions of volunteers from outside, and for that reason, Bill, Lynn, or even Father Al could be treated poorly at times.

Custody could make it difficult for them to enter or leave the prison, and at times they would be denied any access at all. Other times, they were spoken to rudely or sarcastically made fun of for their belief that inmates could be reformed. Visiting the men in prison meant withstanding a lot of ridicule personally but they did it with a smile on their face and a kind word to those who made fun of them. My response to being treated poorly had always been to be aggressive, if not combative, but seeing the examples of my Christian role models of sorts had a transforming quality about how I began to see and treat others.

Although I had been going to church and to Bible studies, I never shared any of that with Lucy. I never shared with her what had happened to me at the county jail either. A part of me felt guilty about hiding those things from Lucy, but a bigger part of me believed she would never understand the reasons for my new convictions. If the roles were reversed, I wouldn't believe it either. On some level, I don't even think I understood my convictions as much as I believed them.

As time went on though, Lucy seemed to be visiting me less and less and I began to question her commitment to me. I became concerned about what she was doing on the street and who she was doing it with. On the one hand, here I was, the guy that had brought negativity into her life, and now I had the nerve to tell her that she couldn't do what I used to do. We were growing in different directions and our relationship was in trouble.

***

In the summer of 1984, an organization by the name of Bill Glass Prison Ministries came to Southern State Correctional Facility. It was a prison ministry that used famous Christian athletes and entertainers to bring the gospel of Christ to men in prison.

While most of the inmate population may not have been believers, they were attracted to the opportunity to meet and mingle with famous athletes and entertainers. But by then, I considered myself a believer, and so I looked forward to hearing the testimonies of the men and women coming to the prison to share how Jesus had changed their lives.

The athletes demonstrated their talents and skills to the inmates but not before they gave their testimonies of salvation through Jesus Christ. We were in the gym and the place was packed. Paul Wren, the world's strongest man at the time, had just put on a pretty impressive weightlifting demonstration. When he was finished, a famous soccer player by the name of Kyle Rote Junior got up to speak.

To the best of my recollection I can remember him telling us, "My life isn't what you all think it is. Sure, you see me on TV playing soccer, a professional athlete, and you think life must be good for me."

He talked about his difficulties growing up and although he was experiencing success in the sport of soccer, he was really a very unhappy man. Then he gave his testimony of how God dramatically changed his life. I listened intently to what he was saying, all the while comparing his life to mine.

He continued, "In order to be forgiven a man needs to repent, and in order to be saved, a man must confess with his mouth that Jesus Christ is Lord and believe in his heart that God raised Him from the dead." It seemed as though I kept being reminded that I had a personal responsibility to respond publicly to what I privately believed.

"For those of you who know Jesus and never publicly accepted him as Lord and Savior, I want to lead you in a prayer," he continued. "Will you please stand up right where you are?"

"You're kidding me, right?" I thought. *"You want me to stand up in front of these guys? Obviously, Kyle never served time in prison. I mean, c'mon! Jesus must know I accept Him. I read the Bible every day now. I go to church on Sunday and I go at eight a.m. at that! Stand up? I can't stand up!"*

I felt that it's one thing to talk about God and go to church with other believers, but it's a different thing to do what Kyle Rote was asking me to do. He wanted me to stand and pray in the midst of a couple of hundred non-believing inmates, and that wasn't going to happen. To me, that was like asking a stray lamb to go over to a hungry pack of wolves and ask, "Hey guys, what's for dinner?"

"The fear of man lays a snare, but whoever trusts in the Lord is safe." (Proverbs 29:25)

I knew what this was. This was God's idea of a joke. Just like the New Testament clogging my toilet and then being sent to a prison where there were no cells. This was God's unfinished business, and now I was going to have to finally answer the question He'd asked me in the county with Lenny and his crew. This was the RSVP to the invitation by God to refine me into a new and improved man. Panic-stricken I thought, *"Why here, God?" Why now? Why are you calling me out like this?"*

As I sat there hoping Kyle would just move on already, I felt like God was trying to tell me, "You've been praying for strength in your life, Mike, and now I am giving you the opportunity to be strong!"

But I couldn't stand up. A very nervous feeling came over me and my legs felt very weak. At that moment, every thought that raced through my mind began with the words, "I can't!"

"I can't stand up in front of these guys."

"I can't take a stance that sets me apart as being different."

"I can't bring that kind of attention to myself."

"I can't risk my reputation in front of all these inmates."

"I can't do this, because people will think I am weak."

"I can't do this because people will crack on me."

"I can't, I can't, I can't!"

Instead, I just sat there disgusted with myself, because I knew I was denying publicly what I had believed in my heart privately.

"For am I now seeking the approval of man, or of God? Or am I trying to please man?" (Galatians 1:10)

The silence in that gym was downright uncomfortable. Not for Kyle though. He continued to stand there as if he had all day. And while I remained seated, an extreme sensation of heat began to overwhelm my body. Suddenly, as if something other than my legs lifted me up out of my seat, I found myself standing alone among hundreds of inmates. As I continued to stand, and Kyle continued to wait, my mentality of "I can't" was replaced by an attitude of "I can."

Then, another inmate stood.

"I can overcome the grip of fear."

Finally, the third and final inmate stood.

The trepidation I felt soon turned to joy when I witnessed the other inmates standing. My daring to stand had encouraged others to do the same. Nothing can compare to the empowerment I felt as I stood there and publicly accepted Jesus Christ as my Lord and Savior inside that prison facility.

When it became obvious that no one else was going to stand, Kyle congratulated those of us who did, and urged us to come and pray with him before we left the gym. He encouraged those who didn't stand to talk to the athletes who would be staying at the facility for the remainder of the day.

Amidst all of the conversations around us, Kyle led us in a prayer where I admitted that I was a sinner, repented for my sins, and committed to change my life.

It's funny how you spend so much time worrying about things that never happen. The fear that I felt in that gym was real but the belief that I should be afraid of the men around me was a lie. No one said a word to me regarding the fact that I had stood and accepted Jesus as my Lord and Savior. I suspect there were some who missed the opportunity.

When I left the gym, I took a walk by myself on the compound to reflect on what just happened. As I was walking, I paused for a moment to look up at the sky. Maybe for the first time in my life, I understood that the sun shining in a bright blue sky with scattered marshmallow clouds was the handiwork of God. As I continued to admire the view from above, the evidence of the prison below disappeared from my sight. It occurred to me that I had just found a way to get away from the prison: I just needed to keep looking up!

That day, I knew I'd never again return to prison. I believed I would never again give in to the pressures of my peers to be someone other than who God wanted me to be. That day, my relationship with God became more important than the force of influence in my life that gave consideration to what others would say, think, or do. *"...choose this day whom you will serve...".* (*Joshua 24:15*)

I was no longer a prisoner of drugs and the tough guy mentality that had rationalized committing the crimes that had landed me in prison. Instead, I took authority over them. I understood that my life was created by God for the purpose of serving God and honoring Him in all I did.

But what was my purpose and how could I honor God? The more I thought about it, and the more I looked around the prison, the more I knew what that purpose was. The prison was a human warehouse of young men, including myself, in their late teens to mid-twenties. Many of them were uneducated and couldn't read or write proficiently. I felt a passion for those guys, because I believed that many of them never had the opportunities in life that I'd had. If they were given another option, if they were taught a skill set, I believed some of them would succeed. That's when I felt God impress upon my heart a calling to work with at-risk youth. Moreover, I understood that I could fulfill that purpose whether I was behind prison walls or not. For the first time in my life, I was free!

Throughout my life, I had believed that freedom was a condition of life found outside of prison walls, a life free from restraint. What I learned in prison is this: I had never before been free, not ever! I had been in prison my entire life. That's right! Concrete walls, steel bars, chains and shackles did not a prison make. Rather, a poor self-esteem that permitted me to engage in the destructive vices that brought injury to my life and the lives of others took me captive long before I ever became inmate number 74590.

There is no prison worse than the prison to which we compel ourselves. In terms of bondage, freedom cannot exist in the midst of an iniquitous or troublesome lifestyle. After all, the condition of peace should naturally accompany the circumstance of freedom, but how many of us living outside of prison walls can say, "I'm at peace in my life." My guess is not many.

Experiencing freedom inside of prison allowed me to enjoy a peace in my life that I had never known. My growing faith began to produce a belief that with God, all things could be possible but only if I continued to pursue God both in and outside of prison walls.

CHAPTER 8

✝

Setting My Mind on Things Above

"Set your minds on things that are above,
not on things that are on earth."
(Colossians 3:2-3)

During the first six months of my sentence, Lucy's visits went from every weekend to hardly ever. By late spring of 1984, she stopped visiting me altogether. I knew it would happen. In fact, I was so sure that it would happen that I had told her to leave me when I got convicted, but Lucy had promised me that she would always love me and that she would come to see me every weekend. Then, I got the letter that every man in prison dreads.

I opened the letter and began to read. "Dear Michael, yak yak yak and Oh, by the way, I really need to have more time to myself." Time to yourself? You're going to be by yourself for three years. That's not enough time to yourself? But then the truth came out: "I want to see other men, Michael."

There I was, sitting on my bed reading the bad news, surrounded by men who I could not allow to see my emotions. "Remember," Derrick had said, "don't appear weak." I wanted to cry, I wanted to run through the razor wire fences and plead with her not to leave me. I wanted to scream, I wanted to hurt something bad, and in the midst of it all, I also wanted to die. I just wanted to stop feeling pain in my life. But if you do whatever you want to do in prison, you'll never leave prison. So I did what most men in prison do. I ate it and showed no emotion at all one way or the other.

"Hey Mike," my friend said as he walked by, "How's Lucy doing?"

"Oh, she's good, man. Thanks for asking."

I got angry (actually, hurt) with her because she didn't understand how badly I needed her in that situation, but then again, I was never vulnerable enough as a man to tell her how I really felt. I just made her feel bad about herself along the way for not keeping her promise to come see me every weekend. Now I got to lie in bed every night and think about who she was with.

It turns out that the excuses she had given me about her car breaking down, or not having gas money to come see me were simply that – excuses. I didn't even write her back. I just took her off my visiting list and planned on never seeing her again.

On the one hand, I had expected Lucy to stop living her life because I was in prison. On the other hand, I never took a minute in my life to think about how my choices had hurt her. I had done nothing to protect her, choosing instead to bring her into dangerous situations where I put her life in harm's way. I can't think of a single way that my life added to her life, but I can think of many ways where I brought harm into her life. Why wouldn't she want to leave me? In one fell swoop, Lucy had lost her father and her boyfriend, and like most all of the losses in her life, they came by way of choices she did not make.

Three or four months after my relationship with Lucy ended, I was lying on my bed reading a book, when I couldn't help but overhear a couple of guys trash-talking about a bet they were making: Each man would send a letter with their picture to the women's prison in Clinton, New Jersey. The winner would be the inmate who received the first response.

When I heard the bet, I commented to the two men, "Ya know, if I were to get in on this bet, you'd both lose." They ended up letting me in and by the end of the conversation, there were four competitors in all.

The stakes were high. Whoever got the first letter back from Clinton could make each one of the other three guys do one thousand push-ups on command. Whoever came in second could make the other two men do one thousand push-ups and so on. If you came in last, you owed three men one thousand push-ups each.

Push-ups on command meant just that. Whether you were eating your dinner, pushing iron, lying in bed, or watching TV, it didn't matter. If the winner of the bet said, "Get down and push," you got down and started pushing. We determined beforehand that visits, bathrooms, and phone calls were off limits. Outside of those areas, you were open game. After the letter went out, the anticipation of who would get the first letter back began.

After a few days had passed, the first piece of mail from the women's prison arrived, and I became the instant grand prize winner of the high stakes competition. A girl by the name of Gerry sent me a letter in which she expressed the sentiment that she didn't think I was her type. Gerry did say, however, that she would pass my letter and picture on to another girl at the prison whom she felt was more my type. But I wasn't looking for a date; I was trying to win a bet, and I did!

I couldn't wait to start collecting my push-ups, so I took my letter, and I waited for the first of my casualties to arrive. As I stood waiting outside of Unit Four, I noticed one of the competitors coming across the compound – a guy everyone called, "Sucker," because he lost every bet I remember him ever making.

"Hey Sucker, give me twenty-five!" I shouted as he got closer, smiling as I held the letter high in the air. "I told you lying about your age wasn't gonna help you." A smile that said, "I can't believe I lost again" came across his face, and he got down and started pushing.

Later that night when the lights went out and Sucker got into bed, I waited for several minutes and then said, "Hey Sucker, did you hear that?"

"Hear what?" he asked.

"Did you hear that voice?"

"No!"

"I think it's Flooreen!" I said.

 "Who?"

"It's your girlfriend, Flooreen, and she wants twenty-five push-ups before you go to sleep. Now give me my money, Sucker!"

Everyone busted out laughing at Sucker, and he had to get out of bed and give me my push-ups. Sucker ended up coming in last in the bet, owing three men one thousand push-ups each. It wasn't easy being Sucker.

A few days letter, I received my second letter from the women's prison, from an inmate named Sharon. It was a nice letter, and the girl sent a picture of herself with two little boys that turned out to be her sons. Most importantly, she described herself as a Christian. She spoke of her experience in prison as being life-changing, and echoed some of the same sentiments I had shared in my letter that Jerry passed on to her. I wrote her back, and it wasn't long before we began writing each other nearly every day.

To hear the story of her young life was heartbreaking, and in many ways, it made my childhood seem like a day at the beach in comparison. Not only did we have, let's say, our custodial circumstances in common, but we also shared a new reverence for God.

The more I learned about Sharon, the more I developed affection for her. In her letters, I read about a young woman who had come from a very abusive home, and I felt sorry for her. She left home as a result of the abuse, and eventually had two little boys by the age of twenty-two. But the boys' father was not in the picture. Sharon had a lot on her plate at that time in her life, and she had made some bad choices that landed her in prison.

But she said that it was good that she went to prison, because it forced her to look at her life differently. We wrote back and forth about our faith and how our relationship with Jesus Christ was changing our approach to life. It seemed as though our meeting was no accident. Sharon promised to come see me when she got out of prison, but I didn't get my hopes up, because she lived three hours from my prison in northwest New Jersey. Visiting me meant spending six hours in the car, and I wasn't counting on that.

Apart from my family, I might as well have been dead to the rest of the world; none of my friends bothered to visit me. Before I left for prison, all of my friends talked about how they had my back and they were gonna look out for me when I was gone. But it turns out that it was just talk. So why would I want to get my hopes up that my prison pen pal would bother to visit me?

By the late spring of 1985, I had served nearly half of my three-year mandatory minimum sentence. While I was working out one day, I got an unexpected call for a visit.

"Are you sure I got a visit?" I asked the C.O.

"You're Number 74590, aren't you?"

"Yeah!"

"Then you got a visit!"

In prison, unexpected calls or visits usually brought with them bad or sad news about an illness or a death in the family. I had seen it a dozen times, if I had seen it once, and immediately, I was anxious.

I put the weights down and headed back to my unit to change my clothes. Inside the visiting hall, I began to scan the room, but I wasn't sure exactly who I was looking for. I just looked for a familiar face, but I couldn't find one. As I searched out the room, I noticed a hand go up to get my attention, and there she was: Sharon had come to see me. I walked over and greeted her with a kiss on the cheek and then sat down across from her. Nervous, I took her hand in mine and told her, "It's good to finally see you in person."

"Yes, I know," Sharon agreed. "I wanted to get here sooner, but the ride is longer than I thought. And then it took me like a half-an-hour to get in here."

"Don't worry about it," I said. "I'm just glad that I finally get to see you."

"Oh, I brought you a food package. I know how bad prison food can be, and I brought you some clothes, too."

"How'd you know what size to buy?" I asked.

"I just guessed. Hopefully it's not an expensive guess."

After nearly a year of writing, here we sat face to face. We talked about her job, her home, and the program that had allowed her to leave prison before her time was up. She seemed to be doing great, but now we had to face reality.

"Visiting hours are now over!" hollered the C.O.

"Thank you for coming to see me, Sharon. You made my day."

"I am planning on coming next week too, if that is okay."

"Sure it's okay."

We kissed each other goodbye and then we both left the visiting hall through our respective doors, hers to freedom and mine back to the reality of prison. We had a great visit but more than that, Sharon had made good on her word to come and see me. Her presence confirmed that the words she had written to me in her letters were genuine.

Sharon started coming to see me nearly every weekend, and every time she came, she brought food packages and clothes. Institutional policy allowed for an inmate to receive ten pounds of food a month from home. It wasn't a lot, but if they were allowing it, I was taking it. There were restrictions on the types of food you could have and how the food was packaged. Eventually fruit was eliminated because a lot of guys were getting oranges from home that had been injected with booze.

I loved the food packages, but I had mixed feelings about the clothes. At the time, street clothes were permitted inside of the prison, but I never felt comfortable wearing them for a couple of reasons. To begin with, I wasn't there to make a fashion statement. I was there to serve time, and wearing street clothes didn't make me feel any less imprisoned. Furthermore, flaunting the name brand clothes that Sharon was bringing conflicted with my desire to add to the lives of the men around me. I firmly believed that such a demonstration of wealth in the midst of an environment as oppressive as prison spoke a silent and elitist message to my peers.

"Can you stop bringing clothes here to the prison?" I asked Sharon.

"Why? Don't you like them?"

"Don't get me wrong. I like them a lot, but the clothes can cause problems for me. Like I see guys eyeballing my locker and I don't want to get in a beef over clothes."

"But I like bringing you gifts. I like seeing you in the clothes and not the prison khakis."

"Sharon, I'm in prison. In prison, I'm gonna wear prison clothes, and when I get home, I'll wear street clothes. It's as simple as that. Some of these guys in here never get a piece of mail, let alone a visit. When they see me walking back from the mail room with these clothes in my hands, they see wealth, and not for nothin' Sharon, people who don't have wealth steal from people who do have it. If I gotta get in a beef over clothes, I'm gonna get more time."

But Sharon ignored my request, and the next time I saw her, she brought more clothes. That bothered me a bit because I felt like she concerned herself more with what made her feel good than with what had the potential to get me more time.

Her stubbornness paid off for the guys around me though. I got a lot of enjoyment when I watched those guys walk out to greet their visitors in my clothes. The only time I wore street clothes inside the jail was when Sharon came to visit.

Sharon continued to visit me nearly every weekend for the next several months and then much in the same way she appeared, she disappeared. By all appearances Sharon had gotten involved with someone else. She was never home when I called. When the operator asked, "Will you accept the call?" a babysitter replied, "No, Sharon is not here."

It hadn't been all that long before then that I had been in the same situation. I wrote Sharon a letter: "I don't know what happened to the girl I used to write, but you're not her. I don't think you should come see me anymore."

That was a difficult decision to make, but this relationship was robbing me of the peace I had come to know in prison. All of the sudden, I found myself sweating the clock on visiting days or the mail call when my name didn't get called for a piece of mail.

What she was doing, or better yet, who she was doing it with were constantly on my mind. I had been there before, and I wanted no part of it. I could do bad by myself. It was easier for me to be alone.

From the time you wake up on a visiting day in prison, you live in anticipation of your visit. Every time the unit phone rings you listen with anticipation for your number/name to be called out. The later it gets in the day and the longer your name isn't called, the more likely you're not going to receive the visit you had anticipated all week.

When Sharon didn't show up for a visit, I was left to do battle with thoughts that left me wondering, *"Is she dead on the side of the road or is she off with another man?"* It would be days before I even knew if she were still alive. But finding out she was with another man was worse.

When I finished writing the Dear Jane letter to Sharon and just as I went to mail it, my Unit officer simultaneously handed me a letter sent by my Appellate Attorney. I knew what it was, and I was afraid to open it. It was the answer to my appeal. The envelope I had waited two years to receive was now in my hands. I knew my conviction would never be overturned, but I had hoped that the appellate court would agree I had received an excessive amount of time for my convictions.

I folded the letter up, put it in my pocket and took it outside near the weight pile where I could read it with some measure of privacy. When I opened it, I noticed there were all of three sentences. That's right – I had waited two years for three sentences! As I began to read, my eyes were drawn right to the word *"Denied,"* and I needed to go no further. I knew everything I needed to know, and the rest was just filler. I took the letter, folded it, and put it back in the pocket of my sweatpants. I pulled my hoody up over my head and began to run, asking God why he had allowed that to happen.

Me and God, we had a lot to talk about. I was furious with God and felt I had a right to be.

"This isn't about the judge or the jury anymore, God, or about what they believed or didn't believe," I told Him. "This is about me believing

Your Word and Your faithfulness to fulfill the promises of Your Word. This is about Your providence and sovereignty and making a way when there was no way!

"I'm no longer the guy who had the Bible-flushing temper tantrum after the judge sentenced me. In fact, God, I'm the guy that just spent the two most difficult years of my life responding to your invitation to refine me, and I did that in the midst of those who criticized and laughed at me for doing it! Now they're really gonna laugh! How did I ever get involved with You?

"Well, what do you have to say for yourself? I'm listening!"

You can't hear God when giving Him your opinion is more important than listening for His answer. Yet the longer I ran – thirteen miles in all, in circles around the compound – and the more I considered the sum of my circumstances, the more I was able to hear something I never heard before. I realized I had never thanked God one time in my life for anything. I never thanked Him for getting only seven years at my sentencing. Instead, I threw a temper tantrum, and I tossed my Bible into the toilet and flushed it.

To the contrary, I reacted to losing my appeal in the exact same way I had reacted to being sentenced, first by getting really angry, and then by blaming it all on God. After sentencing, I saw myself as a victim. I outright cursed God, and told Him to keep His Bible and His religion, too. While my lawyer had said that I should have only served six months, I had never stopped to consider the fact that I could have received a lot more time than I got.

Most of all, the jury had found me guilty of exactly what I was guilty of. Not most of it, not some of it, not more than it, but *exactly* what it was that I had done. That in itself was a miracle, and while I could have easily been found guilty of the lies entered into evidence by the prosecution, I was found guilty of none of them.

The longer I ran, the more it became obvious that God didn't just show up in my cell one day and invite me to change my life. He had been there my entire life, and I never acknowledged Him. In fact, I rejected him! To be even more precise, I lived my life like a fool, and when it all fell apart, I took it out on God.

After running a half–marathon right there in prison, I understood that God had been faithful to His Word long before I knew what His Word said about being faithful, and long before I understood that God's faithfulness wasn't even something I was worthy of. Moreover, God never indicated that He would deliver me from the consequences of my criminal behavior. God simply extended an invitation to refine me. What I did with the invitation was my choice.

I had another year to go in prison, a year I could use to work on the pursuit of restorative change. No more whining to God about what He didn't do for me. No more looking at the glass as half-empty. No more talking and not listening. It was time that I put aside my relationship trials and appellate woes, and focus my attention on the things above. And man, would I need it.

CHAPTER 9

†

A Matter of the Heart

"The good person out of the good treasure of his heart produces good,
and the evil person out of his evil treasure produces 'evil,'
for out of the abundance of the heart his mouth speaks."
(Luke 6:45)

One Sunday morning in the summer of 1985 I had a tough decision to make: Do I skip church and play softball or do I skip softball and go to church? I couldn't do both because by the time church was over, the game would be over, too. It was a make-up game and an important game within the prison that would decide who moved forward in the playoffs.

More often than not, I played catcher because I could throw guys out at second base from home plate. Besides, having a linebacker defend home plate was a valuable asset for my team.

I decided, however, that going to church was more important than going to the game that day. But when I walked out of the building where Father Al had just held mass, I heard screaming coming from across the compound.

"Hey, Palombi!" my teammate Ronnie was running toward me, screaming and cursing like a lunatic. "Hey Palombi? You didn't go to church on the street!"

When he got in my face, I said, "Hey, Ronnie, calm down. It's just a game."

"It's not just a game!" he protested. "We lost because you were in church with a bunch of tree jumpers."

Ronnie was amped up all right. There I was, standing with a Bible in my hand in front of a guy so angry, I was sure was going to hit me.

"Ronnie, I just came from church," I said. "Don't make me do somethin' that I'm gonna have to repent for."

"You ain't gonna do nothin'!" he shouted, adding a popular middle school put-down for good measure.

Finally, I'd had enough. In a calm voice I said, "I'm tellin' ya, Ronnie, either do somethin' or get out of my face, now."

Slowly, he backed away from me, mumbling curse words. Maybe he just didn't think I was worth the extra time he'd have to do for hitting me, I'll never know. But at least I never had to confess to smacking a crazed softball player upside the head just because my new choices were unpopular in prison.

Some of the guys ridiculed my spiritual commitment, saying things like, "You should wear a robe" or "You should be a monk!" Some accused me of being "shot out," meaning that I'd lost my mind. I mean, let's face it: Becoming a student of the Bible in prison was an obvious indication to others that serving time had gotten the best of me. Some guys, however, tried to comfort me, saying, "I went through this on my last bid." Others treated it like the common cold – it would pass.

***

Reaching into his footlocker, my fellow inmate Tony grumbled, "I gotta get me a shot of life." In other words, Tony thought he needed some sex.

"What about you Mike?" Tony asked. "You need a shot of life?"

I knew where this conversation was going, and so I didn't even respond.

"Oh, that's right. I forgot," he said, laughing. "The Bible says you can't have no sex 'til you're married."

All of the sudden Tony, who was now standing in front of me, rolling a joint, knew what the Bible says about what a Christian should or shouldn't do. Tony wasn't a bad guy, he just couldn't believe that I'd bought into that religious stuff. Not for nothing, I'd done to others the same thing he was doing to me. Now that the tides had turned, I didn't like it very much, either. And so I found out yet again what it was like to be my victim.

"Hey guys, Mike says he's a virgin. Ain't that right Mike?" he teased me.

"What are you, beat for somethin' to do, Tony, so you're gonna crack on me about my faith?" I asked.

"You ain't foolin' nobody with this Bible stuff man. You're just fronting for the parole board," he accused, as if the parole board could see me reading my Bible.

"Here's the problem I'm having right now, Tony. My choice to read the Bible isn't gonna hurt anybody on this wing. Not ever! But the minute you light up that joint, you're putting us all in jeopardy," I said. "So you need to stop running your gums and go smoke that joint somewhere else."

"I ain't goin' nowhere."

"Yes you are, Tony."

"What are you gonna do, rat on me?"

"Nope, I'm not gonna say a word, Tony."

Looking at me with his cocky smirk, he lit a cigar that was intended to cover up the smell of the joint he was about to light. As he lifted his lighter to the joint, I cranked the volume on my radio up to ten. He knew that playing my radio that loud would bring a C.O. down our wing in a New York minute.

"Yo, turn the radio down," Tony yelled. Panicking, Tony put the joint in his pocket. "What are you trying to do?"

I turned the radio down for a moment and said, "I told you Tony, I'm not gonna say a word, but you ain't smokin' that joint here."

"You're nothin' but a snitch."

"No I'm not Tony. I just like to listen to my radio loud. What's the problem?"

Walking away, Tony threatened, "You'll see what the problem is."

But this time, Tony was all talk, just trying to save face in front of the other guys. Yet I knew he didn't pack the gear to do anything about it.

A couple of the other guys thanked me, because if a cop had come down the wing, we were all in a jackpot, not just Tony.

The fact of the matter was, there were very few people that I could talk to in prison without walking away from the conversation feeling like less of a man than when I walked into it. A lot of guys in prison like to reminisce about the things they'd done on the street that landed them in prison. You know, the glory days. For many men, much like myself, a large part of their time on the street was consumed with buying, selling, or using drugs.

"Man, look at them veins," a guy I worked out with would say as he tightened his fists. "I couldn't see a single vein when I came to prison." To him, this was a great thing, because it meant that when he went home, as he said, "I ain't gonna have no problem hittin' that with a needle."

"What about parole?" I asked him.

"Man, forget parole," he said. "I'm gonna max out. I ain't peeing in a cup for nobody."

In other words, he was going to refuse the option to be released from prison on parole. He would rather serve every day of his sentence in prison than be subjected to the authority and scrutiny of a parole officer, who would require him to take mandatory drug tests at home. How do you respond to that?

So I didn't.

I was no longer interested in reminiscing and daydreaming about the things that had brought me to prison. There was no future in taking part in conversations that did nothing but bragged about the weaknesses of my past. I had come to a place where, if a conversation didn't add to my life, I walked away from it, and some of the men interpreted that response as me thinking I was better than them. And they weren't afraid to tell me so:

"You can't make it out there, man. It's impossible! How you gonna beat the Man?"

"You got a record. You're a convicted felon! You can't get no job!"

"You got no choice but to commit crime! How you gonna overcome the system? Don't you get it? The system is designed to see to it that you fail! This is a multi-billion dollar business."

"Look at the money these cops are making. They want us in jail because we pay their bills, we buy their cars, and we pay for their vacations and their retirement!"

"You think being saved is gonna overcome the system? Look at you, you're an extortionist, you're a loan shark, and now you want to be saved? Man, you're crazy! You're always gonna be in jail. Get real!"

These guys acted like we were all victims of a conspiracy, when really they'd bought into a mentality of hopelessness. Not one word of encouragement was spoken, not one word of hope, and nothing was said that would inspire any inmate to pursue the change necessary to "beat the Man" or "overcome the system." That is the defeated mentality that nearly every man or woman in prison has to contend with, and that's about as positive as it gets there.

Most people outside of prison believe that overcrowding, violence, and recidivism attest to the inadequacy of our American penal system, but I disagree. Those are merely symptoms inherent to the tragedy of prison hopelessness. But this mentality is common to most any man or woman whose spirit has been broken. Prison is not designed to restore; it is designed to punish, and within that framework, prison nurtures the mentality of hopelessness that is responsible for shattering the human spirit in the first place. The broken spirit of man is the root cause of society's need to confine and punish him.

Pursuing reform and mending my broken spirit in prison was a full-time job that required more from me than just standing clear of the entrapments common to prison life. I literally had to change the way I saw the world. I don't know another way to say it other than I had to raise myself from the dead. The last time I checked, God was the only one who could raise the dead.

As an inmate entering prison, the obstacles before me seemed insurmountable. That's why after sentencing I decided, *"I'm gonna do what I always do. I'm gonna stay high and if I have my way, I'm never even gonna remember I was here."* That was the attitude of a man whose spirit was broken, who believed his existence was for the sole purpose of being punished. But in time, I'd see it a different way. While in prison, I wrote this in my journal:

GRACE

As I lay here in suspended animation,

I look back in time, only to see my life as a blur.

My mind always inebriated, and my body following suit,

simply existed but never truly lived.

I was a living example of the words incomplete and miserable.

My life reflected the likes of Satan, and Satan took me to the depths of Hell

where my only means of escape was the GRACE of a loving and incorruptible God.

It was in Hell that I found Heaven.

It was in Christ Jesus I found eternal Life!

#74590

I never lost sight of the fact that Father Al had said that my reform was a matter of the heart. Teaching me from the Gospel of Luke 6:45, Father Al had spoken to me the words that Jesus said:

"The good person out of the good treasure of his heart produces good, and the evil person out of his evil treasure produces 'evil,' for out of the abundance of the heart his mouth speaks." (Luke 6:45)

If I wanted my heart to change, I had to make a choice to change what went into it. That meant not only policing what I saw on TV and listened to on the radio, but also walking away from negative conversations. When being raised from the dead required more than I had in me, I turned to God for help

Often enough, I found myself in situations where every choice before me was wrong. The confrontation with Lenny, for instance. Paying Lenny the money would have led to more instances of being extorted. Refusing to pay Lenny would have led to anything from injury, to death, or to a life sentence for murder. Without God's intervention and grace, neither choice I had could have ended well. So I learned to give it up to God, something that ultimately meant the difference between parole and serving more time.

Early on in my bid at Southern State, the men in my housing unit nominated me to the Prison Representative Committee (PRC) to be their inmate representative. I don't mean this in an insulting way, but the reality is that I could read and write, and having those skills made me a prime candidate to document and communicate the concerns of the inmate population to the administration.

I accepted their nomination, and carried out the business of making their concerns known to the Superintendent at our regularly scheduled monthly meetings. Unfortunately, the Superintendent didn't respond to the disputes that were respectfully raised by the inmate committee, creating yet another one of those circumstances where neither choice I faced was right.

To begin with, the detail officers were forcing inmates to work in sub-zero temperatures without proper clothing. In addition to that, inmates were not receiving proper medical attention, plus, we were being forced to eat food that was inadequately prepared and lacking nutritional value.

During dinner one night, an inmate noticed that the liver being served was green.

"I ain't eatin' this crap," he lashed out. "You brothers are crazy if you eat this mess. They feeding us the same slop they feed them animals out on the farm."

One by one, men began dumping their meals in the slop bucket that they used to feed the animals. That was all it took. The inmate was written up for inciting a riot, and then he and several others were removed from the prison complex and transferred to Trenton State Prison. Once the inmates arrived there, the cops made them strip naked, and then put them in irons and made them walk through a prison gauntlet of sorts chanting self-deprecating messages for all the inmates to hear. The officers with clubs continually beat the inmates who were bound in irons, killing one and seriously wounding others. You won't read about that in the paper, but J.D. sent me a letter about the men who were beaten.

Hey Mike,

What's doing? I'm still hanging in here. All kinds of stuff going on here at Trenton. The warden has been temporarily removed pending an inves-tigation for allowing the guards to beat up prisoners. The screws are real tough. They get a guy handcuffed and then five of six of them run into the cell with night sticks and beat the snot out of the guys. Pretty tough, aren't they? When fifteen guys came from Southern State, they beat them bad. They put one guy in the hospital (later died) and fourteen others had to be treated at the hospital also but were released. The cops are stool-pigeoning on each other...

Write when you can.

J.D

Meanwhile, all of the representatives of the PRC met to determine what we were going to do about the Superintendent ignoring our concerns. It was decided that a demonstration requiring the participation of the entire inmate population would get the Superintendent's attention. It was also decided that if an inmate didn't participate, he would be dealt with severely.

I couldn't believe that everyone at the meeting supported this decision but me.

"When push comes to shove, guys, and push will come to shove," I tried to reason with them, "we have nothing to negotiate with! The consequences here significantly outweigh the risks."

But they weren't trying to hear any of it.

"What are you, a punk? You down with these crackers?" they shouted.

"Look, I'm going to support you in whatever you do," I said. "I just think this is a good time to remember the guy that got beat to death *over liver*. What do you think these screws are gonna do if we turn this place upside-down? They ain't gonna be comin' in here with no clubs. They'll be comin' in here with firepower. You ready to die? I'm not. Not over freakin' liver!"

But they wouldn't listen. The demonstration was to take place in just forty-eight hours. Even though there were only two ways that I could respond to it, once again, neither choice was right. Yet after accepting the Lord, I chose to live my life in a way that would cause others to rethink their attitudes concerning me, particularly the parole board, who would be making decisions concerning my release. Participating in the demonstration would sabotage any chance I had for proving I'd truly experienced sincere reform.

On the other hand, if I didn't support the inmate cause, I may be seen as a punk or a snitch and that was the least attractive option to me. While the inmate cause was a worthy one, it was clear that the battle they intended to fight could not be won through an inmate demonstration. Life in prison was hard enough, but refusing to participate would definitely put a target on my back inside the prison. I felt like I was back in the county jail all over again struggling with the decision, *"Do I stab him or do I pay the money?"*

Before bed that night, I prayed to God, asking Him for wisdom and direction, now a part of my daily routine in prison. This time, I needed direction more than ever.

The next day, there was a buzz among the inmates about what was to take place the following day. The more I heard the inmates talk, the less hope I had for a positive solution. Fortunately there was one distraction to the impending demonstration: A football game.

That evening, the prison flag football team had a game against neighboring Leesburg State Prison. I was on the kickoff team, receiving team, offensive line, and a linebacker. The games were big events that usually brought out the entire inmate population. Guards and inmates alike bet on the games, and when the game was in your house, you had a definite home field advantage. For one thing, the referees for the game were the same guys we were jailing with every day and we could count on the penalty calls being made in our favor. Even though it was just "flag" football, it was competitive and some of the roughest football I ever played. I am sure many of the guys playing were also former athletes who loved the fact that we could legally unleash the stress and frustration that had accumulated over time in prison out on the field.

As soon as Yard was called, we headed out to warm up for the New Jersey penal system's version of the Super Bowl. This game was going to decide who would remain undefeated, them or us. Whatever was going to happen with the demonstration the next day was gonna have to wait for the next day. It was game time!

I felt right at home as I lined up on the field for the kickoff. I could hear the noise of inmates who had come together and lined the field to cheer for our team. Even the guards were pulling for us as the fate of their bets rested on how well we would play. But this football game was unlike the games I'd played before prison.

To begin with, there were no cheerleaders shouting or bands playing. Family, friends, and football fans did not fill stadium bleachers, nor were there any concession stands where fans could buy snacks during the game. The field of battle was surrounded by razor wire fences and armed men in towers watching for any wrong move. Nothing about the conditions of the field resembled the turf of my former gridiron days. Rather, the field was pure dirt with rocks everywhere. In the absence of yard lines, there stood two inmates holding chains that would mark our position on the field.

The whistle blew and it was game on. As we kicked the ball to Leesburg Prison's team, I headed down the field with my eyes fixed on the opponent that would pay for the last two years of my life. When I reached full running speed, however, I tripped over a rock and landed knee-first on another rock. Immediately, I knew I'd hurt something in my knee really bad. I made my way up on all fours, and began to stand. But one of the Leesburg players greeted me like a freight train hitting a stalled car on the tracks. He drove me viciously backwards and into the ground. There I lay with my legs folded under me. When I looked up, I saw three images of the guy who had just hit me.

"Nice hit!" I complimented the middle image.

The Leesburg player reciprocated with a tongue lashing that attacked my race, and questioned my manhood. Satisfied with his assault, (both physical and verbal), he let a smile replace the scowl on his face. To add insult to injury, my rival spit on me as he walked away.

I jumped up and shouted, "You haven't seen the last of me!"

While laughing, he turned his back on me and said, "Bring it, cracker," which is exactly what I intended to do.

Two plays later, he and I would meet again, only this time I wouldn't be defenseless. As I was leading the way on a screen pass, I saw the bully bearing down on me full speed, and I was determined to give him a lesson in how to get up close and personal. Though I wore no pads, I banked my next decision on the fact that history had proven with Nicky Newark's hand: I had a really hard head. This guy's poor attempt to bully me on a football field was about to come to a painful end.

Running at each other was like a game of chicken, only neither one of us ever intended to back down. Anticipating the oncoming fierce collision, a wild and violent scream erupted from deep within me. As the scream carried across the prison yard, I leapt off of my feet and launched myself, head-first, like a missile, aiming right for his face. SMACK! We collided, head-to-face, after which I saw an amazing light show before we both fell to the ground.

Though dazed, I jumped up, and as he continued to lie there, I flexed my arms letting out another violent scream. The inmates erupted with shouts and screams of their own, showing their approval for the outstanding hit. Reaching for my forehead, I noticed a golf ball-sized egg that matched the one on my knee. As I turned to find the bully, he was still lying on the ground. So I went and stood over him, hoping he was seeing three of me.

I erupted with the same venom he spewed at me and I made sure I didn't walk away before he knew what it felt like to be spit on by another man.

In the end, we won the game. Leesburg had the ball first and goal when the guards called game over on account of disappearing daylight (nudge, nudge, wink, wink). But I could barely walk. I didn't know what needed more attention, my aching head or my throbbing knee. Both injuries did earn me a well-deserved trip to the hospital and frankly, I was looking forward to a change of scenery.

After the game, I was sorry for the way I handled the bully when it came to returning hate for hate. I had let my emotions get in the way of what I knew to be right, and therefore, I set a bad example for everyone who was watching me. I had wanted to be known as a Christian, but I failed miserably in my responsibility to be better than what I was that day.

Later on that evening, a friend of mine who referred to himself as "Self," said, "You know, Mike, you come across like this nice easy going guy, but when you play football, you turn into another person. I don't even know who you are!"

"The person you see on the football field is the person I have always been," I replied. "The man you see walking around this prison is a man that God is trying to rescue."

Self wasn't a believer but he was a very good friend to me. He respected my beliefs and how I was trying to change my life for the better. He even told me that he could see how my faith had changed me from the time he first met me when we would get high, drink hooch, and reminisce about the things that had brought us to prison. I explained to him that, without God, "none of us has the capacity to treat with honor that which God cherishes most – other human beings."

"That's deep, Mike."

Turns out, I had a nasty concussion and a knee injury that would require surgery. Yet the doctor at the hospital simply gave me two Tylenol, no crutches, and nothing in writing relieving me from my work detail. I returned to the prison disturbed by his apathetic response to my injuries. It wasn't like I had never been injured before and didn't know what proper care was. On the one hand, I could understand why the doctor didn't want to give me stronger pain meds, but his refusal to give me crutches and a note relieving me from my construction work detail for a couple of days was ridiculous.

Soon, I went from reminiscing about the game to worrying about the demonstration the next day. Again, I started considering my options: participate or sit out. That's when it occurred to me: *I don't have to make a choice; the choice has already been made for me.* No one would expect me to take part in in the demonstration with a bum knee and no crutches. My injuries had become an answer to my prayer!

Tripping over rocks at kickoff wasn't a matter of fate, luck, or coincidence. It was divine intervention that had caused me to fall, and caused my knee to hit that rock. In other words, it was God's will for it to happen. I could have never come up with a strategy like that on my own. And believe me, I had spent a lot of time considering the options to participate in the demonstration or sit it out, and I never came to a place where I said, "That's it! I know what I'll do! I'll get a concussion and tear the cartilage in my knee, and that way I won't have to participate in the demonstration." In all of my infinite wisdom, I could only consider and dissect the options to participate, or not participate, and then make my decision based on which choice would end up hurting me the least.

The knee injury alone was a great answer to my prayer, but the knee injury without crutches was the perfect answer to my prayer. Had the doctor issued crutches to me, the other inmates would have expected me to participate. This way, I didn't have to suffer the legal repercussions of participating in the demonstration, nor the physical retaliation for sitting it out.

Sometime around noon of the next day, I was summoned to meet with the Superintendent. As I hobbled over to the "Administration" Building with the help of a couple of inmates, I spotted the president of the PRC coming out.

"What's going on?" I asked him.

"Somebody snitched to the Superintendent about the demonstration," he said.

"So, what did he have to say?"

"If anything were to jump off tonight, I'd be the first one sent to Trenton."

"What did you tell him?" I asked.

"I told him to gas up the bus and give me two minutes to pack!"

I entered the Administration Building, where I was searched and brought in to see the Superintendent, who made it clear that he was aware of our intentions to stage an inmate demonstration. As he pressed me for information, he promised to hold my comments in the strictest confidence.

"If this thing does jump off tonight," he warned me, "you and the other members of the PRC will be sent to Trenton State Prison with new charges. You will ultimately receive more time."

When the Superintendent finished speaking, I looked him in the eye and said, "I have no plans to participate in an inmate demonstration this evening. If you have knowledge that there is going to be a demonstration, then you should do what you gotta do to make sure everyone is safe. Beyond that, I can't tell you anything about a demonstration taking place this evening."

I went back to the unit, and I tried to call home. I wanted to let someone in my family know what was happening in case they didn't hear from me for a while. But when I went to make the call, I discovered that all the power to the phones had been shut off. I knew they were preparing for the worst, because the phones only went down when the administration felt that there was the possibility that the security of the institution could be at risk.

Shortly after dinner, just as planned, men started pouring out onto the compound. With the exception of only a couple of men, nearly every single inmate was out on the compound – a recipe for disaster. Soon, men began throwing rocks at the windows of Center Control. The institution responded to the inmate protest swiftly and aggressively, surrounding the prison with what appeared to be several hundred S.W.A.T. Team members dressed in all black and helmets and carrying weapons. Some of the S.W.A.T. guys were situated up on the rooftops with machine guns pointing down at the men on the compound. The show of force was impressive and persuasive, and ultimately all of the men retreated back to their housing units. The S.W.A.T. Teams remained at the prison for a few days. I told the guys the Superintendent wouldn't be responding with clubs, and I guess nobody was ready to give up the ghost over liver.

We were put on lock-down, after which the administration went over the videotapes of the demonstration. Unit by unit, they came and began removing inmates that they felt led the demonstration or had become aggressive during the event.

Yet the demonstration did accomplish something: It pressured the Superintendent to meet with us and forced him to begin to answer our meetings. After all, the demonstration was his fault to begin with, and later, I told him so. He called together the remaining members of the PRC the day after the lock-down. That's when I gave him a piece of my mind.

"You men got what your hand called for," the Superintendent told us. By that, he meant we were going to be locked down for many months to come. As he continued, I interrupted him.

"You got what your hand called for? This situation is your fault and you could have prevented the whole thing by simply answering the meetings. You provoked these men with your silence, and they responded in the only way they knew how. We're not here because we made good choices in life, but I can tell you this: I'm gonna make a good choice right now. I'm done with this."

At that, I got up and went back to my unit. And that was the last PRC meeting I ever attended.

Later in the day, the Superintendent called me back to his office. He encouraged me to stay on the PRC committee, telling me he felt I demonstrated real leadership qualities. He assured me that in life there will always be resistance to leadership and that you can't lead people problem-free.

"This could be a good experience for you," he said.

"If I am leading people on the street and they don't listen," I replied, "I'm not going to spend another five or ten years in prison for their choice not to be led! I'm not willing to take that chance here but I do appreciate your encouragement."

Despite the demonstration, I didn't receive any new charges or additional time. Instead, I got praise from both sides: the Superintendent and the inmates.

I can't take credit for the variables I couldn't control. I can't call what happened a coincidence. I can't dismiss it to chance or fate or even luck. Only arrogance would allow me to believe that I could so perfectly oversee and influence the external circumstances of my life. That I give up to God. Only God can cause a man to change his heart, and only God can redirect his path so perfectly. Prison didn't reform me. God did.

CHAPTER 10

†

Homeward Bound

"Many are the plans in the mind of a man,
but it is the purpose of the LORD that will stand." (Proverbs 19:21)

I should have been out of prison and into a halfway house by April, 1986. Instead, I was denied those opportunities by the State of New Jersey because of the *"nature and circumstances"* of my crime. The circumstance to which they referred, of course was Vinny's murder. Let's face it: That was the same "circumstance" that had persuaded the judge to send me to prison to begin with.

Now, Southern State made an internal decision to move me to the Ocean County Jail in Toms River. It was common practice for prisons to relocate inmates who were short in time in order to open up bed space for men who had just been sentenced to significant amounts of time.

But this was the worst-case scenario for me because no matter how few they may have been, I was about to lose all of the privileges I had earned at Southern State. Other than outright refusing to go to the county, I had no other choice that was free of receiving more time. I wanted the quickest path to physical freedom, and refusing to go to the County Jail wouldn't bring me that.

I had seen a lot of men leave Southern State Correctional Facility, but I had never seen as many people come to bid a person farewell as I did when it was my time to go. Some of the same guys that had ridiculed me and rode me hard about my pursuit of change were the same guys that came to wish me well upon my departure. And Tony was among them.

"Hey Mike, represent when you get out there. If anyone's not coming back to this toilet bowl, I know it's you. I want you to know that I don't think you're frontin'. I know you're for real." Laughing, he added, "You'd have shanked me a long time ago if you weren't."

"Don't think I never thought about it Tony," I laughed.

Tony must have said to me a thousand times when he was breaking my chops, "Hey Mike, what would Jesus do?" That was decades before the popular bracelet W.W.J.D. came out. Talk about missed opportunities.

"I learned a lot from you, Mike. I can't believe I'm sayin' this but I'm gonna miss you."

"Who would have ever thought you'd say that?"

"I don't know, maybe you're convertin' me."

"Take care, Tony."

But the warm farewell that surprised me most of all came from an inmate who hadn't liked me very much when we first met. In fact, Shaheed was a militant Muslim who slept in a bed literally six inches away from me, and he made no bones about the fact that he hated all white people. He had told me outright, "White people are the devil!" On the day I left, however, he walked up to me with a big smile and put his arm around my shoulder.

"Mike Palombi, now that I met you," he said, "I can never say again that I hate all white people." He gave me a big hug and insisted that he help carry my stuff to the van that was waiting for me outside.

"Mike, I want you to write something in this book. I know you're gonna be famous someday," he said, handing me what appeared to be a journal.

After I finished writing, Shaheed opened the book and immediately read out loud what I had written.

"Shaheed, In all you do, consider death. Death can be escaped by no man! Consider it, Shaheed, because you will give an account for this life and keeping that in mind it will be a safe guide towards that which has eternal value. Never forget, folly is for fools. Let wisdom be your blanket. Jesus loves you, Shaheed!

Signed, Michael Palombi, April 4, 1986."

After reading every word on the page, a big smile came across Shaheed's face.

"Mike Palombi, this is deep." Patting me on the back as we walked toward the van he concluded, "Only Mike Palombi can write that kind of stuff."

"Not true, Shaheed. You can write stuff like that too. It's a matter of the heart."

"What's a matter of the heart?"

"What comes out of your mouth is a matter of the heart, I explained. The Bible says, '*For out of the abundance of the heart his mouth speaks.*'"

"What does that mean?"

"Ask Father Al. I gotta go."

Throwing my belongings, which amounted to a paper bag with my state clothes and a couple of pictures, in the van, Shaheed turned to embrace me and said goodbye.

An officer walking by us commented, "You're leaving us, huh, Palombi?"

"Yeah. Today's the day, Officer Graucho. Take care of yourself."

"Oh, I'll be right here when you get back."

Shaheed said, "Ain't no way Mike Palombi's comin' back to any man's prison. I know that for a fact!"

My gang minimum status meant that I no longer had to be shackled to be transported. I climbed into the front seat next to the officer driving the van. As we pulled away from the prison, I didn't look back at the place I had called home for the previous thirty months.

Within a couple of hours, we pulled into the Ocean County Justice Complex. I wasn't looking forward to being there, but it was a step closer to freedom. Unfortunately, moving to the county meant I would be locked down twenty-four/seven again, and lose what little privileges I'd earned at Southern State. Before I went inside I took a couple of deep breaths of fresh air. I knew it might be a while before I'd see the light of day. This time around, I was jail-wise and able to make my way into population without any hassle at all, though there was one anxious moment the first night I arrived.

The bell rang indicating that the shift change of the guards was complete and all inmates were accounted for. It was time to lock in for the night, and as I walked up the stairs towards my cell, I noticed that the cop locking me in had been a teammate on my high school football team. I did my best to hold my head high and greet him, but it was obvious to me that from where he stood, we weren't on the same team anymore.

He was standing at my cell door waiting for me to lock in and that's when we first made eye contact. As I walked into my cell, he didn't even look me in the eye.

"Hi Norman, how are you?"

Looking past me he grunted, "Good." He locked me in and began to walk away.

"Have a nice night."

He didn't even respond to me. I don't know what his problem was, but from what I remembered of Norman and his drug use back in the day, I should have been locking him in.

I was one of three state inmates now locking in with county inmates. With the exception of befriending James, one of the state inmates, I didn't interact with the county inmates at all. Everything was like a big joke to them, most probably because many of them were serving nights and weekends or a couple of months at the most.

One night, a couple of men from a local prison ministry came into the cell block to talk to anyone who might listen to them. I sat down with them for a while and we talked about everything from sports to scriptures. When the conversation turned to the Bible, one of the county inmates sitting next to us playing cards kept telling his friend, "I don't want to hear this nonsense. I don't believe in God. I shouldn't be forced to hear this garbage."

I felt like he was disrespecting the men who had come into the jail to volunteer their time, but I still didn't say anything. I was trying to work on that turn the other cheek lesson. Then he called the three or four of us inmates talking to the volunteers what is the equivalent of a female dog.

There are certain things that you just can't let go in jail, and that was one of them.

"You know what I think bro?" I said. I think your mouth's writing a check that your butt can't cash, and if I keep hearing your shuck and jive you're gonna catch a bad break. That's what I think."

Then out of nowhere I heard, "And I got his back!" James threatened. He wasn't even sitting with us. He announced that while looking down from the tier above. Then he came down the stairs and got in the young guy's face, and challenged him, "You ain't no real convict, white boy. How do you think you gonna talk to a man like that and not get hurt?"

The guy ended up walking away with his tail between his legs.

Aside from dealing with the social issues of the day, the lack of fresh air and physical movement in the jail left me with headaches. Much of the time, I felt extremely lethargic, so I began a regimen of exercises that I would do in my cell, mainly jumping jacks, toe touches, squat thrusts, pushups, sit ups, and dips. I did a thousand repetitions of all but the dips and squat thrusts every day. In addition, I would use a mop bucket filled with water to do several different weight-training exercises. Yet with all of the exercises I did, I still found myself with hours upon hours of idle time on my hands.

I decided to use that time productively, and so I turned my attention back to the State's decision denying me the opportunity to go to a halfway house. I had never responded to that decision, because I was fighting the institution's more pressing decision to send me to the County Jail.

So I wrote a respectful, but strong letter to the State of New Jersey, and condemned an authority who had rendered decisions originating from speculation. I put forth the sentiment that the *"nature and circumstances"* of my crime were more the cause of my incarceration than any crime I had actually committed. Furthermore, the phrase *"nature and circumstances"* had become the speculative standard of measure governing every decision related to my case during all of my time in custody.

It didn't matter how well behaved I was. It didn't matter what I had accomplished during my time there. It didn't even matter that in nearly three years of investigation, nothing pointed to me being involved in Vinny's murder. There were no charges, there were no indictments, there was nothing! When it came to earning privileges, the only thing that anyone ever considered was the *"nature and circumstances"* of my crime.

I closed the letter by stating, *"You have denied me everything you can deny. My release date is but a matter of time now, and freedom is already mine. For what is most important to me I have, and that is my relationship with Jesus Christ. Neither prison walls nor speculative decisions can deny me of that."* After signing the letter, I sealed it in an envelope and mailed it out, assuming I would never hear back from them.

A couple of weeks later, I received a letter from the State of New Jersey approving me for the Volunteers of America (V.O.A.) Halfway House in Camden. I couldn't believe it! I had basically told them to keep their halfway house privilege and resigned myself to the fact that I would be going home from the Ocean County Jail. The decision by the State of New Jersey caused me to consider more clearly God's role in my transfer to the county jail in the first place. Had I not gone there, I more than likely would not have fought the state's decision that had denied me halfway house privileges.

A couple of days before I was supposed to leave for V.O.A., an officer I'd never seen before woke me up at six a.m. and told me, "Palombi, you'd better have these guys clean this day room when they get up for breakfast or none of you will come out of your cells today."

Still half asleep I'm thinking, *"Six a.m.?"*

"Officer, I'm not telling these guys to do anything. That's your job."

"You'll do what I tell you to do."

I got out of my bed, and, standing in my boxer shorts, I asked him, "Are you a rookie?"

There's no way a veteran cop would wake me up at six a.m. and tell me to tell these guys to do anything.

"You're not allowed to do that officer," I fired back.

"I'm writing you up for refusing a direct order. I'm also aware of the fact that you just got approved for a transfer to V.O.A. You might as well know I'll be taking that away."

"You're not doing anything. You're nothin' but a rookie!" I shouted as he walked away. I was mad at myself for feeding into that nonsense. I should have just ignored him, but what he was asking me to do would get a guy hurt in jail.

I could see from my cell that the officer went to talk to the Lieutenant down in sally port, a secure area right outside of the cell block. He pointed up at me and when the Lieutenant looked up, I began yelling to him, "Crack the gate! Crack the gate open!" I wanted to go speak with him, because I knew this cop was not telling him the truth about what had happened. The Lieutenant cracked the gate, and signaled me down to sally port.

"What's your version of what happened?"

"I was sleeping and this officer woke me up at six a.m. and ordered me to tell the guys to clean the day room. You know he can't do that, Lieutenant! When I refused to do it, he told me that he was going to take away my transfer to V.O.A."

Looking firmly at the officer, the Lieutenant asked him, "Did you do that?"

"Yes," the officer answered. "He kept calling me a rookie."

"You are a rookie!"

The Lieutenant turned to me and said, "I'm sorry for the misunderstanding, Mr. Palombi. I'll handle it from here."

I turned, and went back to bed.

***

The evening of April 23, 1986, was the last night I would spend in prison. It was the last time that I would go to bed or wake up in a jail. The next day had a lot of promise, but as I laid there on my bed, I experienced nothing that vaguely resembled a spirit of celebration. Instead, I was scared, and my mind was consumed with doubt. I couldn't believe it, but the reality was that I had come to a place in prison where I felt confident and secure in my surroundings, and the thought of my release made me anxious.

I considered what it was going to be like to live a normal life, and from those meditations, I drew some disquieting conclusions. To begin with, I had now spent the better part of three years in confinement and it was that condition and those experiences that defined what was normal to me. Before prison, a normal life included committing crime, doing drugs, and giving my life foolishly to the attitudes and behaviors that had sent me to prison in the first place. It became clear on the eve of my transfer to V.O.A., that I had no idea what a normal life looked like, and perhaps more importantly, how to effectively live one.

Sure, I had made great changes. In prison, I overcame my addiction to cocaine. I even quit smoking cigarettes. I got in great shape, and I became somewhat of a student, getting straight A's in community college classes I had taken in prison. I changed my tough guy attitude, and became a man who pursued God and wanted to live a life that pleased Him, but I wondered: *Was my desire to do so going to be enough to see me through the trials that life was sure to hand me?* Only time would tell.

I considered the many men that had returned to prison after being released over the couple of years I had been inside. There is no doubt that many of them left determined never to return to prison again, but one by one, most of them did return. It seemed that those returning to prison somehow legitimized the lies that so many prisoners seemed to live by – that the system is designed to ensure their failure.

As I lay there in my cell in the quiet of night, I considered how I had lived for this moment and now that it was here, I was fearful of leaving. I wondered how many men felt the exact same thing on the eve of their release. A part of me worried that I would end up the same way they did.

The next morning, after spending nearly a month in the Ocean County Justice Complex, I left having had very little sleep. I stopped by

James' cell on my way out to say goodbye and give him my Walkman and the couple of packs of cigarettes I had left.

Soon, I was on my way to the V.O.A. in Camden. After perhaps an hour of driving, we came into North Camden near the Ben Franklin Bridge, which leads to Philly. It was a rough-looking area right in the middle of the inner city. On every corner, I could see drug dealers or prostitutes hanging out, looking for business. Then the van came to a stop in front of a group of row houses on State Street. On the front of one of the homes was a sign that read, "Volunteers of America," and it was right smack dab in the middle of one our nation's most violent cities. Perfect!

I grabbed my belongings from the van, and then the officer and I walked up the concrete stairs and headed inside. As I stood there waiting to sign in, I looked around the place, and the first thing I thought was, *"Wow, they have couches here!"* After three years of sitting on steel chairs, I looked forward to relaxing on a nice soft couch.

When Ms. Greene, the Director of V.O.A., came in, the officer handed her an envelope of money from my inmate account at the county jail.

"Hold out your hand," she said, and as I did, she began to count the money, laying forty-three dollars and forty-seven cents in the palm of my hand. With my hand stretched out, I waited for someone to tell me what to do with the money, because waiting for someone to tell me what to do had become routine in prison. But no one said anything.

"What should I do with the money?" I finally asked.

"Put it in your pocket," Ms. Greene sternly instructed. As I pushed the money down into my pocket, I felt like I was doing something wrong. And yet, the privilege of holding money once again felt good.

We went into the Director's office, where I was introduced to my case worker whose name was also Mrs. Green, and that is where we got down to the business of talking about rules and expectations of the halfway house. For me to succeed there, I had to stay clean, and I had to find a job. I had already been clean for two years, and I felt no temptation at all to use, but finding a job, that was gonna prove to be a little more difficult.

After completing the intake process, I was allowed to go out and explore the city for two hours. I wasn't sure that I wanted to after what I had seen driving in. Fortunately, there was a guy there that I had served time with at Southern State, and he offered to come out with me to show me around. I followed his every move as if I had just arrived from another planet and was experiencing everything for the very first time.

At first, it was overwhelming. When we went into a store, I felt like everyone knew where I had been for the last three years and that I should walk around with my hands up in the air. Everyone was friendly enough. I just felt very out of place, and I lacked confidence when it came to going into a public place. My friend said he had experienced the same thing, and assured me that I would be fine in no time.

I ended my first evening at the halfway house eating an ice cream cone, sprawled out on the couch in front of the television. It was an amazing relief to sit alone and to watch a TV without all of the commotion of prison.

The next day, Mrs. Green asked me if I felt like I was ready for a furlough home. That was a no brainer. "Of course I am!" Mrs. Green picked up the phone to call my sister, as her house would be my home when I was to be paroled. She went over the details about what time she could pick me up and what time I had to be back at V.O.A.

There is no other way to explain it other than going home just felt good. Colleen picked me up in her little red Toyota pickup truck, and we drove to her house with the windows rolled down and the wind blowing in our faces. It was a beautiful sunny day, and I took in all of the colors of the tulips blooming and the smell of the fresh spring air. I thought how appropriate it was that I should be coming home when everything was coming back to life.

I was looking forward to getting to my sister's house, especially since I had never seen it before. While I was away, she had gotten married, and she and her husband bought it together. I had met her husband only a couple of times before going to prison, so I appreciated his willingness to let me stay there while I was getting back on my feet.

It was good to see my family again outside of prison walls, but as the day went on, I felt more and more like I didn't belong. I never anticipated such a feeling. At first there was no shortage of things to say. I talked about the halfway house and all of the privileges I had there. I went on a tour of Colleen's house and saw where I would be staying when I came home on overnight furloughs.

But as the day went on, the conversation shifted to times and memories I had not been a part of. It was like I was sitting there with a family I didn't know and one who certainly didn't know me anymore. I felt like a stranger in the company of my own family. Our lives shared nothing in common.

It wasn't anybody's fault; it was just a matter of having been separated for so long. It was awkward being around people who were laughing and enjoying themselves. I had lived with my guard up for so long, I found it difficult to even let it down and relax in an environment that was safe and welcoming. Colleen later told me I looked like a deer caught in headlights. I don't know what I expected from that day, but I never dreamed I would be returning to the halfway house feeling so detached and alone.

When Monday morning came, I arose early and optimistically set out on foot to find a job. Each day until I had a job, I had to bring back evidence in the form of applications and signatures of potential employers that I had in fact aggressively pursued employment. After going to a couple of places, though, I realized that finding a job was going to be a lot more difficult than I had thought.

To begin with, once I learned whether or not a particular business was accepting job applications, the V.O.A. required me to show them my prison I.D. and then introduce myself in the following way: "My name is Michael Palombi and I am participating in a pre-release program from prison. Are you taking applications?" Talk about sabotaging my chance to be hired!

How could they expect me to get a job when they required me to tell my potential employer, "I'm not quite out of prison yet, but I expect to be in the near future, and oh, by the way, here's a mug shot of me holding my prison number. I know I'm not really smiling in that picture but that was a really bad day for me!" Are you kidding? Who's going to give me a job after hearing and seeing that? I'm thinking, I wouldn't give me a job! I only wish I had a picture of every person who held my prison I.D. and listened to me speak those words. The very same people that I asked to employ me began to fear for their lives, only hoping they would make it home to see their families again.

In those moments, I finally understood why so many guys returned to prison. In many cases, the men leaving prison have no education, no trade skills, and poor social skills. On top of that, we are sent back to a place like Camden that is impoverished and crime-ridden with drugs and violence.

Every day, we have to walk past drug dealers and prostitutes through the temptations of a city filled with crime to go look for a job. Every day and every week that our sincere efforts to get a job are shot down, discouragement gets deeper, and a *"What's the point of trying?"* mentality kicks in, and the temptation to return to what you know best gets stronger. Finally, the condition of hopelessness is revealed, and the consequence of the broken spirit of man begins to thrive. The recidivism cycle's completed. In my eyes, I was the gauge for the success or failure of the parole process. I had an education, I had trade skills, and I had pretty good social skills when I needed them. On top of that I had another advantage over many of my peers. Others won't say it or perhaps simply don't believe it. But the fact of the matter was being white was an advantage. None of that meant a thing because as soon as a potential employer hears "ex-con," the interview's over.

When I went back to the V.O.A. that evening, I was feeling really discouraged, so I pulled out my Bible for some encouragement. I realized how distracted I had become by the transfer to the halfway house, the furlough home, and looking for a job. It had been days since I had read my Bible, and just as long since I had met with God in a time of meditation and prayer. I was hungry to read God's word.

The thing about reading the Bible is that everything comes back into perspective for those who believe it. *"Come to me, all who labor and are heavy laden, and I will give you rest. Take my yoke upon you, and learn from me, for I am gentle and lowly in heart, and you will find rest for your souls. For my yoke is easy, and my burden is light."* (Matthew 11:28-30)

I needed to be able to go through this process of finding a job and at the same time find rest in the fact that God's will for my life would ultimately prevail. In other words, if someone rejected my application for employment, my response shouldn't be, "Woe is me, I'm never gonna get a job." My response should be, "Thank you, Lord, for having a better plan for my life."

The next day, I went out looking for a job and again, had no luck. While I was watching television that evening, Mrs. Green told me that I had a visitor. It turned out that Sharon had come to visit me. The afternoon before I left Southern State Correctional Facility for the County

Jail, I got a message from my social worker that Sharon wanted me to call her. When I returned the call, Sharon explained she had been in a bad place at the time we'd parted ways and claimed that the stress of raising two little boys and the pressure of family and friends telling her she was making a bad decision coming to see me were the reasons she had become so distant. Sharon insisted she had not been in another relationship. Her story seemed reasonable to me, especially since my family felt like I was making a bad decision getting involved with her. I did call her a couple of times from the county, and that's how she knew I was going to the V.O.A. in Camden.

As I walked up to greet her, I took her in with my eyes. I thought to myself, she looked beautiful. I felt the most comfortable in her company, because we shared very similar pasts. Sharon had a good job, drove a new car, and provided a nice home for her two young boys. She seemed to be extremely independent, and, despite her troubled past and prison time, her life appeared to be in order. We were allowed to visit for a couple of hours and then Sharon had to leave.

A couple of days later, I found a job working at Cherry Hill Pools. I didn't get the job because I had an education or trade skills. I got the job because only someone as desperate as an ex-con would take it. I was given the responsibility of washing the concrete walls of built-in swimming pools with muriatic acid. "*Thanks, God,*" I thought, sarcastically. Is this my plan for a hope and a future? I'm not finding a lot of rest in working with toxic chemicals. But that was my nature – to run my mouth before I knew all the facts.

Whew, it was nasty breathing in the hydrogen chloride, and dangerous, too, but this was one job you'd never fall asleep on. It was like having smelling salts for an air freshener in your home, only worse. I was paid five dollars an hour, which at the time was a buck sixty-five higher than minimum wage. It wasn't much, but it was a job and it was a beginning for me.

Later, I'd learned the real reason God had brought me to Cherry Hill Pools. The owner of the company wrote an outstanding letter of referral for me to take to my initial parole hearing. Among other things the letter said:

"I would heartily recommend that he be permitted to go back to society as I'm certain that's where he belongs… He is a hard worker, a gentleman, a leader, intelligent, and honest. …Michael Palombi is a good man and to continue his incarceration, in my opinion would serve no useful purpose."

This letter was more valuable to me than the money I'd earned working at Cherry Hill Pools. Finally, I had proof from someone else – a business owner, a family man, a tax-paying member of society – that keeping me in prison would serve no useful purpose!

Here, I'd gone to that company with tunnel vision, looking to earn money and satisfy a requirement for the V.O.A until I was paroled. Eventually, however, I'd learned that God had brought me to that company for a season to position me to receive a recommendation for my parole hearing, after which, I continued to clean pools, completed the outpatient drug program that the V.O.A. required me to do, and earned my driver's license. I began making plans for the future, plans that included a life with Sharon.

By now, I was getting to know her sons, Mark, four, and Tony, two. They were as different as night and day. Mark was quiet and reserved and liked to sit on my lap, while it was all I could do just to get Tony to sit still for a moment.

It seemed that Sharon couldn't do enough for me, and that her doing for me made her happy. In turn, I cared about her all the more. I talked to her about starting my own business in the ceramic tile trade because I knew how to do it well and I wouldn't have to tell anyone about my past. I had done it on a very small scale before, and I knew I could succeed if I put the same energy into building a business that I'd put into committing crime.

Sharon took it upon herself to pay off debts from my past so I could establish credit. She bought the tools I needed to start the business, and finally, she purchased a van for me, which was essential to running my own business.

Eventually, I changed my parole plans from my sister's house in South Jersey to Sharon's house in North Jersey. Everything was falling into place for me. The only thing I was waiting on now was October Second – the day of my parole.

PART THREE:

He Makes All Things New

CHAPTER 11

†

The Sick Find the Sick

"Do not be unequally yoked with unbelievers."
(2 Corinthians 6:14)

My family wasn't happy about the plans I was making. They had met Sharon and sensed she was not the woman she claimed to be, and felt she was intentionally smothering me by not allowing me any time with them on my weekend furloughs home. Meanwhile, Sharon could sense my family's objection to our relationship, and she felt like they were judging her.

I understood that my family was trying to look out for me, but I figured, why would Sharon do for me the things she was doing if she did not experience a genuine love and affection for me? Strangely enough, my family thought the same exact thing. Well, except they thought Sharon had a hidden agenda. They wondered why she would do the things she was doing for me unless there was something in it for her.

As my parole date drew nearer, I could tell Sharon was feeling anxious about our relationship and my long-term intentions. Was I in this relationship for the long run, or was I just jailing off of her (using her) like some of her friends said I was?

I figured out how to assure her uncertainty about our relationship…I moved into her house. I struggled with that decision spiritually, because I knew what I was doing did not line up with what I knew the Word of God to be. But I became more concerned with proving my intentions to Sharon than with proving to God I would live a life that honored Him outside of prison.

In time, my decision to move in with Sharon cost me my relationship with God. Not because God didn't love me anymore, but because of the guilt and shame I felt by choosing to dishonor Him. How could I stand before God and ask Him to bless a life and a relationship that discredited the sanctity of God? Essentially, that's what I did!

In the months following my parole, I learned some things about Sharon that had not shown up during our jailhouse visits.

"Why are you going to the gym?" she'd ask.

"I'm goin' to work out. Why don't you come with me?"

"Because you're really going to look at the women there."

"What?" I couldn't believe she said that and what's more, I couldn't believe she believed that.

"Sharon, I've gone to the gym most of my life. I'm an athlete."

"You don't need to work out for me to love you. I love you the way you are." Which, I felt, was another way of saying, she shouldn't have to go to the gym to look good for me. I should have just loved her the way she was.

"Well, I'm not gonna stay the way I am if I don't go to the gym."

"Fine. Go to the gym then. I know what's more important to you."

When I went to the gym, Sharon would show up to check on me, or she would send Mark and Tony with me to play at the gym, which was just another way of keeping an eye on me. Ultimately, Sharon bought workout equipment for the house, and because I didn't want her to feel insecure about my going to the gym, I worked out at home.

I didn't take it personally. I understood it was hard for her to trust anyone after enduring an abusive childhood. Instead, I made excuses for her behavior and believed that it would improve over time, because I would be the guy to help her change it.

So, I asked Sharon to marry me, and we set a date for May 3, 1987.

It wasn't long after we got married that many of Sharon's "I do's" became I don'ts:

I don't want to go to your family's house for the holidays: "I know they hate me."

I don't like your friends: "They mean more to you than I do."

I don't like your church: "I'm Catholic. I don't believe in being reborn."

I don't want a Bible study at our house: "All of the people are weird."

Every time we got in an argument about any one of those things, she was quick to remind me about the gifts she had given me, the debts she'd paid off, or how she provided the means for me to start my own business, claiming, "You're nothing without me!"

She became like a loan shark collecting the vig on a loan. I wasn't in a marriage at all. I was paying off a debt! Only, I believed I owed her a debt for all she had done for me, and believing that lie was the evidence of my own emotional injury.

Unfortunately, I had walked out of one controlling environment and right into another one. I began to think about my marriage in the same way I'd thought about prison.

"How could anything good come from a method of operation that intended to demoralize its occupants as a means of controlling them?"

It entered my mind on more than one occasion that Sharon had a lot in common with the judge who had sentenced me: They both intended to control my life.

When the judge sentenced me to seven years in prison, he never expected me to get in my car, drive down to Southern State, and knock on the front gate and say, "Hi guys, I'm here!"

Rather, he had me chained like an animal and forcefully taken to prison. The judge had me secured in a facility surrounded by razor wire fences that would cut me to shreds if I tried to climb them and escape.

And just in case I did climb those fences, there were armed guards in towers ready to shoot me dead on sight.

Much like the judge, Sharon never expected that when I was paroled I would get in my car, drive to North Jersey, knock on her door and say, "Hi Sharon, I'm here!" On the other hand she didn't have the resources to bind me in irons and whisk me away to her house where armed guards would prevent me from leaving her. So, Sharon manipulated our relationship, and instead of using force she took me "captive" through kindness. Finally, she said all the right things, convincing me that she was a woman of faith. By all appearances, Sharon was everything I'd ever wanted in a woman.

***

Right away, we agreed that Sharon would control the finances. She worked as the controller of a successful wire and cable company where she would oversee all of the financial matters of the company. That arrangement made perfect sense to me, particularly since the only money I ever managed was my thirty dollar-a-month inmate account.

When it came to the cars we owned or the home we eventually purchased, she convinced me that we should only list her name on the bill of sales and the deed to the house, reasoning, "If something goes wrong on your construction jobs, the homeowner can't take our cars or house, because they're not in your name." That sounded reasonable to me, too, but then again, so had strong-arming people.

She worked hard to keep me away from family, friends, and the church, seemingly because she didn't want me around people who were trying to point out what I couldn't see – Sharon wasn't the person she portrayed herself to be. Sharon gradually and methodically took control my life, and I let her do it.

I have heard it said that the sick find the sick, and Sharon and I did just that. We were two emotionally damaged people who found each other and then decided to get married. Had I been an emotionally healthy man, I would not have made excuses for some of the things she said or did prior to getting married. I probably would have never made it past our first Christmas.

Our first Christmas together was anything but what I had imagined it would be. Mark and Tony opened their gifts first. Tony's goal was clear: Open as many gifts as he could, as fast as he could. But Mark took his time, carefully opening each one, studying the gift before moving on to the next. When they were finished I was excited for Sharon to open the gifts I had gotten her, but she insisted that I open mine first.

Wow! She gave me more gifts in one Christmas than my parents had given me in five. Growing up, there was no extreme gift-giving in our home, so this was new to me. From new skis to a Nikon camera, a pocket watch, and tons of name-brand clothes, she had to have spent a small fortune. After opening so many expensive gifts, I felt embarrassed to hand Sharon such a small stack of gifts.

"I didn't have a lot of money," I apologized.

"Don't worry about it," Sharon said. But I could tell by the strained smile on her face that she felt let down by the small number of gifts I handed her. Still, I couldn't wait for her to open them.

"Don't open the small gift until last." That was a special gift.

As Sharon opened her gifts she criticized them. "This size is too big. I'm not that fat," or "I don't wear this brand. It's cheap." What a buzz-kill on my first Christmas home, but I was still confident that the special gift I'd gotten for her would be my redemption of sorts.

"This better be a necklace," Sharon said as she began to remove the wrapping paper from the gift. Well, it wasn't exactly a necklace but it was the beginnings of one. I knew that Sharon loved sapphire gemstones, and so I'd gone to a jeweler and I bought a loose sapphire gemstone in the shape of a heart. The stone cost me over nine hundred bucks, which was a big purchase for a guy who, just a few months before, was making a dollar a day. I figured I would get the stone and then we could shop together for a nice necklace.

As Sharon opened the box with the stone in it, I had a big smile on my face, like, *"That's right. I'm the man!"*

After opening the box though, Sharon removed the sapphire and began screaming and swearing at me in front of Mark and Tony, "This isn't a necklace! All I wanted was a freaking necklace and you couldn't get that for me? After all I do for you, was that too much to ask?" Sharon threw the sapphire at me and began crying.

"I spent thousands of dollars on you and what do I get? Clothes that don't fit! You must have been thinking about your female customers when you were shopping, because you couldn't have been thinking about me!"

Suddenly, I felt guilty for not measuring up to my fiancée's expectations. I had wanted to keep the heart-shaped gemstone a surprise for her. Now, I thought twice about telling her how I was able to afford it – by setting aside cash from the money she gave me for a weekly allowance.

For weeks, she'd lashed out at me because I couldn't give an accounting for all of the money she'd given me.

"What are you doing with all the money I give you?"

"I put gas in the van?" I'd reply.

"Well the van shouldn't need gas if all's you're doing is going to your job and besides, the receipts don't add up to that amount anyway. Nice try."

What a disappointing holiday that first Christmas was for me. In prison, I didn't open a single gift, but I came to love Christmas day for what it meant in terms of a Savior being born. But in this house, Christmas was clearly all about the gifts.

Even though I had been saved spiritually and although I had changed my life behaviorally, I never took the time during my incarceration to focus on and console the deep emotional wounds of my inner being, but why would I? To begin with, I didn't even know they existed. Next, I was the offender of the crime and as I understood it, the act of consoling was reserved for the victims of a crime.

Besides, I believed that when it came to my emotions, I was expected to suck it up and walk it off like a man. Well, that's what a man does, isn't it? That's what Mom and Dad taught me, that's what football taught me, and that's what prison taught me. So why pursue emotional healing?

It would be years before I understood that when I went to prison, I was both offender *and* victim. Like most of the men and women serving time, my offender status was directly linked to the emotional wounds of my victim status. And, left untreated, emotional wounds can be just as fatal as physical wounds.

The fact is this: If you don't know the truth, you can't see the lie. And my mother wasn't about to stand idly by and watch Sharon work her son like that, either.

"She's got you whipped," my mother said. "She's not paying your debt and buying you tools and a van because she's madly in love with you. She's buying you tools and a van because she expects you to support her and the kids for the rest of your life. For crying out loud, take off the blinders, Michael, she's using you!"

But I believed that Sharon genuinely loved me for who I was.

I had just come home from prison when I put myself in a situation where I had an instant family, and as a result, a lot would be expected of me. My mom was worried about how the pressure of having those responsibilities would affect me.

After all of the warnings by my mother and others, and after excusing behaviors that contradicted the words that Sharon spoke, I realized that the sick had married the sick, and within six months, I left her.

Unfortunately, leaving Sharon meant saying goodbye to Mark and Tony, the two little boys who had come to know me as Dad. I had begun to teach them right from wrong, gave them responsibilities like cleaning up their toys, and I disciplined them if it was necessary.

The two of them would tag-team me in their Spiderman underwear. They'd jump from the couches on top of me, growling as they used their favorite Hulk Hogan and Randy Savage moves to try and force me to submit. I got a kick out of watching them giggle and glow when I let them beat me. I was excited about being their father, but when it came to doing what would have been in their best interest, I let them down.

I didn't set Godly examples for them to follow. In truth, I did just the opposite. I moved into their home and took up residence with their mother before I was married to her. That's not part of God's plan for anyone's life, let alone the example God wanted a Christian man setting for two young boys. Had I not moved in with Sharon, but just dated her, I more than likely would not have married her.

For a couple of months after I left, I visited the boys on and off, but seeing them meant I had to see their mother, too, and because of the confrontations we would have, I did not see them as much as I would have liked to.

We had had some big fights, alright. There was yelling and screaming and swearing. Sharon would break things, and at times she would throw things at me. Once, she got fired up over something I said, and started yelling at me, "Get out of my house!" And then she slammed the bedroom door behind her.

"I'm not going anywhere," I replied. Then Sharon came out of the bedroom with an oversized coffee mug, and winding up for the throw, she screamed like a convict, "I said get out of my house!"

I high-tailed it out of there, and as I was running away, I remembered that I'd left my van keys in the house. I turned to go back, but it was too late. Sharon had locked the door.

Knocking on the door I said, "Sharon, I need my keys."

"Go away. You're not getting the keys. They're my keys. I bought the van."

I stood on the deck for a while thinking about how I could get her to give me the keys. Then I looked in the window of the kitchen door, and I could see my keys sitting on the counter nearest to the door. They were so close, and yet so far away. The window I was looking through was made up of nine individual panes of glass, and looking through it, I could see that Sharon was nowhere in sight.

SMASH! I broke the pane of glass nearest to the doorknob. I reached in, unlocked the door, opened it and snatched my keys in about one second flat, but not before Sharon came trucking around the corner with that coffee mug in her hand. As she wound up to make the throw, I slammed the door behind me, and then, leaping down the stairs three treads at a time, I sprinted to the van like I was running from the law, only faster.

As I opened the van door, I could see Sharon at the top of the deck, and with a look of determination, she launched the mug at me. I dove into the van to take cover from the flying coffee mug, and at the moment I landed on the seat of the van, I heard the sound of breaking glass. Sharon had thrown the coffee mug so hard that it embedded in my windshield without breaking and simultaneously blasted the rear-view mirror off of the windshield and right into my hard head.

Not only did the mirror cut my head, but I couldn't move because I had pulled my back out when I dove into the van. I ended up having to go to the hospital to get treated for severe back pain. Embarrassing as it may have been, it was Sharon who took me to the hospital.

Obviously, it was better for everyone involved if I just stayed away.

***

After we separated, I worked on trying to restore some of the things my relationship with Sharon had required me to surrender. I began reading my Bible again, and I tried to rebuild my broken relationship with the Lord, but it was difficult. I felt hypocritical running back to God, and I suffered from an unrepentant heart.

When I was locked up, I'd think *"If I can survive the struggles of serving time in prison, anything else will be easy."* But soon after my release, I realized that wasn't exactly true. Serving time had its struggles, but living life responsibly had its struggles, too.

My relationship with Joey began when he stole my brand new 1988 GMC Jimmy. I had stopped by my buddy Ray's house and left the car running while I went inside. A minute later, I went back outside and my SUV was gone. At first, I thought Ray was playing a joke on me, but when he called the cops to report the vehicle stolen, I knew it wasn't a joke.

When the cop arrived at the house, he suggested I get in the police cruiser with him so we could take a ride around the neighborhood to search for my car. I went to the back door of the cruiser and the cop told me to get in the front. As I grabbed the handle on the front door of the police car, I turned to my friend Ray and said, "I never rode in the front seat before."

It was a cloudy winter day and snow had been predicted in the forecast. In preparation for the snow I had put the plow on the GMC. Good thing, because it made it easier to find.

Within five minutes of our search, I spotted my Jimmy, and that's when me and Joey made eye contact for the first time. Joey hit the gas hard and took off. The officer called in for back up and the chase was on. We followed Joey closely through the streets of Jefferson Township with lights flashing and the sirens sounding, but it didn't make him stop.

At the town border, the Roxbury cops had set up a barricade across the road using two of their police cars. The nervy sixteen year-old literally plowed right through the seam of the two police cruisers. With three cars now chasing Joey, the pursuit took us into Wharton Township, where we picked up two more cops, and then to Dover Township where we picked up a couple of more cops. Finally, Joey brought us into Rockaway Township, and added two more cars – nine cop cars in all – in the five-town chase.

By now it had started to snow, and the road conditions were getting slick. It appeared that Joey was trying to make his way back to Jefferson, and that's when he made his boldest move yet: He started heading north into the oncoming traffic of southbound Route 15. A few of the cops followed him into the southbound lanes and others stayed side by side in the northbound lanes. It was obvious that Joey had no intention of stopping the vehicle on his own.

Suddenly, Joey made another risky move and cut across the grass median and began heading south in the northbound lanes. Cars were dodging Joey's daring attempt to escape the long arm of the law, but time was running out. The snow was getting harder, the roads were getting slicker, and it seemed to be just a matter of time before he would crash. Joey made one more desperate attempt to outmaneuver the cops near the entrance to the Picatinny Arsenal, but it backfired. One of the cops took the opportunity to ram my mini SUV into the rock ledge of the mountain.

I watched in disbelief as my brand new GMC Jimmy hit the wall, and one of the tires broke off the frame and headed in a different direction. The Jimmy was destroyed, and that meant the chase was over. The cops couldn't get to Joey fast enough to drag him out of the totaled Jimmy and give him a token beat-down. Even though the kid had destroyed my SUV, I couldn't help but feel for him as he covered up to protect himself from the onslaught of blows from the officers.

After Joey was arrested and later released, I went to his house to talk to him and his parents.

"Is your son home?" I asked. "I'd like to speak to him if that's okay with you."

"Sure it is. Hey Joey? C'mere for a minute. Somebody's here to see you."

Joey came walking out from his bedroom, and I greeted him. "Not havin' a good day, are ya?"

"No."

"Remember me?"

"Yeah."

"Who am I?"

"You're the guy that was with the cop who was chasing me."

"I asked you when you got arrested, why did you steal my car? Well, you never answered me, so I'm here to find out."

"I wanted to go see my girlfriend. I wasn't planning on stealing it but when I saw it sitting there and running…"

"You couldn't help yourself, right?"

My sarcasm broke the tension, and Joey cracked a smile.

"I don't think you're a bad kid, Joey, but you definitely made a bad decision today. I came here to make you an offer. You interested?"

"What's the offer?"

If you come with me for one day, Joey, I won't press any charges against you. In fact, I will come to court and speak on your behalf.

"What do I have to do?" Joey inquired.

"I'm gonna take you and your mother to Rahway State Prison. I have some friends I want to introduce you to."

I intended to bring him to see the Lifer's Group at Rahway State Prison. They were known for their Juvenile Awareness Program called "Scared Straight" that used the natural environment of the prison to confront at-risk teens and the behavioral issues surrounding their circumstances of delinquency. In other words, prisoners tried to scare them straight.

When I was in high school, one of my teachers had taken a group of us to the same program. It was a class trip for our criminal justice class that just happened to have an unruly group of kids in that very class. We weren't in trouble with the law, but we were doing things that could have definitely interfered with attending our graduation senior year.

On the day of our tour of the prison, I wore jeans and a denim shirt and not by coincidence. I knew that was what the inmates were wearing at the time. I thought I knew something about prison because my uncles had served time, but I was in for a rude awakening. It was all a big joke to me on the way up to the prison, but the minute the steel doors closed behind me and I was standing in front of inmates serving life sentences, nothing was funny anymore.

"Hey," one inmate said. "Look at this guy, he's already to go."

"Get your butt over here. Hurry!" he screamed. "You wanna be like us?"

"No."

"Then why are you dressed like us? You think this is funny?" Then he got real close to me and said, "Look at my eye. You see my eye?"

He was holding his eyelid open with his two fingers. Again he yelled, "Look at it!"

But it wasn't there.

"I lost my eye over a cigarette. Another man stabbed me in my eye over a lousy cigarette. And you want to come to prison right?"

"No."

"What do you mean, no. You're here! Look at you. Take a good look around. You're in prison right now. Where are all of your friends?"

"In school."

"Where are you?"

"I'm in prison."

"What do you see when you look at me?"

"An inmate!"

Frustrated, he threw his skull cap on the floor and began screaming at me again.

"When I look at you, I see myself, and when you look at me you should see yourself, because you're lookin' in the mirror! This is your life if you don't change!"

All I was thinking at the time is, *"I'll never be like you!"*

I just couldn't understand how partying and smoking a little weed could be compared to the life sentence that he was serving for murder. But he knew what I didn't: My behavior would escalate over time if I kept approaching life with the same bad attitude.

But this time, I was going to see the Lifer's group for a different reason. The young man who had stolen my car agreed to go with me to Rahway State Prison to be confronted by some of the same guys who'd warned me a decade earlier that I'd wind up like them.

When I got to Rahway Prison there were a couple of guys among the Lifers that had been in Essex County Jail with me. I also saw some of the same men that had been in prison when I went to the program in high school.

My pals from the county worked Joey over. They double-teamed him.

"What do you think's gonna happen to a white boy like you when you come here? Take a look around. You're the closest thing we have in this prison to a woman!"

Joey was afraid for his life.

"You like to steal cars? Answer me!" Kevin screamed. "Do you like to steal cars?"

"No."

Kevin got next to Joey's ear and said in a quiet voice, "If you lie to me one more time I swear I'll knock every tooth in your pretty little mouth right out of it." Screaming in Joey's ear, Kevin asked, "Do like stealin' cars?"

"Yes."

"That man who brought your sorry little butt here, Mike, he's my associate. You stole my man's car and now you in prison with me. Man, you're in a world of trouble."

Then Howard jumped in. "Turn around and look at your mother. DO IT! Look at her, she's cryin', and why? Because she's worried about her son, but you don't give a rip about her or you wouldn't be doin' this drunk stuff you're doin'. Tell your mother you love her. TELL HER!"

By now Joey was crying, too. Truth be told, it was hard for me not to cry, but it was exactly what Joey needed. Kids like to talk back to their parents, but they don't normally talk back to men serving life sentences, and so for a change, they listen, and Joey listened.

In exchange for his visit to the Lifer's group, I agreed to appear in court and speak on his behalf. Joey's attorney opened up the hearing by telling the judge, "Your Honor, we have a unique situation here. The victim of the crime is here to testify on behalf of my client."

The judge asked me, "Do you have something you want to tell the court today?"

"Yes, Your Honor. Joey's a good kid who's made some bad decisions. His parents are recently divorced, and he has taken it hard. After stealing my truck, I took him to Rahway State Prison to participate in their juvenile awareness program, 'Scared Straight.' If he didn't know where his behavior was leading before he stole my truck your honor, I have no doubt that he is clear about that now, and he can no longer say, 'I didn't know.' I believe Joey is going to take the advice of the inmates and turn his life around moving forward. I have spent three years in prison myself, your Honor, and if there are any options available to this young man that do not include incarceration, I would ask the court to grant him those options one last time."

"Thank you, Mr. Palombi." Then the judge asked Joey to stand and he began to interview him. "This isn't your first time in front of me, son. Mr. Palombi has been very kind, but now I need to hear from you."

After completing his interview with Joey, the judge imposed a sentence of custodial time, but suspended it and sternly warned, "If I see you back in front of me again, there are no more chances."

Joey was smarter than I ever had been, because he received the message and advice the Lifer's Group had given him: "Get an education, make something of yourself. That's how you tear down these walls." To the best of my knowledge, Joey never got in trouble again. In fact, I saw him eleven years later when he was married with a son and was running his own tree-cutting business. He was just the first of many young men I'd take to the Lifer's Group at Rahway State Prison.

***

A year after I separated from Sharon, I'd gotten off parole, and for some reason I wanted to share that good news with her.

"Why are you calling me?" Sharon asked.

"Because you went through a lot of that with me, and I'm just excited that's it over."

"Well, I'm very happy for you, Michael. You deserve it."

"I've also been thinking about our marriage lately and perhaps I hadn't given our marriage much of a chance."

I thought with good intentions, *"Maybe if I worked as hard on our marriage as I am working at my job, maybe we would have had better results."*

"I haven't always made it easy on you," she chuckled. "It's my fault, too."

Soon after, Sharon and I began to see each other again. One day, around two months after we started seeing each other, Sharon called and said she wanted to see me. She had something important to tell me, but wanted to wait until we were together.

"I'm pregnant," she told me.

"What?"

"I'm pregnant."

"You did this on purpose!" I was angrier with myself than I was with her. This is a trap! How could I have let this happen? We weren't divorced, we never even officially filed for divorce, but yet again, I used poor judgment.

Sharon was crying and appeared to be genuinely upset and so I began to settle down. I didn't know what to believe or not to believe, but it didn't make a difference. I was going to be a father, and more than ever, I wanted to try and make our relationship work.

I formally returned home for Christmas in 1988, when she was five months pregnant. It was a good Christmas and things were going very well between us. Many of the issues that we had fought about, we no longer fought about. I was doing some Bible studies again, but I was not going to church. I had been going to the gym, but I began to use the equipment at home when I moved back in.

It seemed that being pregnant was good for Sharon. I mean that in a good way. I had never seen her happier, and I had never seen her emotional state more settled.

On April 14, 1989, Sharon and I went to the hospital to have our baby, but the delivery was anything but typical. The umbilical cord was wrapped around the baby's neck, and the doctor panicked. The midwife literally pushed the doctor to the side and took over the delivery. She kept turning Sharon from side to side and eventually our baby girl came out.

They took her immediately out of the room for some tests, but then brought her back shortly after. The nurse placed Christina in my arms and immediately I felt pure joy. I stared at my daughter in amazement of what I had just witnessed – the beginning of life! I don't know that I have ever witnessed anything in life that can compare to the miracle of birth.

Christina weighed nine pounds and twelve ounces and was delivered by natural child birth, and yet Sharon never made a sound during the entire delivery process. She even returned to work on the following Monday morning, just three days later. Talk about walking it off!

During the year Sharon and I were separated, I was working with my friend Ray. We built new homes, completing the entire building process from the excavation of the job site to finishing the construction of the house. Working with him was like a crash course in residential construction, because he put a lot of responsibility on me in a short amount of time.

To begin with, I had to learn how to read construction plans and how to use them to build a house. I worked alongside the masons building the foundations, the framers constructing the house, and with most of the other tradesman to install roofing, siding, windows, doors, trim work, and of course, ceramic tile. When you do that every single day, you become efficient at what you do.

But Ray pulled an underhanded move that caused us to lose a two-and-a-half acre parcel of land that had been purchased with the help of a group of investors that my brothers had pulled together. It wasn't pretty when I had to tell them that the money they had invested was lost. My days with Ray were over.

For the next couple of years, I installed ceramic tile and marble with my sights set on completing additions and renovations. I understood that in order to make more money in the construction business, I had to be able to provide more services. It was difficult at first to make money on some of the bigger projects because, while I had the experience of performing the labor, I had no experience in bidding the costs of a job. More often than not, my bidding mistakes were related to underestimating the costs of materials and how long the job was going to take. And those mistakes caused some of the most serious arguments Sharon and I had.

I mean, it wasn't like I had gone to school for this, and yet Sharon was anything but warm-hearted and understanding when I made bidding mistakes. She behaved as though I'd intentionally made them, when the truth of the matter was, most men in construction made those same bidding errors when first starting out. The one person whose support and encouragement I needed most, ridiculed and belittled me when jobs did not turn out to be as profitable as I had originally estimated.

"Are you getting paid today?" Sharon asked.

"Yeah, but there isn't gonna be as much profit as I estimated."

"Why not?"

"I underestimated the waste on the cedar clap board. I figured fifteen percent waste, and I should have estimated forty percent waste because of the reveal of the siding."

"So what does that mean?"

"It means I under-ordered the siding by twenty-five percent, and I've got to go buy it and I need the money that's coming in to purchase the siding."

"You're going to charge them for that, right?"

"I can't charge them for that. I should know how to bid a job, Sharon."

"What, are you stupid? You're gonna pay to do their job? I can't believe you're that stupid!"

And you know what, that's the same exact phrase the customer would use if I told them they owed me more money because I'd bid the project wrong.

When it came to the business, I needed my wife to be my partner but it always felt more like she was my adversary.

Ultimately, I learned how to bid jobs the same way I had learned how to do everything else in life – the hard way! Like most things, if you do it long enough, you can't help but get good at it, and in time I got good at bidding jobs and closing the deals. I began to make more and more money at construction, but the money came at a personal price. I had to work more and more hours of the day and more and more days of the week. I went on the estimates, I prepared the proposals, I picked up the materials, and I completed much of the work on the projects, and to do that, it took all of my time, from sun up 'til sun down, there was no time for my family and no time for me.

CHAPTER 12

†

Iron Sharpens Iron

"Iron sharpens iron, and one man sharpens another."
(Proverbs 27:17)

My first surgery came after I'd repetitively bench-pressed heavy amounts of weight, but the second surgery came by way of swinging a twenty-eight ounce framing hammer. Hammering ten to twelve hours a day caused the first repairs on my rotator cuff to tear again, so I couldn't work for a couple of months.

Although I couldn't work in the trades for a while, I could volunteer at an alternative school in Pompton Plains. I had gone there on a couple of occasions to speak to some of the young men who'd had run-ins with the law. I took those same kids to Rahway State Prison to meet the Lifer's Group, and hoped that it might have had the same impact on them as it had on Joey.

When I arrived at the school, I asked a counselor there if the owner was available to talk to me. She pointed in the opposite direction and said, "Oh, you just passed him on your way in. He's the man over there feeding the fish."

I looked in the direction she was pointing, and saw a slight man dressed in dungaree overalls and a white T-shirt. He had a pair of bifocal glasses resting on the end of his nose, and he was holding a can of fish food in his left hand. I thought to myself, *"This guy owns a school? He looks like he owns a farm!"*

Nevertheless, I introduced myself to him, but he never took his eyes off of the fish he was feeding.

"Are you Richard Sheridan?" I asked.

"Yeah, whadda you want?" This guy had an edge like the wise guys I hung with on the street.

"My name is Mike Palombi. I've been to the school a couple of times to speak to your students and take them to Rahway State Prison." I explained, "Many of your students are going down a path that I have already gone down and I think my life experience can help those particular students."

He never looked at me once while I spoke. He seemed to be more engaged with the fish attacking the food falling into the water than he was with the words I was speaking. I felt like I was wasting my time.

"I want to volunteer at your school while I'm recovering from shoulder surgery."

In the instant I said "volunteer," he stopped feeding the fish, turned to face me and, looking up at me over top of his bifocals, he said, "Absolutely not! You're not going to volunteer at my school!"

He put the fish food down, removed his glasses and continued, "I'm gonna pay you to work here. In fact, you're gonna run my Juvenile Awareness Program and in order to do that, you must have spent at least three years in prison!"

Richard was a tough guy of sorts himself. He'd spent much of his childhood from about the age of three living in a group home after his parents split up. Sometime around his twelfth birthday, Richard's father remarried and came to the group home to take him home to Roosevelt, New York. But his new home was anything but warm and fuzzy, and by his eighteenth birthday, Richard, a stand-out high school wrestler, decided to quit high school and join the marines. That decision came on the heels of his high school principal telling him he wasn't going to graduate.

Richard went from strolling the hallways of his high school to surviving the jungles of Vietnam, where he was a field radio operator, who were often strategic targets and therefore, among the first to die in battle. Without the field operator, there were no calls for backup.

After four years in the marines, Richard came home to his father who callously asked, "What are you doin' home?"

For a tough guy, Richard sure showed a lot of compassion. Had I been confronted with the same set of circumstances, I can't say that I would have responded to the likes of me the same way. I mean, he didn't even know me. I was an ex-con whose character would always be in question, and where everyone else used that status to condemn me, this stranger immediately used it in a way that absolved me.

Even if he didn't, I realized immediately, he was risking everything he'd ever worked for in his life on his one decision to take me into his program. In other words, if I wasn't who I said I was, he could kiss his school goodbye. I was truly stunned. When we parted ways that day, I was set to start working three days a week at Chancellor Academy beginning the following Tuesday.

I couldn't wait to get home to tell Sharon the good news about what had just happened. After all, she knew it had long been my dream to work with at-risk kids.

"You're never gonna believe what happened today when I went to Chancellor Academy," I told Sharon, excited. "The owner of the school not only said I could work there while I am recovering, but he said he would pay me to work there!"

I could tell by the look on her face that Sharon wasn't nearly as impressed or excited as I was.

"How much is he going to pay you?" she asked.

"Twenty-one thousand dollars per year as a teacher's aid."

"What are you, stupid?" she asked. "You're making a lot more than that doing construction."

"That's not the point, Sharon." I explained. "I'm an ex-con who went there only hoping he would let me volunteer while I recover from surgery, and now this guy Sheridan made me a paid member of his staff!" This was the door I needed to be opened in order to have any hope to work with the student population I had dreamed to work with. There was no doubt in my mind this was the opportunity of a lifetime and an opportunity like this may never cross my path again.

At the end of the day, though, Sharon didn't care about opportunities. She didn't care about dreams. She didn't care about the bigger picture. She only concerned herself with the bottom line, and the bottom line was that this job wouldn't line her pockets with cash.

"You're never gonna go anywhere at that school," she insisted. "I don't know why you want to work with a bunch of derelict kids anyway."

"This isn't a surprise to you, Sharon. You've known that I wanted to work with troubled youth since I was in prison."

"Just do whatever you want, Mike. That's what you always do anyway. You could care less about me and the kids. Maybe I should just kill myself and you would be happier without me. You can find yourself a new wife at the school and start a new family."

But this situation was non-negotiable for me. I was not turning down this opportunity to work at the school, but I would have to handle the situation skillfully. In order for me to work at the school and simultaneously maintain some measure of peace in our home, I was going to have to work two jobs once my shoulder healed. Although Sharon's salary as controller of a wire and cable company could have supported us while I took some time to get a degree, she wasn't trying to hear that I was going to give up my construction business, which was becoming a lucrative endeavor. At least not for starting a career in teaching that paid twenty-one thousand bucks a year.

Five years had passed since I'd begun this dance in construction, and by now I was doing a lot more than installing tile and marble. I was completing a lot of roofing projects, and it wasn't by design either. Roofing was really hard work, but I had met a guy through a friend who was a good roofer, but didn't have enough work to keep busy all of the time. So, I got the roofing jobs, and he taught me everything I needed to know about roofing, and it became very profitable.

I was also beginning to get a lot of work replacing windows. I had made a couple of good contacts with a major window distributor in Springfield, and they took a liking to me. It wasn't long before they began referring me for jobs ranging from replacing windows to major additions and renovations.

In light of Richard's offer, my plan was to work construction all day from Friday through Monday, and then on Tuesday through Thursday I would work at Chancellor Academy as a teacher's aide. Richard gave me the luxury of leaving the school at 2:00 pm on those days to head over to my construction jobs. I told those customers up front that I was very busy, but I could squeeze their job in if they didn't mind me working from 3:00 pm until 10:00 pm to complete their projects. Most people agreed to those terms because they wanted me to do the work. Thank God for halogen lights!

I knew the opportunity at the school was much bigger than the salary it offered, and that's why I was willing to go through the grind of working the two jobs. To me, my shoulder injury had been a blessing.

When I began working at Chancellor Academy, I drove to school full of anticipation, believing that my life experience and my desire to help at-risk kids would be an invaluable resource at the school. I knew what it was like to stand in the shoes of those young men, looking at the future and feeling like I don't stand a chance. That's why I decided that committing crime was a good idea in the first place. Hopefully, I could use my life experience as a means to empower the students I was about to meet.

But after a few days, I realized this wasn't school at all – at least not how I remembered school. This was war, and the battle that I had just begun to fight had nothing to do with the academic abilities or potential of the students; it had everything to do with a dysfunctional stronghold on the hearts and minds of the students in that school, a stronghold that in many instances resulted from a dysfunctional upbringing.

As a teacher, I was emotionally tried and tested in every way a human being can be. So much so, that I finally came to a place after the first week on the job where I thought to myself, *"And I want to do this, why?"* Here I was, right where years ago I had asked God to bring me, and now I questioned my ability to serve in such a capacity. There are no words, no tests, and no experiences in life that can prepare a new teacher for the moment when the classroom door closes, and you find yourself for the first time face to face with a group of students who could care less about receiving an education. I don't know which was more frightening to me the first time it happened…A cell door slamming behind me, or the sound of the door to my classroom closing me in with those students who society says are hopeless.

My desire to help the students was there, but I felt more like a target for their mutinous antics than I did an educator. From swearing at me to threatening to cause bodily harm to cracking on me for purely recreational and time-passing purposes, these students had what every socially maladjusted student longed for, a new teacher who took their behavior personally. That's right. It's a lot more fun for the students when their inappropriate behaviors get a rise out of their teachers and trust me, they knew exactly how to get a rise out of me.

During my first week on the job, I politely suggested to one of the male students to put his hair brush away and get involved in the gym class. It was then he suggested to me that I get involved with a particular part of his anatomy. And that's when I learned Rule Number One of working with kids with behavior problems: Do not challenge a student in front of his peers.

"What did you say to me?" I asked him.

"You heard me," he snapped back.

Oh yeah, "If you said what I think you just said, we're gonna get busy!"

He smiled a goofy smile that revealed his missing teeth – and the evidence of tooth decay – and he suggested yet again that I get involved with a particular part of his anatomy, only this time he addressed me using the mother of all expletives. The entire class burst out laughing at me, and I stood there feeling completely helpless.

I couldn't believe the level of disrespect, and on top of that it seemed there was no expectation by these kids that anyone could do anything about their disrespect. In other words, if you don't like it, then too bad!

I was brand new at this. I had no strategy, no skills, no plan to follow, but truth be told, I had no patience for that type of disrespect either. After all, had he treated me like that at any other point in my life, I'd have knocked whatever teeth he had left right out of his face.

"Get up and get out of my gym!" I yelled. To my surprise, he got up, and as we walked out into the hallway, Richard was there, and he could tell that I was really upset.

"What's wrong, Lumpy?" Richard asked me.

I told him what the kid had said to me, and that's when Richard told me to take the kid for a walk and tell him a little bit about myself. I knew Richard wanted me to tell him about my criminal past, only I think he may have had a different approach in mind. Still, I did as Richard said and took the kid outside.

When I knew I couldn't be seen, I put my hand around the back of his neck, grabbed his pony tail and then, pulling him in close, I pointed to my truck in the parking lot and said, "Do you see that truck over there? The first thing you need to know, young lady, is I have another job so if you ever in your life disrespect me like that again, I'll knock whatever teeth you have left in your mouth right out of it! Got it?

"The next thing you need to know is I spent three years in prison watching little girls like you getting traded off for cigarettes. Don't think your goofy long hair, no teeth-havin' butt is intimidating anybody, 'cuz it ain't! I'm not gonna have this conversation again! You understand me? Now if you got somethin' on your mind, say it or do it now…not inside the school when you're in front of your little girlfriends…right here, right now!"

He stood there in utter shock, and with a look of fear on his face. He said nothing, but tears began falling down his face.

"Yeah, that's what I thought. You're not so tough after all!"

I can assure you that you won't find that approach in the latest edition of "Behavior Modification Techniques for Teachers."

Later, Richard pulled me into his office and explained to me that I was taking things too personally.

"Someone telling me to do what that kid told me to do was personal!" I asserted.

"No, it's not personal! Their behavior has nothing to do with you. It's simply a manifestation of their personal problems. That's why they are here! If you take everything these kids say and do personally, you won't make it until the end of day, let alone the end of the year!"

I needed that conversation with Richard, because until I understood that their behaviors had nothing to do with me, I would always be ineffective as a teacher. I had a tendency to think, *"What am I doing wrong? Why don't these kids like me, or why do they treat me differently than the rest of the staff?"* As I watched the students interact with other teachers, it became obvious to me that the kids didn't necessarily treat me differently. It was that the more experienced staff responded differently to the same behaviors that upset me.

Essentially, we were called together as a staff to do with these students what their district teachers could not afford to do – tolerate their inappropriate behavior with the hope that our investment of time and energy would bring about positive emotional and social change. This was something I could get on board with, but I still had a lot to learn when it came to interacting with students.

One day, Richard had me outside with a student who was performing what we referred to as "hard labor," something the students could do in place of the more traditional approach to punishment that came in the form of out-of-school suspension. At any rate, Richard thought it would be a good idea for me to spend some quality time "investing" in a young man by talking to him about my life and the consequences of some of the poor choices I had made. The student I was with was filling in holes with dirt around the school barnyard where Richard kept the animals from the Animal Care Program.

"Why did you get hard labor?" I asked.

"Because I cursed at Smitty. I hate his class."

"Was it worth it?"

"Yeah, it was worth it. Now I don't have to be in his sorry class."

"Hey Darryl, I don't mean this in a bad way, so don't take it personally, but is his class sorry or are you sorry because you're almost eighteen and don't know how to read?"

As Darryl worked with shovel in hand, he listened intently to what I shared about my personal life.

"I never read a book from cover to cover until I was twenty-three years old," I told Darryl.

"What?"

"That's right, and the only reason that I read it then was because I was in prison. There was nothin' else to do. I didn't care about an education. Studying was too much work. It required too much effort and besides, I wasn't very good at academics anyway."

"What did you go to prison for?"

"For the same reason you're out here digging holes and shoveling horse manure. I had a bad attitude and it all started with the same type of nonsense you're doin' – cuttin' up in class, disrespecting teachers, and wanting to be part of all the wrong things."

For whatever reason, Darryl began to find a great deal of humor in what it was that I was saying, and he started laughing.

"What's so funny?" I asked.

In hindsight, I should have never asked that question, but I did and Darryl's answer was nothing short of X-rated, the result of watching too many prison movies. I thought to myself, *"The nerve and disrespect of this kid,"* and that's when I learned Rule Number Two: Don't share personal information with emotionally disturbed students for any reason if you can't handle them using that information to perpetually taunt you.

I responded to Darryl's taunt with a phrase I had heard years earlier while watching the movie, *"The Blues Brothers"* :"It's tough to eat corn on the cob with no freakin' teeth!"

That's when I learned Rule Number Three of working with kids with behavior problems: Don't provoke a student who has a shovel in his hand!

Darryl started laughing even harder but he said nothing back to me. He simply put his shovel to the dirt and stepped on it, sinking it deep into the pile. Once the shovel was full, he lifted it up and threw the dirt right in my face and took off running.

We were off to the races. He got a good jump on me, because I wasn't expecting it, but knew I would catch him if he didn't run inside of the school. It was just a matter of time.

As I was chasing him, I could only think about how good it was gonna feel to drag his sorry little butt back to that pile of dirt and rub his face in it! He rounded the corner of the building and out of my sight only momentarily before I came rounding the same corner. I must have looked like a deer caught in the headlights of an oncoming truck, because standing there was not only the student I was chasing, but also Richard, a Child Study Team, and a family who had come to visit the school.

The chase abruptly came to an end. As I stood there looking at the student cowering behind Richard, all eyes were on me, silently awaiting a valid explanation as to why a two hundred and thirty-pound man was chasing down a fifteen year-old kid who was half my size. I knew this didn't look good, and as I breathed heavily and covered in dirt, Richard broke the awkward silence.

"What are ya doin', Lumpy?" he asked in a tone that matched the aggravated look on his face.

"This meathead just threw a shovel full of dirt in my face!" I complained. Richard just looked at me like, "What's wrong with you?" and then he said something to the effect of, "Get over it and go make yourself useful."

Later in the day, Richard brought the two of us together, and we ended up shaking hands and moving forward. But when I later took Darryl to Rahway Prison, I couldn't help but tell the inmates what he had done to me.

"He did what?" they asked.

I hate to admit it, but I had a big smile on my face in the prison auditorium as I sat watching Darryl get worked over by the Lifer's Group. It was a smile much like the one he had just before he threw the dirt in my face.

Not only did I have a difficult time getting along with the students, but some of the veteran staff were not all that fond of me either. Some of them thought Richard had lost his mind when he hired an ex-con to work at the school. The nerve of Richard to take notice of a man whose credentials for employment he considered an asset included the time he served in prison!

Richard understood that while academia has its value, life experience has value as well. No matter how educated and experienced his staff may have been (and they were very good), he knew they did not have the social, emotional, behavioral, and consequential experience of having lived in prison. You simply cannot glean that experience from a book or a classroom. Besides, teachers aren't knocking down the doors to work with at-risk youth, and here Richard had a man who was passionate about doing such a thing.

Whatever the reasons were behind Richard's decision to hire me, he obviously saw something in me that he valued. He was patient with my inexperience, and invested a significant amount of time instructing me how to be skillful in the art of working with the non-traditional student population his school served. Richard understood that my life experience, combined with my skill of carpentry, could compliment what he was already doing well — affecting positive social and emotional change in students who traditionally failed. Together, we worked at using that experience and skill in a way that was appropriate and relevant to his students.

While I worked for Richard, my relationship with him took on many forms. He was an employer, a mentor, a counselor, and at times he was a father figure to me. He instructed me, he advised me, he corrected me and, when necessary he even reproved me. Ultimately, my life is better for having known him. Richard is and will always be my best friend. Not only did he give me the chance to fulfill my dream to work with at-risk youth, but in time and with his support, I became very good at it.

I learned that the students whose behaviors got the best of me were the students who reminded me most of a younger me, a young, criminal me. I found myself standing in the shoes of the inmate at Rahway State Prison. The inmate with one eye, who sixteen years earlier tried to warn me that looking at him, was like looking in the mirror. It had been sixteen years since that moment, but something rather profound had taken root and I finally got it.

I was looking in the mirror again, but this time I wasn't looking from the eyes of some punk kid who hadn't begun to experience life. Now I gazed in the mirror with the eyes of experience, and I saw in my students what that inmate had seen in me years earlier. I had come full circle, and just like the inmate before me, that which the mirror reflected frustrated me.

The mirror reflected images of disrespect, arrogance, defiance, and indifference for life. I had a hard time getting past it all. I concentrated more on the behavioral enemies of my past than I did on the heart of the injured kids before me. As much as I cared about the students, I'd had it all wrong. I tried to prevent the inevitable consequences of their deviant behavior rather than purposefully sow and nurture seeds of caring and change into the lives of my students. I mistakenly tried to change the external behaviors of the students without challenging them to bring about permanent change from within. For the first time, I understood how deeply that inmate had cared about my life. Furthermore, I could identify with the level of frustration he'd felt when we met up that day at the prison. As an adolescent, I didn't care about my life, so why would I believe anyone else cared about it? More than likely, my students felt the exact same way. The inmate had two hours to get his message across to me before we would part ways and, hopefully, never cross paths again. But I had the luxury of years to help influence positive change in our students.

Richard's approach to positive change took on many forms. Each week, for example, Richard had the school psychologist review with his staff the social backgrounds of the different students enrolled at the school. Those meetings disclosed critical information regarding the home life and family structure of our students, and by reviewing that information with the school staff we had a better understanding of the behaviors each student displayed. When you know where the behavior is coming from, you to tend feel more compassion for the student. And the more I was exposed to the social backgrounds of our students, the more I came to recognize a measure of dysfunction in my own home.

CHAPTER 13

†

A Quarrelsome Wife

"It is better to live in a corner of the housetop
than in a house shared with a quarrelsome wife."
(Proverbs 21:9)

"In Jimmy's case," the doctor noted, "there are a variety of factors contributing to his overall poor mental health." The shrink emphasized that abuse and dysfunction is not limited to extreme violence and sexual abuse in the home but that "genuine dysfunction" covers a much wider range of negative behaviors.

"Jimmy goes home every day to an environment where he is belittled and ridiculed by one parent or both. Nothing he does is ever right and if he questions their authority, if he shows emotion, he pays the price in the form of physical discipline."

"Does Jimmy act out at home like he does in school?" one teacher asked.

"Usually he doesn't, because he is afraid of his father, but recently he has tried to fight back when his father hits him. His dad is a big man, and he controls Jimmy with fear." Doc began referring to his notes in front of him, and he read Jimmy's response to a question he had asked him about his parents.

"They're hypocrites! They yell at me and punish me all the time for doing the same exact things they do." When the doc asked him for an example of what he was talking about, Jimmy had no shortages of examples. The most telling may have been the following: *"They yell at me for fighting*

and hitting my sister, but my father fights with my mother and hits her all the time."

In Jimmy's life, I saw my own. The abuse. The hypocrisy and the fear. Apart from Jimmy's father hitting his mother, the doctor could have been describing my own home back when I was Jimmy's age. No wonder I tended toward self-destruction in my life.

In prison eight years earlier, I had begun my initial search to understand my tendency to self-destruct, but that search was fueled by remorse and regret. A serious guilt trip left me looking at myself as the intrinsic cause of all of my problems. I never considered for a minute that my experiences as a child may have contributed to my propensity to gravitate towards negative behavior. At the age of twenty-four, I very simply reasoned: I rejected the good advice of others, I chose to forfeit an education, I chose to use drugs, I chose to commit crime, I chose to do or not do the things I did or didn't do. As far as I was concerned, I needed to look no further – It was all my fault!

I had always believed that my story was a case of a good child gone bad. That type of accountability served me well when accepting the consequences of my personal choices, but it was an ineffective approach to understanding and changing the foundational flaws by which those personal choices were made.

Many nights I laid awake in prison thinking, *"I should have just listened to the good advice my parents and others tried to give me. If I would have just listened to them this never would have happened to me! How could I have been so dumb?"*

Over and over again, I blamed myself. But then the Chancellor Academy made me rethink my thinking. My tendency to make poor choices had nothing to do with being dumb. In fact, making poor choices had nothing to do with my intellect at all. It had to do with the fact that, like

Jimmy, those who had given me their good advice never equipped me with their "good example" to give their good advice my full attention.

On more than one occasion, I heard my parents use this old saying, "Do as I say, not as I do." In other words, don't imitate my behavior, but listen to my instruction. Oddly enough, whether it was smoking cigarettes, punching holes in walls, disrespecting one another, extreme physical discipline, or even road rage, they had an expectation that I would show restraint when it came to participating in the exact same destructive behavior they did over and over again.

Without question, my parents were appalled by my criminal behavior, but I just don't know if they ever understood how the poor examples they set in our home contributed to my negative behavior outside of the home.

The quandary that I found myself in now was that I was already guilty of perpetuating some of the same exact dysfunction in the lives of my children. In fact, my sons could make some of the same claims about me as I did about my father. Regrettably, I have no doubt there were times when my boys were growing up when they felt either afraid or beaten or unloved and perhaps even worthless as a direct result of the words I spoke or the poor examples I had set.

I can recall times when they misbehaved, and I would make them stand in front of me with their hands at their sides. I would address the behavior whether it was drawing all over the walls, ruining something so they could get the newest and latest version, or whatever annoying things it may be that kids do. I yelled at them and I scared them, because I wanted them to listen to me, but I didn't know how to accomplish that short of instilling fear in them. That technique by my father got my attention, and so I figured it would work on them and besides, that was all I knew. I understood punishment, not discipline.

After yelling at them, I would smack them in the face, and if they flinched or moved and I missed them, I would make them stand with their hands at their sides and do it again until they didn't flinch.

There were times when I verbally emasculated my sons in an effort to get them to do what I wanted. I may say something to them like, "Stop whining. You're acting like a girl." Or at times I called them stupid. One of the things that most amazes me is that my instruction encouraged my sons to be violent in the same exact way my father's had encouraged me.

When my son Tony was six or seven, he was being picked on at school by a bully, who was kicking him in the groin every day. And every day when Tony told his teachers what the kid was doing, they did nothing about it. Tony finally told me about what was going on during recess and how his teachers just kept talking and drinking their coffee and did nothing about it. This is where I excelled; I knew exactly how to make it stop.

"Listen to me, Tony," I said. "I'm going to make you a promise right now. The very next time that kid kicks you or touches you in any way, you punch him as hard as you can right in his face. You have my word that he will never touch you again." In a brave little voice he said, "Okay, Daddy." Rubbing his head as I walked away I said, "You'll see Tony, everything is going to be fine."

The next day while I was at work, I got a call from Tony's principal.

"Mr. Palombi, we need you to come pick up your son. He is being suspended for hitting another student." I thought to myself as I hung up the phone, "Atta boy, Tony! You did it!"

When I got to the school, the principal warned, "Mr. Palombi, we can't have your son hitting other students. If it happens again he will be expelled."

"Are you finished?" I snapped back. "Sir, Tony did exactly what I told him to do. My son comes to your school every day afraid because you don't protect him from that bully. This kid has been kicking my son in the groin for two weeks and your coffee-clutching staff does nothing about it. Today, something was done about it, so if we're finished I'm going to take my son out for ice cream."

I left him speechless.

It was just like I'd said: the bully never bothered him again. Let's face it, nobody likes getting punched in the face, but punching the bully in the face should not have been my instruction to my son. My instruction to my son should have included an example that attempted to settle things between him and the bully peacefully, and in that example teach them to resolve their conflicts without the use of violence.

Beyond those examples of poor parenting, I have listened with my sons to inappropriate things on the radio and watched inappropriate things with them on television hoping that my kids would think I was cool. I've been drunk in front of my children and my children knew that I smoked pot. Somehow I reasoned that telling them the truth about smoking weed was honorable, because I wasn't lying to them. I set poor examples for my children in every way a man can, but I thank God there's a Father in Heaven who is faithful.

I can remember as a child thinking about my dad, *"I'll never be like him when I grow up."* What I meant was, I would never be as harsh a man as he was but that is exactly what I had become. That's certainly not the way I wanted to be remembered by my children. So how does it happen? How do you end up repeating history?

Until somebody opposed the way I did things, until somebody gave me new information and until somebody set a new example (and I was willing to listen), there was no reason for me to rethink the dysfunctional approach of my parents. And like me, my children paid the price.

By June of 1992, I completed my first full school year at Chancellor. It was very clear by then, as a father, I had to change my ways, particularly where it came to corporal punishment. I needed to employ in my home the behavioral strategies that I learned at school. I never gave my children orders not to cry during a spanking nor did I ever beat them with a belt. However, that is not a lot of consolation to the man I am today and knowing the truth about training a child up in the way he or she should go.

All of my life I'd heard the words and felt the brunt of a highly misquoted and misunderstood biblical reference that expressed, "Spare the rod and spoil the child." I had spouted those words myself until I eventually learned otherwise. Yet "Spare the rod and spoil the child," is not even a verse in the Bible. It's actually from a verse in a seventeenth century poem written by Samuel Butler called "Hudibras." Unfortunately, too many parents have elevated the verse of a poem to a biblical truth and a green light to physically beat their children.

What the Bible does say in Proverbs 13:24 is *"Whoever spares the rod hates his son, but he who loves him is diligent to discipline him."* Lest anyone think that God intended for parents to beat their children with a rod, nothing could be further from the truth. That would be in direct contradiction to verse four of Psalm 23 where the psalmist says, *"Your rod and your staff they comfort me."* The rod to which the Bible refers comes from the Hebrew word "shabat," and describes a rod used by a shepherd to compassionately care for his sheep. I've never seen anything in the Bible where the shepherd used his rod to beat down his sheep.

A parent's discipline is for such purposes as instruction and correction and in whatever form discipline comes it is to be executed in a way that is loving, un-provoking, and in the end, allows your child to grow in wisdom, insight, and understanding.

Yet there was nothing un-provoking about the way I had been disciplined as a child, or the way I disciplined my children early on in their lives. That type of discipline never intended to inspire wisdom or give moral instruction to my children in a loving way. Contrary to what I may have believed at the time, it was purely for the sake of exacting punishment and served no corrective purpose whatsoever. One could argue that such a dysfunctional approach to disciplining my children had been beaten into me at a very young age.

Finally, the weekly meetings with the school psychologist that often drew parallels between the family structure and the behavioral dysfunction of our students made me alarmingly aware of the effects of Sharon's verbally abusive assaults on both me and our children. In the same way that I could not make excuses for my inappropriate behavior when it came to the examples that I set as a man, I could not make excuses for the destructive words surrounding Sharon's verbal onslaughts of our family. No matter who the target was – and more often than not it was me – everyone in the family paid the price for Sharon's emotional abuse.

Many of her attacks had to do with the lack of intimacy in our relationship, but I no longer felt intimate with Sharon because she had become my abuser. At home or in public, Sharon would disrespect and emasculate me on a daily basis. She routinely referred to me as "a piece of crap" and she hardly passed up an opportunity to remind me, "Without me, you're nothin!"

The fact is, the thought of being intimate with a woman whose words and actions disparaged and disregarded our family became emotionally painful for me. In her mind, if I wasn't being intimate with her, it must have been because I was being intimate with someone else and Sharon had no problem explicitly accusing me of that in front of the kids. Sharon could not grasp the fact that my lack of interest in her romantically was due to nothing other than the hurtful and harmful words she spoke to me nearly every day of my life.

I had finally come to a place where I understood the provocation of my unpredictable corporal punishment and yelling out of frustration. I also understood the impact of words being spoken that served no purpose other than to injure the individual on the receiving end of those communications. The challenge for me was trying to get Sharon to understand the same thing in order that we could begin a new legacy for our family.

Our family was still young, and we still had a chance to turn it around but her excuse, "That's just the way I am," sabotaged our chances to do so. I came to understand the manipulation and motives behind her verbal abuse, and I was frustrated that other people were always paying the price for her just, "being the way she is."

Yet it seemed that the more I pushed for change in our house, the worse the behaviors became.

"Sharon, you can't keep speaking to me and the children the way you do. It's abusive. We have been talking in school about the long-term effects of verbal abuse and how that will negatively affect our children for years to come."

"I'm sure that you can find a new wife at the school who will talk the way you want!" she replied. "You can marry her, and I'll just kill myself and then you'll all be happy!"

"Why does it always come down you killing yourself and me starting a new life with a new woman? Why can't you just try to do what would be best for you, our relationship, and our kids?"

"Because that's what you want! You want a new wife!" she complained. "Ever since you've been at that school, you've changed."

Over time, I resented Sharon for, among other things, her refusal to do what I believed would be best for our children and our relationship. I strongly considered leaving her again, and I had many conversations with Richard about doing that during our daily two-mile jog. I told Richard, "I think I'm gonna leave Sharon."

"Now hold on a minute, Lumpy. Not so fast. You know this decision is gonna affect a lot of people, particularly the kids."

"I know, Richard, but I can't take it there no more. We fight so much that it may be better for the kids if I weren't there."

"How old is Christina now?"

"She's seven years-old."

"And Mark and Tony?"

"Tony's thirteen and Mark is fifteen."

"Mike, you have to try to get into counseling with her. You haven't done everything you can do yet."

We did end up going to counseling, and it was great right up until the conversation turned to Sharon. She got up, walked out, and never went back again.

Throughout my time at Chancellor Academy, Richard purposefully, selflessly, and skillfully helped me navigate my way through a turbulent life. In other instances, Richard's help came inadvertently through a conversation we had. Every day during lunch, Richard and I, along with some of the students, would run two miles. It was during those runs when Richard would share with me his life experiences, thereby equipping me with the wisdom necessary to overcome the difficult challenges that I found myself battling at home.

***

By 1996, I was burning the candle at both ends. I had been working at the school full-time and working construction full-time without a vacation for six years. I was working seven days a week, and there were many times I would work through the night on a construction job, and come to school to teach the following day. Meanwhile, I was also taking correspondence courses to earn a degree, so I could potentially earn more money in education.

The fatigue of that grueling schedule and the constant confrontations with Sharon about my job at the school became too much for me to take. Even though I was willing to pay my dues to get where I wanted to go in life, I couldn't do it coming home to a woman whose verbal assaults crushed me on a daily basis. So after six years of working at the school, I told Richard I was finished.

"No," he said. "You're good at this. This is where you belong!" I knew he was right, but my decision to quit was about placating Sharon, and keeping the peace at home. Just like when I told my father I'd broken the chair in order to make his screaming stop, I told Richard I quit to make Sharon's screaming stop. I guess old habits really do die hard.

For the next eight years, I chased the American Dream. I would rise early in the morning before any of the family was awake, and I came home often times long after they were asleep. If I did get done early, I was either picking up materials for the next day or working at the computer preparing proposals for potential clients late into the night. There was no time for family, to hang out with friends, visit relatives, or go on vacations. Weekdays, weekends, holidays, it didn't matter. I was always working and something inside me believed that this was what Sharon wanted.

On the one hand, it seemed that the effort I put in paid off because my home improvement business grew from earning tens of thousands of dollars a year to earning hundreds of thousands a year. On the other hand, despite all of the money I earned, our family lived in poverty. We lived without heat and hot water for four years and at times the electric would be shut off as well. During those times we were always in danger of losing our home.

To an outsider looking in, that may not have seemed to be the case because we had a big home, nice cars, and we even had a boat. Unfortunately though, there arose in our home some critical problems.

To begin with, Sharon's employer from the wire and cable company accused her of embezzling a large sum of money, and that led to a criminal indictment. Although the specific charges were later dismissed for lack of evidence, the cost of those accusations took their toll on the family both financially and emotionally.

In addition, Sharon developed an unhealthy passion for lady luck in Atlantic City. In the beginning, I was a willing participant. In fact, before we landed on hard times, we won more often than we lost. Eventually though, the gambling tides had turned for the worse and when that happened, Sharon's compulsion with gambling manifested itself in a big way.

Don't get me wrong. I was right by her side all the while she did it. I was there getting the comps, going to the shows, staying in the best hotel suites and gambling, too. The difference was, I didn't want to be there. But I didn't stop Sharon from going. Honestly, I was too scared to cut her off from gambling.

I had been a football player, a linebacker at that. I had met with some pretty tough men on the field. I was an inmate incarcerated for three years with hardened criminals and even encountered some difficult times on the street before my incarceration. I didn't fear God, I didn't fear man, but now I lived my life in fear of how my wife would respond to opposition.

I became unwilling to confront a temperament that seemed to have no regard for the pain it caused, and most particularly, when that temperament would negatively impact the lives of our children. My reluctance to confront Sharon essentially gave her control over my life. But people controlling my life was all I knew.

For all practical purposes, I might as well have been back in prison. Marriage was no different. In fact, in many respects it was worse. Even in prison, I could make some choices, and because of those choices, I grew as a man. From the moment I left prison and started my relationship with Sharon, however, I regressed.

In return for her kindness and generosity while I was in prison, I felt compelled to give up the things Sharon had required me to surrender to prove to her I loved her until eventually there was nothing left to part with. From my relationship with God, to my relationships with friends and family, to a calling on my life to work with at-risk kids, I surrendered it all because I could no longer contend with the extreme consequence of Sharon's torment for non-conformance. The torment wasn't always violent and aggressive. Actually, some of Sharon's more subtle strategies to control me alarmed me more than her aggressive outbursts.

I may have gone alone to a friend's house six times in the twenty years we were together. Each of those times, Sharon showed up to make sure I was there, and she made sure that I knew she had checked up on me. If I purchased something at the store, within minutes, Sharon would call and ask me what I purchased. Sharon would ask what so-and-so had to say on the phone that day, subtly informing me that she even knew who I talked to when she wasn't there. She made herself appear to be omnipotent, and that feeling that I was always being watched left me feeling paranoid and trapped. Eventually, I did the only thing she would allow me to do in peace, and that was work. My only problem now was what to do about it.

CHAPTER 14

✝

There Are No Fairytales!

"For what partnership has righteousness with lawlessness?
Or what fellowship has light with darkness?"
(2 Corinthians 6:14)

I was forty-four, overweight by sixty to seventy pounds, clinically depressed, and taking medication for high blood pressure and high cholesterol. I had been smoking two packs of cigarettes a day since I had left teaching, and on top of that, I began to court a couple of old friends I used to go out with when I wanted to forget about things for a while.

What's more, I left Sharon.

I was crashing each night on the third floor of a construction project I was working on for a doctor in Montclair. There, I would sit in silence late into the evening, smoking pot and drinking alone. I would think about the nightmare that was my life. How I worked like an animal for nearly twenty years and all I had to show for it now was a blow-up mattress with a slow leak. I was tired, bitter, and angry. I was worn down and I was worn out in every way a man can be.

What happened to the life I was supposed to have? What happened to the man I was supposed to become? How did I lose my heart, and where did I lose my desire and fire for life? Why was I such a failure? What is the point of living when living just hurts so darn bad? I went to bed without having answered a single question.

The next day when the doctor showed up at the building, she yelled to me up the stairs.

"Hey, Mike!"

"Yeah, Doc?"

"The painter is coming today to start the painting on the third floor. Keep an eye on her for me."

"You got it, Doc."

The painter turned out to be a girl named Heidi who was actually an actress who worked as a stand-in for *"The Sopranos."* This was her downtime, and she helped make ends meet by catering and painting.

As I was working, I could hear music coming from the room Heidi was painting in and so could the rest of the guys. She was listening to Star 99.1, a radio station that played Christian music. She sang along with the music beautifully, but it wasn't long before the guys began yelling, "Hey Mike, tell her to turn that lousy music off!"

"Guys, leave her alone and get some work done."

I had never heard music like that before, and while I know it was like fingernails on a chalkboard to the guys working with me, the music had a calming effect on me. Christian artists who I had never heard of, guys like Matthew West, Casting Crowns, Third Day, and Mercy Me, were becoming my favorite artists to listen to, but of course only when Heidi had it on. The rest of the time in front of the guys, I felt like I had to disguise my true feelings about the music or pay the price of getting cracked on about it.

Many of the lyrics in the music took me back to my days in prison where under the most difficult of circumstances, I was able to experience genuine peace. I could find calm in the midst of extreme chaos, and most critically, I knew exactly what I wanted my life to accomplish. Perhaps the words from "Sing a Song" by Third Day recalled best for me what had been my heart's desire:

"I want to live my life for You, Lord

Lord, for You I want to live my life."

But you know that never happened, and now eighteen years later I couldn't even begin to recognize that man.

Despite the fact that I liked listening to Heidi's Christian music, we didn't hit it off so well, Heidi and I. Heidi felt like I assisted the owner of the building in trying to get her to do the work she had already quoted, for less money.

In a meeting one day the doctor asked me, "Do you think Heidi's price for painting the third floor is too high? It seems high to me."

"Based on what?" I asked the doctor. "Forget about painting, this girl has days of caulking and filling to do." The trim work in the building was intricate and quite frankly, it was more work than Heidi had expected. "If anything, Doc, I don't think she charged enough. I don't see how she's gonna make any money."

"Well," the doctor said, "I'm going to try to get her to come down on her price anyway."

After Heidi met with the doctor, she called me into the room where she was working.

"Michael, I would like to have a word with you," she said.

"Uh oh," I commented to my guys on the way in. "The principal wants to see me!" The last thing I wanted to hear from Heidi was an attitude about anything.

"You know, I really want to work with you, but you can't undermine me like this," Heidi said.

"What are you talking about?"

"You told the doctor that my price for painting was too high and she wants me to come down on my price."

"I never said that. In fact, you undermined me! You told the doc that we used the wrong paint and if you read the plan, we used the paint that the plan called for."

"Well, it's the wrong paint for walls."

"Well, it's the paint the plan said to use! Are we done?"

A few weeks later, I began to notice a sub-contractor named Arthur on the job spending a lot of time talking to Heidi. So much so, that I confronted him in front of her.

"What are you tryin' to do, get a date with her? Go on, get outta here. You have a beautiful wife and daughter at home!"

After he left, I went outside to my truck to make some phone calls in private. It wasn't more than ten minutes later when I noticed Arthur going back inside the building. The same guy was working on another project two buildings away, so it was easy enough for him to walk over.

It was the day before Thanksgiving in 2004 and Heidi was finishing up some work before the holiday. Something in me said to go inside the building, but as I headed toward the door, Arthur and Heidi came walking out.

"Is everything okay?" I asked Heidi.

"Yes, I'm fine," she said with an agitated look on her face.

I wasn't convinced that everything was fine and so I asked, "Are you sure?"

As Heidi answered yes, Arthur interrupted and said, "I'm just helping her carry her tools out."

"Okay," I said. "You guys have a happy Thanksgiving."

When they left, I locked up the building, shut my phone off and called it a day.

When Friday morning came I turned my phone on and began listening to messages. Heidi had left a message on Thanksgiving Day that made me furious. As it turned out, everything wasn't okay when she and

Arthur came walking out of the building.

"Hello Mike, it's Heidi. I hope you are having a happy Thanksgiving. I'm sorry to bother you on a holiday but I wanted to let you know of something that happened yesterday so you can address it before I return on Monday. I know I said everything was okay when Arthur and I left but they say it's a woman's prerogative to change her mind, so I wanted you to know what happened. Arthur has been pursuing me to go out with him and I only learned recently that he was married. I made it clear in no uncertain terms that I do not date married men. He has been calling my house despite my requests to stop calling. When I finished yesterday he walked up with me as I put my tools away and like an idiot I decided to take the elevator down. Arthur followed me and when the doors closed he pushed me into the corner and tried to force himself on me. I pushed him away with my arm and told him that you were downstairs parked facing the elevator and as soon as the doors open you were going to see what he was doing and be very upset. I didn't want to make a big deal about it when you asked, but I don't want to have to deal with him anymore. I will finish the job but I just don't want to be in the building when he's there so if you can, please schedule us at different times. I would appreciate it."

Heidi ended her message by telling me that she would wait to hear from me.

That morning before work began, Arthur came by the doctor's project, and asked if we had seen Heidi.

"No we haven't. Why...what's up?" I asked.

"Heidi needs a man really bad!" he replied.

"And you're that man, right?"

Then Joe, one of the younger guys joked, "I'm available!"

"You don't know how to treat a woman like that," Authur insisted. "She needs a real man."

"Get outta here with that nonsense," I said, reminding him that he had a wife and daughter at home. Everything in me wanted to kick him as hard as I could right between the legs, but I was waiting for a better opportunity. I had a real difficult time with men who tried to force themselves on women, and I was going to deal with it, just not right then.

I told Arthur I wanted to show him some additional work in the doctor's office once he finished up what he was doing over at the other project. He wasn't going to be working for me anymore, and I didn't want to confront him before he finished what amounted to be a couple of hours of work at the other job.

"When he comes back," I told my son and another employee, "and you see me go with him into the doctor's office, follow in behind us. Once we are inside, close the door and nobody leaves." My plan was to put the fear of God in him.

A few hours later, Arthur came by. I invited him into the doctor's main office, where I turned my cell phone on, set it on the mantel over the fireplace, and listened as it began playing the message Heidi had left me on Thanksgiving. I paid close attention to Arthur as I walked over and picked up a wooden club I had tucked in behind the fireplace after the house had been broken into during construction – likely some local junkies trying to steal tools for drug money.

Arthur had an arrogant smile on his face as the recorded message continued to play.

"Is somethin' funny?" I asked.

"No, you don't understand...she wanted it! She came on to me!" he insisted.

"Ya know, Heidi admitted to me that she liked you, right up until the part where she found out you're married."

Arthur didn't say anything.

"Look, you're not denying what she said, and I'm not here to debate this thing," I said. "You're nothin' but a sexual predator. You know what happens to sexual predators in prison?"

"No."

"Oh, you don't know? Well you're gonna find out right now! You have two choices. We can either call the cops and press charges for sexual assault, or you can catch a beatin' right here, right now. What's it gonna be?" As I moved in closer with the club, Arthur tried to explain his way out of the beatin'. But it only made me impatient, so I lifted the club and asked again, even more loudly, "What's it gonna be?"

"No, no, wait a minute!" he pleaded, hands raised.

"Now you understand the word 'no,' but you didn't understand the word 'no' when Heidi told you no, did ya? Get out of this building before I hurt you. Get outta here!" I screamed. As he was walking away, he had the nerve to ask if I was going to pay him.

"Yeah, I'll pay you Arthur......when you bring your wife and daughter to the job and tell them what you did to Heidi, then I'll pay ya!"

The next day Arthur called me. He told me he wanted to apologize to Heidi for what he had done. He said he couldn't sleep all night because of all that had happened. I told him I would call Heidi and see if she even wanted to hear an apology from him. Heidi agreed to meet with him as long as I was there. After Arthur finished his half-hearted apology where he claimed to be a praying man, Heidi laid into him.

But first Heidi told me, "Bring Joe in here for a minute." Then looking sternly at Arthur, Heidi began, "So, I heard you said Joe's not my type. As if you know what my type is? This eighteen year-old is more of a man than you are at forty-two years! He's respectful, kind, and has always been a gentleman. I wanted him to hear me say that to you because I don't want him thinking you're the example of what I'm looking for in a man." Heidi thanked Joe for coming in and then excused him before laying into Arthur.

"Now as far as your apology is concerned, I don't believe a single word of it. I don't think you're sincere at all. The only reason you came here today is so you could get paid! I don't know what NO means in your country, but in our country, the word no means NO! Not maybe, but NO! Where do you get off putting your hands on me when I repeatedly told you I'm not interested in you? You said you were a 'praying' man. You're a 'praying' man alright…P R E Y I N G on women! I am a daughter of God. How do you think He feels when you put your hands on me? Where do you get off thinking you can treat women like a piece of flesh! How would you feel if someone did that to your daughter? You should be ashamed of yourself. Yes, I liked you in the beginning but as soon as I found out you were married, all bets were off. I told you I am a Christian woman, and I don't date married men, and I didn't appreciate the fact that you kept that information from me. I forgive you, but I don't believe a single word that is coming from your mouth, and so I don't accept your apology."

But Arthur responded to her dress-down with apathy, making it clear he never intended to make a sincere apology in the first place. More than likely, Heidi was right. He was just trying to patch things up in an effort to get paid, but that was all for naught.

"You didn't get charges filed against you for sexual assault, and you didn't get a beatin' like you should have," I reminded him. "Heidi and the men working for me need to know that in no way do I condone this type of thing going on at my jobs. Here's what's gonna happen. To begin with, you'll never work for me again," which at the time was a big earning loss for him.

"I am going to pay you an amount of money that I believe you pay your men and I am also going to pay for the product you installed. But what I owe you, I am giving that money to Heidi to donate to a charity of her choice.

"As far as receiving any of the money I am going to pay you, don't call me for that money until after Christmas. When you don't have the money to buy your kids presents, I want you to remember why you don't have the money to buy them presents. If you don't like that arrangement, sue me!" After Arthur left, Heidi and I went back to our personal responsibilities, and Heidi later donated Arthur's pay to Shelter Our Sisters – an organization that houses and helps women of domestic violence – in honor of her great aunt Brunhilde who suffered abuse at the hands of her husband.

I don't recall if it was later that day or the next day, but at some point shortly after the meeting with Arthur, Heidi pulled me aside down in the rear entrance foyer where she was painting and I was completing trim installations. She never knew until Arthur's apology that I had confronted him the way I had in the doctor's office. Once she knew how I was going to deal with the inappropriateness of his behavior, Heidi said something to me that cut to the core of a lifetime of emotional wounds.

"You're a good man, Michael." At the instant I heard those words, I broke down sobbing. I never ever expected to hear those words. The truth was I didn't believe those words. My wife had verbally abused me for so many years that there was nothing about the man I was that felt good. I had come to the place where I believed her lies. I felt guilty to be called a good man. Where many men may have said thank you after hearing those words, I told Heidi, "No, no. I'm not a good man." She said it again, "Michael, you are a good man." It sounded so unnatural to hear those words she'd spoken to me that I couldn't receive them without instantly bursting into tears.

I was embarrassed at the way I reacted to what Heidi said to me. I had never showed that kind of emotion to anyone, anywhere that I could recall, but for the next month, I cried. It was like my body just began to release the pain that had gone unattended for most of my life. There was nothing I could do to stop it. Even when I was working, tears would flow from my eyes. I explained it away as allergies, but it took about a full month for that to stop happening.

In the meantime, I continued listening to the words of the music Heidi played. I also listened to some of the Christian teaching tapes she played by Joyce Meyer, and it seemed that when Heidi wasn't singing, she was listening to those tapes.

I liked Joyce because she said things how they were. She didn't sugar-coat things, even when it came to the shortcomings in her own life. Whether it was her bad attitude, an unruly tongue, or destructive thoughts, Joyce told it how it was. I'm sure her approach offended some people, but she didn't offend me. She had already been where I was, and so I was willing to listen – in secrecy that is.

After some time, I began to engage Heidi a little about her faith, telling her how I used to be a Christian, but that I had been backsliding in a big way. She encouraged me to go back to church but I told her, "I don't have in me what it would require to do that again."

My sorry life had made me bitter, and beyond that, my hardened heart combined with a guilty conscience would not allow me to call on the name of Jesus after having turned my back on him eighteen years earlier. Besides, there's nothing easy about living the life of a Christian in a culture that opposes most everything that's in agreement with God's word anyway. Johnny Cash perhaps said it best in his song, *"The Wanderer."*

"They say they want the kingdom, but they don't want God in it."

When a person says, "I'm a Christian," there's a responsibility to live as a Christian, and there was no way I was ready to do that.

I had been staying in Montclair for several months, and I needed to come to terms with what I was going to do about my marriage. The time away from home allowed me to deal with it, and it came down to Sharon's refusal to pursue a path of healing for eighteen years of marriage.

It was clear to me years before when she walked out of counseling that Sharon would never pursue a path of healing as long as I was with her. As a result, her abusive behavior would continue to escalate as it had in the past. There was no end in sight to the gambling, nor the poverty that came along with it, and there was no end in sight to the extreme emotional abuse and violence in our home.

So, I called a family meeting and went back to the house to address my wife and our children, Christina, who was fifteen, Tony, twenty-two, and Mark, who was twenty-four. We sat down together as a family for the last time at the kitchen table.

"I didn't come here tonight to point fingers. But what's going on in our home is crazy, and it has to stop, and tonight it is going to stop. I have allowed things to go on that no man should allow."

"Oh, it's my fault right?" Sharon blurted.

"I'm not saying it's anybody's fault. I'm just saying that things have gone on in this house that should have never happened and I allowed it. I should have been a better man. I should have been a better father and because I wasn't, I failed you kids." I promised my children, "You're going to see a new man in me. I'm going to set a better example and I will never stand by and knowingly allow to go on what I have seen go on in our home."

"So you're saying you're not coming home anymore, right?" Sharon asked.

"That's what I'm saying. It's time that we begin to heal. Everyone here needs counseling and I will make arrangements for you kids to go if you want. I know I can't force you but you should seriously consider it. I'm personally gonna go. I only ask that you all forgive me for how I may have failed you. I just wanted to come here and tell you to your faces like a man. I'm gonna go now."

Sharon began to cry and pleaded with me not to leave. Tugging on me as I walked toward the door, she promised, "I swear, I'll get help for my gambling problem and I will get help for my emotional health. Please don't leave."

"Don't do this in front of the kids, Sharon."

"Don't leave, I swear, I'll go for help!"

"Sharon, you're not gonna go for help. You never go for help."

"I will. I promise I will."

"I have to go. Please let go of me now."

It took everything in me to walk out of our home. All I can recall as I drove away is a vision of Sharon standing alone on the front porch, crying. Alone in my car, I fell to pieces as I drove away. This was now the lowest moment in my life.

Of all of the mountains I'd climbed in my life, none were more difficult to climb than the mountain that would bring me into a loving relationship with my wife. But it seemed the harder I climbed, the more extreme the conditions became, and the more extreme the conditions became, the more I lost sight of why I attempted to climb that mountain in the first place. Somewhere along my ascent to the top, my focus changed from winning the love of my wife to surviving the extreme conditions of the climb.

You could have never told me when I got married that I would one day be divorced. I'd stood there on my wedding day with the best of intentions, confidently making my vows until death would we part. By the time it was all said and done, I could only recall welcoming the experience of death. At the age of forty-four, I had failed even in marriage.

Many around me celebrated the fact that I left Sharon because they saw the way she had treated me. In fact, some of them had been the targets of Sharon's verbal abuse in the past. When that happened, they held their tongues out of respect for me.

But there was one person who seemed to understand more deeply the impact of divorce on my life. As I was completing trim and cabinetry installations, Heidi was right behind me caulking, priming, and painting. Unlike many of my friends, Heidi had regard for the loss I was experiencing. There were kids involved, there was a home involved, there was the loss of a family.

Heidi witnessed some of the difficult times to come, and through it all she never stopped speaking words of encouragement to me. Day by day, my life fell apart more and more. Financially, I was in a hole due to gambling, court ordered payments, and unbeknownst to me, Sharon had not filed our taxes in ten years.

Further, shortly after I left Sharon, I ruptured several disks in my back when on the job we were moving a twelve hundred pound steel I-beam. One of the discs exploded into pieces that traveled up my spinal cord and had to be surgically repaired. After that, I needed my hips replaced and then several shoulder surgeries followed. Physically, emotionally, financially, and relationally, I had never been through more difficult times.

Heidi had been divorced for ten years herself, and though I didn't know her well I wondered, "Why is she still single?" The truth was, she seemed like she would be a good catch for somebody looking for marriage, so why wasn't she married? I reasoned there must be something wrong with her. Heidi kept saying she was waiting for her fairytale, but I didn't mince any words when I told her, "If you're waiting for a fairytale, don't hold your breath. There are no fairytales!"

Ultimately I found out what was wrong, that is, why Heidi wasn't married: She didn't believe in premarital sex. Men, even Christian men, had a difficult time agreeing to that. I pressed her further about her strong stance on the issue, and she said something I found to be quite remarkable.

"I pray for my future husband every day," she said.

"How do you pray for someone you don't know?" I asked.

"God knows who he is!"

"*Gee,*" I thought. "*This woman is an incredible woman of faith, or she's nuts!*"

"I have a responsibility to my future husband," she continued. "My body belongs to him, and I have a responsibility to protect and save myself for him." I couldn't believe what I was hearing. This woman showed more regard for a man she had yet to meet than my wife showed for me during our entire marriage. Her faith and her commitment to what she believed were truly inspiring to me.

But I wasn't looking for a relationship with Heidi. In fact, after my failed marriage, I vowed to never be in a relationship again. Besides, Heidi and I were too different. She was an upbeat, warm, and encouraging person, and I, well, I wasn't that. I used salty language, I smoked cigarettes, smoked pot, drank, I didn't do church, and what's more, I didn't believe in fairytales.

CHAPTER 15

†

Touched By An Angel

"Every good gift and every perfect gift is from above..."
(James 1:17)

One night while working late and trying to finish the Park Street project, Heidi and I ordered food from the corner pizzeria. During the course of eating our meal, I told Heidi a story that left her laughing very hard.

I explained that me and my daughter had gone to Dunkin' Donuts one night. As we pulled up to place our order at the drive-through window, Christina said, "I know the guy taking orders at the window." So when her friend greeted us I began...

"Hello, welcome to Dunkin'....," he said.

"Loser says what?" I interrupted.

"What?" the employee asked.

Christina and I started cracking up. "Nothing" I said, "Go ahead please."

"Welcome to Dunkin' Donuts, may I....?

"Loser says what?" I interrupted again.

"What?"

We laughed even harder. I did that like five times before we decided it was enough and finally gave the young man the order. As we pulled up to the window, Christina said, "Oh my God, that's not who I thought it was."

"You don't know him?" I asked

"No!" The poor kid didn't know what to make of us two clowns as we pulled up to the window laughing hysterically, I told Heidi.

Heidi's laughing abruptly turned to panic when a piece of Italian bread got lodged in her throat. Suddenly, she started motioning with her hands, 9-1-1, but I couldn't understand what she was trying to tell me. I was still trying to tell my story, not realizing she was choking. Finally, I caught on.

I used the Heimlich maneuver several times, but I couldn't dislodge the bread blocking her airway. She wasn't breathing at all, and when I felt her body becoming limp in my arms, I turned her around to look at her.

"Oh my God!" I said. Her whole face had swollen and the whites of her eyes were blood red. At least a minute had gone by since the bread had gotten stuck. If I didn't do something fast, she would die. I picked her up and turned her upside-down, pressing her chest hard onto the edge of a nearby chair. Holding her body in place with one arm, I began pounding on her back with the other. I had hoped that the forceful blows in combination with being upside-down would shake something loose in her throat. Also, with her chest up against the edge of the chair, the blows to her back were so forceful that it was like she was receiving compressions from the front and the back.

On the one hand, I didn't want to hurt her, but on the other hand she was going to die if I didn't dislodge the bread, and so I let it rip. Finally something dislodged and came out onto the floor. Heidi began gasping for what little air she could get and I continued to administer the forceful blows that eventually cleared her airway.

After she caught her breath and began breathing on her own, she just sat on the floor weeping, and I sat there relieved that I didn't have to explain a dead body to anyone.

"It's not that I was afraid to die," Heidi explained. "I'm sad because I haven't fulfilled what I was created to do. What would my legacy have been had I died tonight?"

It entered my mind to hug her, but I didn't do it. I just sat there with her while she collected herself. A smile emerged on her face. She said jokingly, "You know you're in trouble when the guy doing the Heimlich maneuver looks at you and says, 'Oh my God!'"

The near-death experience left Heidi visibly shaken. She got up and went to the bathroom to clean herself up. When she came out she asked, "Why didn't you tell me I looked so bad? When I looked in the mirror I scared myself!"

We were so happy that she didn't die and that she was breathing normally on her own that it never occurred to us that Heidi should have gone to the hospital.

"Can I stay here tonight and sleep on the couch in the lobby?" Heidi asked. "I'm afraid to go home and be alone." Doc had just gotten brand new couches that day for the waiting room, and I told Heidi that it would be okay to stay on one of them.

Afterwards, I went up to my construction suite and air mattress waiting for me on the third floor, but not before I caught a buzz out on the balcony. Something Heidi had said that evening had struck me, and I considered the very same question that she had asked herself: "What is my legacy? If I died tonight what greater purpose has my life served?" But all I could hear screaming inside of my head was, *"NONE!"*

By Christmas Eve, everything had settled down at the project in Montclair, and, thanks to the doctor, Park Street had become my permanent residence. Heidi stopped by to wish me a Merry Christmas and invite me one more time to come to her church for the Christmas Eve service, but I wasn't feeling the holiday spirit.

When Heidi left, I went out and got some booze and some weed and took my place out on the balcony of the third floor. Some people go to the park, others to the mountains, and even others to the beach when they want to get away from it all, but for me, the Park Street Balcony was the perfect place to escape the reality that was my life. In the cold December air and under the cover of darkness, I began to self-medicate. The more I consumed, the more a battle deep within me began to rage.

A voice inside me said, *"It would be better for you to end your days than to stand and fight such a hopeless battle. Look at you! You've done nothing with your life! What about the promises you made? You've made good on nothing, and more than that Michael, you're good for nothing!"*

Deception had a lot to say to me. It was as if Deception sent marching before me an army of demons whose end I could not see. Each demon carried with him a sign declaring an accusation against me.

First to show his sign was the demon of Failure.

"Guilty!" Deception declared.

Disgrace.

"Guilty!"

Then Shame, Dishonor, Regret, Poverty, Hostility, Stubbornness, Indifference, Rage, Depression, Misery, and on and on as far as my eyes could see.

And Deception levied its verdict, "Guilty!"

On the eve of Christmas 2004, eighteen years since I'd left prison, I sat alone on the balcony of my Park Street residence bitter and angered by the evidence of my disappointing life. As I continued to drink and smoke, I could only think about the fact I was better off in prison.

Why? What was it about prison that made me feel like I was better off? Because in prison, I grew more substantially as a man than during the other forty-one years of my life combined. It came down to my love and pursuit of a relationship with God, a relationship that my marriage to Sharon required me to surrender.

Sharon never came out and said she didn't want me going to church or she didn't want me having Bible studies. She just made my life miserable when I did do it by continually criticizing the church that I liked or the people whom I befriended. And when one of the men coming to my Bible study borrowed a thousand bucks from us and the same week ditched his wife, left town, and never paid us back, that was it. Sharon had all of the ammunition she needed to prove her case that people of faith are phonies.

When I was in prison, Sharon had portrayed herself to be a woman of faith. After our wedding however, she rapidly moved from portraying herself as a woman of faith to a woman who did nothing but find fault with those who claimed to be people of faith. It felt like pure Deception.

So now I was left with a choice: Do I choose God and constantly have confrontations about faith, or do I choose Sharon and hope that over time it will get better? But sitting on the balcony, I realized that to continue in the way I was going would certainly lead to death, but the road to life looked too difficult to follow. Once again my life came down to a choice: Do I live or do I die?

I started considering the option to go to Christmas Eve service. There was still time enough to make it if I hurried, but Pride suddenly rose up in me and quickly pointed out, *"You've broken nearly every commandment there is to break, committed every sin there is to commit! Certainly God can't forgive you considering all you've done, and furthermore, pursuing God now would make you look like nothing other than a hypocrite! What if the guys on the job were to find out you have a heart for God? They would laugh at you until next Christmas, that is, if they are still working for you by then! In any event Michael, didn't we go down this road years ago?"*

Pride knew me all too well, using my worry about what people would think as a tool of persuasion. Then Surrender abruptly cut short Pride's guilt-ridden offensive against me and asked, *"Do you recall the day in your cell when we first met? Today is no different because depending on your choice, your end is not very far away. Your opponent today is the same as your opponent then. Defeat him and you will experience Life!"*

In that moment I put my beer down, I put my cigarette out, and lifted my sorry butt out of my chair. Leaving Pride and his harsh indictments of my life behind on the balcony, I went back inside the house, took a shower, got dressed, and headed off to church. In the parking lot of the church, I began to have second thoughts about going inside.

"What am I doing here anyway?" I thought. But just like something lifted me out of my seat that day in the prison gymnasium, something helped me to open the door to my car.

It had been many years since I had been inside a church. Nonetheless, I got out of my car, but not before I practically took a bath in cologne hoping no one could tell I was under the influence.

As I opened the door to the church, a man with greying hair greeted me with a welcoming smile. I could hear the music playing and people singing.

But Condemnation shouted at me, *"Run! You don't belong here! You don't deserve forgiveness! Everyone's gonna know you're stoned! Don't go in!"*

I managed to fight off the voices in my head and opened the door to the sanctuary. An usher signaled me to take a seat about three rows up, but near the very back of the church. As I moved to my seat, I could see people with their hands raised high and singing along with the Christmas choir. The music sounded just like the music Heidi listened to on that Christian station, only it was live. I'd never heard anything like that in church before. In the churches I had gone to, you sang from the hymnal while the piano or organ player played along, but here, there was a whole band on the platform, like you would see at a rock concert. Despite the music, I stood there lifeless among the worshipping congregants, hoping no one would notice me.

When the music ended, everyone took their seats, and Pastor Don James began to speak. As I recall, he did not speak for very long, but when he did, it was as though I was sitting in the church all alone and he was speaking directly to me. Even being high didn't keep the word of God from penetrating the depths of my soul. I was reminded on that Christmas Eve that Jesus had come to bind up the brokenhearted and to set the captives free. But why was God mindful of me? I had turned my back on Him and He was willing to pluck me yet again from the ruin that comes natural to living the life of a fool.

At the end of the service, Pastor Don asked everyone to stand. As the musicians started playing background music very lightly, he began speaking again, describing the very prideful and arrogant life I was leading, and had been despite having forged a relationship with God in prison.

As he spoke, I tried my hardest not to cry. I knew I had just heard more truth spoken in thirty minutes of that service than I had heard in the previous eighteen years of my life. Perhaps that is why I was so fearful of going to church in the first place. Perhaps I just didn't want to hear the truth about my life!

Yet it was for me the equivalent of a starving person receiving food within minutes of dying. At once, I received words of life, words of hope and encouragement. There was a promise of freedom from a life of dysfunction, abuse, and poverty, and I wanted that so badly. I wanted to experience the peace and joy that came with the promise of freedom.

I mean, when was the last time drugs or alcohol had brought peace and joy into my life? When did sex ever satisfy the need to experience the joy of being loved? When did gambling ever satisfy the hunger and desire of greed? When did owning a big home ever determine the happiness of the family living in it? The answer is never!

I had tried everything there was to try in life and none of it had brought fulfillment. All of it left me empty and wanting or craving more. There was a void in my life that no matter how hard I tried, no matter what I put in it, the void remained empty. Sadly enough, I'd spent years filling that void with poison and expecting a cure for what ailed me. It remained empty, I learned, because that hollow in my life was only meant to be filled by one thing – a relationship with God!

The peace I'd found in prison was the result of my relationship with Jesus Christ. The Bible described it as a peace that surpasses all understanding, and having experienced that peace, I can testify to the truth of such a description.

On Christmas Eve of 2004, I was in the process of filing for divorce. I was sick, and I was in financial ruin. My home was in foreclosure, and I owed hundreds of thousands of dollars in taxes. If that wasn't enough, the machine that could earn the money to pay those debts – my body– had become severely arthritic. I would undergo at least one major surgery every year for the next seven years.

But I decided that Christmas Eve service to take a stance against Deception, who was devouring my life. To do that, I'd have to do what I'd told Heidi I didn't have the strength and courage to do: Restore my relationship with Christ.

Having been there before, however, I was well aware that Christianity wasn't magic. Personal problems wouldn't disappear and character flaws were not going to vanish simply because I made a decision to follow Christ. In order to experience a life-long relationship with the Lord, I was going to have to deal with the emotional dysfunction that in the past had helped me to rationalize making choices that dishonored God. I'd set out to start the new year by renewing my relationship with God and by finding a way to contend with a lifetime of dysfunction.

That January, I'd learn there was nothing easy about confronting decades of heartache. Where do you begin, and how do you deal with the fact that your wounds were caused by the very people who'd claimed to love you? How do you learn to validate and treat those emotional wounds when your whole life, you were taught to walk them off? How do you begin to value your life when your whole life, you believed it had no value?

You do it by exposing the lies. And Eleanor Buscher would be the one to help me do that. Most times I walked into Eleanor's office feeling a lot better than I did when I walked out. The reason is this: You don't know where you're going until you know where it is you've been, and therapy with Eleanor, a social worker and licensed clinical counselor, always required me to go back and focus on where I'd been in life. So we didn't start off therapy talking about my divorce, prison, or using drugs. Rather, Eleanor wanted me to tell her about my life as a child.

"Well, I think I had a pretty normal life growing up," I told Eleanor.

"Tell me about your dad."

"He was a tough man."

"What do you mean by tough?"

"Well, my dad's father was an alcoholic and from what I understand he had it pretty rough as a kid. He told me a story about when his dad tied him to a post in the basement and beat him. I also heard that he was never the same person when he came back from the Korean War."

After some silence, Eleanor prodded, "Does your father drink?"

"You know, my father doesn't drink but he seems to have the temperament of an alcoholic. I mean, he gets frustrated easy, he's really impatient, and he has an explosive temper. When I was a kid, he used to scare me a lot."

"Do you have any fond memories of a time you spent with your father?"

The silence was awkward. I couldn't remember a single time that just me and my dad had done something together other than work together, and I wouldn't describe our work environment as warm and tenderhearted. The truth was, I couldn't think of a single tender moment with my dad.

When I couldn't give Eleanor an answer, a look of curiosity came on her face and she asked, "Have you ever heard of Focusing?"

"No, I haven't."

"Focusing, it's a method of therapy that involves something called the felt sense. The felt sense is exactly what it sounds like. It is a feeling or a sense in your body about something that you have never verbalized externally, but internally you are fully aware of. By Focusing on the 'felt sense,'" Eleanor explained, "we may be able to get some answers that you're looking for." And the answers I was looking for had to do with the fact that everything in my life ended in the same way, in failure.

"If she's looking for feelings," I thought, *"she's got the wrong guy. As soon as I'm on to the fact that she's trying to get me to show emotion, I'll come up with distractions. This is a piece of cake!"*

"So, how do we start?" I asked.

"Well, you're the focuser and I will be the listener. When you say something I will repeat back to you the thoughts you verbalize."

I'm thinking *"This is nuts! What does she have me doin'?"*

"Okay Michael, I want you to relax. Be silent and just pay attention to your body. Tell me what you feel when you think about your dad."

With my eyes closed, I began to focus on my dad. After some time, I told Eleanor, "I feel my jaw clenching down and I feel tightness in my chest." I guessed that was the felt sense.

Eleanor said back to me, "You feel tightness in your chest and your jaw's clenching down."

Then again, there was silence for a while.

"What is your earliest memory of your dad? Can you remember that?"

As I focused on her question for several moments, I saw a young boy sitting on the couch with his mother watching television. It was Memorial Day in 1963.

"Yes, I remember."

"What do you feel now?"

"I feel fear."

"What are you afraid of?" Eleanor asked.

"I'm afraid of my father. I want to go to the parade but I am afraid to ask him. He's really angry. He and my mom just had a fight."

Eleanor said, "You're afraid of your father. He's really angry because he was fighting with your mother."

"Yes."

"Did something happen?"

"Yes."

"Do you want to talk about what happened?" she asked.

"I went to ask my dad if I could go to the parade. He was in the bathroom spackling sheetrock. When I walked in, he looked angry, but I asked him anyway because my mother assured me that he wasn't mad at me. He never said a word to me, Eleanor. When I asked him if I could go to the parade, he just smacked me in the face with a trowel full of spackle. It went in my eyes, up my nose and in my mouth, and I started to cry."

"Can you just sit with that feeling for a minute?"

So much for distractions. As I sat there with my eyes closed, I could feel tears streaming down my face. I could hear Eleanor's voice acknowledge my pain as I sat there in front of her weeping for that little boy.

That was the beginning of my journey into Focusing about my life. Focusing ultimately revealed the emotional provocation of both of my parents, provocation that had long-lasting effects. The provocation that taught me to show no emotion, forced me to endure beatings in silence, treated me as though my life had no value, caused me to live in fear, and taught me to be violent. Whereas before I couldn't, now I could sum up my childhood experiences and do it in as little as six words: detached, beaten, worthless, afraid, unloved, and violent.

It was beginning to make perfect sense why everything I put my hands to ultimately failed. Where Christianity was leading me into a loving relationship with God, Eleanor was helping me develop a loving and healthy relationship with myself. The special thing about Eleanor was that she always prayed before our sessions. She invited God to be present in our therapy, to give us wisdom and understanding as we set out to discover and expose the origins of my emotional wounds.

The Bible says that the Spirit of truth will guide us in all truth (John 16:13) and so it was important for me to call upon the Spirit of truth when Focusing with Eleanor. Emotional healing was going to transform how I viewed myself as a man, and that particular transformation would be the starting place to maintaining a life-long and fruitful relationship with God.

In the midst of all of the difficulties I faced, I found Heidi to be a true friend. In fact, I don't know what I would have done without her. It was like one minute she wasn't in my life, and then in the next minute she was caring for my life. She never focused on my inadequacies as a man and though this church-going lady saw a man who smoked cigarettes, weed, drank a bit, swore, etc., she still treated me with regard. She spoke to me gently with words that were affirming and compassionate. And whether she was taking me to the doctor's, bringing me a warm meal, changing my bandages, or just being a support to a guy who had hit rock bottom, the burden that my circumstances presented for her were never larger than her desire to care for another human being. Her presence in my life had a healing effect on me. God had truly sent an angel to watch over me.

I'd sworn that I would never be in a relationship again but I was developing feelings for Heidi. Would a girl like Heidi even go for a guy like me? I did save her life, and I did have her back when that guy tried to get cute in the elevator. That would have to earn a guy some kudos, right?

But more importantly, what about my kids? What would they think about their father in a relationship with another woman? How would I explain it to them?

I did the only thing I could do. I went to Heidi and I told her how I was feeling. Heidi confided she had feelings for me, too. But we both decided that there could be no relationship beyond our friendship until Christina was out of high school two years later. If by then we still felt the same way, then we would cross that bridge when we got to it.

I wanted more than anything to be a man worthy of the calling of God. I wanted my life to accomplish things that had eternal value. I also wanted to be a man worthy of a woman of the likes of Heidi. So for the next couple of years, I continued to press deep into the personal challenges of changing my life. As the weeks and months went by, I gathered together what had become a large collection of greeting cards given to me by Heidi. The cards were filled with beautiful messages and words of encouragement, and she wrote about how proud she was of me and how my effort to restore my relationship with God inspired her. To know that my example could inspire the person who inspired me filled my heart with joy. She would always write at the end of her cards, "You're a good man, Michael Palombi." And every time I read those words, my eyes would fill with tears until eventually I could receive them without crying. Those words served to expunge all of the lies I had once believed.

By January of 2007 – the year Christina would graduate from high school – I sat down to write a note to Heidi. I wanted to express to her my deepest gratitude for all of her support and encouragement during the most difficult times of my life. Trust me, there was nothing attractive about the man I was that would have drawn a woman like Heidi to me apart from her divine desire to represent God well. In other words, if Heidi looked at me through the eyes of the world, she would have run for her life.

I don't think Heidi ever considered how God was using her in such a supernatural way, and it was important for me to tell her that her life was accomplishing all that God created her to do – Heidi's legacy was a heart of compassion. The example she set as a woman, for a man as broken as me, was nothing short of inspiring. When I sat down to write the note, God poured from my heart a poem that intended to communicate those sentiments to her. After completing the poem, I decided to have it framed and then gave it to her for a gift on Valentine's Day of 2007. As I watched Heidi read the poem her eyes filled with tears.

Touched by an Angel

I recall the day we met,
I recall the smile on your face as you extended your hand and said,
"Hello my name is Heidi!"
I recall extending my hand to politely make your acquaintance
At that time never realizing,
Forever, my life would change.

That as our two spirits drew nearer, one to another

By the touch of our hands,

The birth of a divine intervention had taken place.

For out of nowhere you came

And have touched my life in a way that only God could have sent you.

Only God could have known how badly I needed you!

For I was a man broken and laid to waste.

By all accounts my end was near and more so, the end I welcomed.

Far easier would it have been to surrender this life

Then surrender my will to the Lord our God.

But with your hand extended and a smile of encouragement

God touched me as with the hand of an Angel!

As a messenger of God and by way of your lips

He has spoken salvation and rescued me from myself.

And with your arms wide open, God embraced and comforted me

So the rivers of life should flow freely from my eyes as never before.

With your mouth the Lord breathed the breath of life into my soul.

With great thanksgiving to the Lord our God

It is to His glory that I commit all of my love and affection

That our Joy will be made full.

CHAPTER 16

✝

Experiencing the Blessing of God

"The blessing of the Lord makes rich, and he adds no sorrow with it."
(Proverbs 10:22)

"Have you ever been convicted of a crime that included the use of force on another human being?" That was the obstacle I was facing in the spring of 2007, when applying for a Certificate of Eligibility for Teacher of Carpentry.

Answering "yes" would automatically disqualify me from teaching for life, but I wanted to teach, and Richard Sheridan wanted me to teach, too. He'd told me that it was time to start a vocational program at his school, something other alternative schools didn't offer. What's more, he wanted me to run it! But I would need a teacher's certificate for the job.

"I am going to sell the school within a year, and I want you in here before I leave," he explained.

Getting permission to work as a teacher's aide with a criminal conviction was difficult enough, but would the State of New Jersey really issue a Standard Teaching Certification to a man who had been convicted of a violent crime?

Heidi was excited for me, because she knew it had always been my dream to work with at-risk kids.

"I don't know if I can still do it," I told Heidi. "How am I gonna get past my criminal convictions and besides, I don't even know if I'd be good at it anymore. You need a lot of patience to work with these kids and trust me, they're gonna try my chin. They always do when you're new."

"Listen to me, you were great at it before and you will be great at it again," Heidi said. "Remember, God is in the middle of all of this. If this is what He called you to do, He will see to it you get that certification. The word of God does not return void!"

With Heidi's encouragement, I began the process of applying for my Certification of Eligibility. I went to the Morris County Department of Education, where a woman named Anita Colatta walked me through the process of filling out the initial application where I answered yes to the questions surrounding my criminal convictions, and then arranged for me to come back to take a basic skills test. All I needed to do now was document four years of employment as a carpenter using my tax returns and pray for the best. It seemed to be as simple as that.

A couple of months passed and I didn't hear anything, but according to Anita, I should have heard by then. I called to tell her that I had yet to receive an answer to my application and she said she would get back to me.

When she called me back later in the day, she told me that the Department of Education changed their eligibility requirements so it ended up taking me a bit longer to complete the application process. Unfortunately, I wasn't going to be approved before Richard retired and the school was sold – that's if I were even going to be approved at all. Now I had to come up with several letters of reference from former customers detailing the work I'd performed on their homes. Unfortunately, people were busy and didn't get to the letters of reference as quickly as I may have liked, and for that reason, the process of applying for a Certificate of Eligibility took a full year.

Worse, when I submitted the application, the Department of Education disqualified me from teaching for life. As part of my application, I had to go for fingerprinting, and of course, the fingerprint search conducted by the New Jersey State Police and the Federal Bureau of Investigation revealed my criminal convictions. It's not like I didn't expect the fingerprint search to disclose those convictions. After all, I'd checked "yes" to the first question.

Some said it would never happen, that is, I would never be able to overcome the criminal convictions, and now they were right. Even though twenty-five years had passed since the day of my arrest, I was still being punished for a debt I had paid long ago. Vinny's murder wasn't even an issue any more. I had read in a newspaper in the mid 1990's that the cops discovered who did do it, and it wasn't me and it wasn't J.D.

But I noticed that the letter disqualifying me now was signed by the same man who, sixteen years earlier, had determined I could continue my employment at Chancellor Academy as a Teacher's Assistant despite results of a similar fingerprint search.

At that time, I had appealed the decision by the state, by using evidence related to rehabilitation, and sent it to the Manager of the Criminal History Review Unit. In the appeal, I sent a copy of my Judgment of Conviction and every Classification Report from Southern State Correctional Facility which detailed all of my work assignments and behavioral infractions during the time of my incarceration. In addition, I sent copies of any and all achievement awards I received at S.S.C.F., a certificate of completion for a substance abuse program, and eight notarized letters of recommendation from people in the community. Finally, I was required to write a letter detailing all of the circumstances pertaining to my arrest and conviction, as well as explain why I considered myself to be rehabilitated.

I remember well the first words I heard coming off the bus at Southern State Correctional Facility: *"You are not here to be rehabilitated. You are here to be punished!"* There is no doubt that every convict, including me, who comes before the parole board will be armed with umpteen reasons why they consider themselves rehabilitated.

But the reality is, extended periods of isolation and severe punishment do nothing to restore the broken spirit of man. Earning a G.E.D. or completing a substance abuse program or even learning a trade skill in prison will not generate the emotional and social growth you need to survive an abusive upbringing or a prison stay. My life is living proof of that, plus, that's why there's such a high recidivism at American prisons.

When I'd addressed the topic of rehabilitation with the case manager back in 1991, I challenged the assumption that rehabilitation could be achieved in an environment as hostile as prison. I spoke out about the "destructive" qualities of the prison environment, and pointed to how, *"...I beat the odds of the prison system!"* After reading my letter and reviewing the documents I'd sent him, he determined, *"...you are qualified to continue your employment in the public schools of New Jersey."*

But this time, I was pursuing a Standard Certification as Teacher of Carpentry. No longer was I asking to be employed in a capacity where I would work with students under the direct supervision of a certified teacher. Now, I was asking to work in a capacity where there would be no supervision of my interaction with students in a classroom.

So I wasn't shocked by the determination of disqualification in the spring of 2008. In fact, I kind of expected it. When I wrote the case manager this time, I reminded him that we had gone through this process in 1991 when he had determined I could continue my employment at Chancellor Academy. I asked him, *"How long does a man have to pay for his crime? I have lived my life without incident since my arrest in 1982 and that statistic alone demonstrates what happened in 1982 was a mistake and not a way of life."*

If I had been charged in even one incident during the twenty-six years I had been paroled, I would have understood fully the mentality to disqualify me from teaching for life. On the contrary, I recalled for the case manager six amazing years of teaching without incident at Chancellor Academy under the guidance of my mentor, Richard Sheridan.

Yet not only were there no incidents, I was actually a positive influence on these kids. For example, during a graduation ceremony in 1996, a student by the name of Greg Snyder presented me with a plaque that read, "Thank you for saving my life." There is no football game, nor any home I've ever built that could surpass the sense of accomplishment I felt when I read the words on that plaque, particularly when I had lived my life in the shadow of the words of an appellate judge who said about me, "It's a shame that people like him even exist." That simple plaque had been the highlight of my life.

I went on to detail for the case manager my relationship with the Lifer's Group at East Jersey State Prison (formerly Rahway), a relationship that had spanned nearly twenty years. I tried to demonstrate to the case manager that I had a passion to work with at-risk kids. I wanted to work with the kids that society claimed were hopeless.

A few weeks later, I received a letter back from them that stated *"...you are approved for school employment in accordance with N.J.S.A. 18A:6-7.1; N.J.S.A. 18A:39-19.1."* Immediately, I called Richard to tell him the good news.

"You've got the blessing of God all over you!" he said, and he was right! The letter the case manager had sent in 1991 had simply stated that I could continue my employment in New Jersey schools. But this letter said I was approved to teach in New Jersey schools despite a law that essentially disqualified me from teaching for life!

It says, in part:

"An individual, except as provided in subsection g. of this section, <u>shall be permanently disqualified from employment</u> or service under this act if

the individual's <u>criminal history check reveals a record of conviction for any</u>
<u>crime of the first</u> or <u>second degree</u>; or

c. (1) A crime involving <u>the use of force</u> or <u>the threat of force to</u> or upon <u>a</u>
<u>person</u> or property including, but not limited to, robbery, aggravated assault,
stalking, kidnapping, arson, manslaughter and murder; or

(2) A crime as set forth in chapter 39 of Title 2C of the New Jersey
Statutes, <u>a third degree crime</u> as set forth in chapter 20 of Title 2C of the
New jersey Statutes, or a crime as listed below:

<u>*Terroristic threats N.J.S.2C:12-3*</u>" Bam! I got four years for that sucker
alone. Everything underlined represents a crime that I was convicted of
having committed. Apart from challenging the accuracy of the convictions, there is nothing as I understand the law that would exclude me from
being permanently disqualified from teaching. Once again, I saw evidence
that God is sovereign and that God truly holds the heart of the king in
His hands. The case manager is to me the king whose heart God held.

If I read the statute above as a man without faith, I'd see the impossible standing before me. I would see four reasons to disqualify me from
teaching for life, and I'd see no reason to keep pursuing what I believed
I was called to do. But I read that statute with faith, believing that God
would overcome the things of which I have no control, specifically, the
decision that was the case manager's to make.

Finally, at the age of forty-eight, I realized my dream to do what others
had thought would be impossible to do. Everything was in place for me
to start teaching that September.

There was another big day coming for me as well: Heidi and I were
getting married! As I thought about the June wedding and our time
together, I recalled a conversation we had early on when Heidi had told
me that she prayed every day for her future husband. I can still see her
with the paint roller in her hands.

Never in a million years would I have believed then that the future husband Heidi was praying for would turn out to be me! Even today, it is an amazing thing to consider.

What a turn of events in my life. It hadn't been all that long ago when the enemy of Deception was urging me to end my days, claiming the battle before me was hopeless. But now, four years later there stood a new man, a man nothing like anything I could have ever imagined I would be.

In fact, I was on my way back to Southern State to take care of some unfinished business. I went back to the same prison gymnasium where years before, I had publicly accepted Jesus Christ as my Lord and Savior. The gym, filled with inmates for the annual Christmas celebration, was exactly the way I'd left it twenty-two years earlier. Even some of the guards were the same, just older and probably preparing for their retirement.

During the Christmas dinner, Heidi got up and sang for the men and then, much in the same way Kyle Rote Jr. gave his testimony, I was called forward by the pastor to give my testimony of God's mercy and power to transform lives.

"Twenty-two years ago," I told the inmates, "I sat where you are sitting tonight. I sat in your seat because I believed lies, I chased after lies, much like the lies that brought you men to prison. I thought I was a tough guy. I knew it all, and like many of you, you couldn't tell me nothin.'"

Then I told the men the story about Lenny and me gambling in the Essex County Jail.

"I didn't believe in God, I wasn't looking for God, and my plan was to stab Lenny, but God had a different plan for my life, a plan with a hope and a future. I believed that promise privately in my heart – I swear I did, but publicly, I was ashamed to show it. I was afraid of what the other guys in here would think of me."

By now all of the side conversations had stopped. The gym was silent and I had everyone's full attention. I continued, "In the summer of 1984, a man by the name of Kyle Rote Jr. came to this prison, and he was standing right here in practically the same exact spot where I am standing tonight." Pointing to my left I said, "I was sitting in those bleachers over there among a couple hundred inmates listening to the words Kyle spoke. When Kyle finished speaking, he did something that I never saw coming or I probably never would have come to the event. He asked that anyone seated who believed that Jesus Christ was Lord and Savior but never publicly accepted Him to stand.

"Immediately I was consumed with fear. I was paralyzed in my seat. All I could think was, '*I can't do this. What will people think of me?*' Out of nowhere my body became consumed by an overwhelming sensation of heat that seemed to lift me to my feet, and there I stood all alone among a couple of hundred inmates. As I stood there among my peers, my stance of trembling and fear became a stance of confidence."

I emphasized, "Now look at me. Listen to what I am going to say to all of you. That moment, when I stood, was the most empowering moment of my life. God is a God of empowerment. That is why He said to the apostle Paul, '*My grace is sufficient for you, for my power is made perfect in weakness.*' (2 Corinthians 12:9)

It was clearly an encouragement for those men to see one of their own come back after twenty-two years and stand before them and say, "*I am proof that you can do all things through Christ who strengthens you.*" (*Philippians 4:13*)

We held two services, and at the end of those services more than forty men responded to an altar call, an experience that was nothing short of overwhelming for me. God had brought me back to the exact place where the fear of man had paralyzed me. In the midst of those trials, I never dreamed that one day I would stand in that very gymnasium and boldly offer a message of hope and redemption despite what other people thought! My greatest joys in life were uniquely tied to the most difficult times in my life. Today, I refer to those instances in my life as God's signature moments – the moments when the inconceivable became reality.

***

Talk about inconceivable – Heidi and I began working together with at-risk youth at an alternative school outside of Atlantic City. Heidi was so excited about working with the kids she could hardly wait for her new job to begin. The principal assured her that she'd be a great fit for the few girls that did attend the school. But after just ten days, not only did that great fit unravel, Heidi unraveled as well.

"You is a fat ho," one girl told Heidi. "Why don't you just quit. You ain't even good at this."

Those may have been the kindest words spoken to Heidi during the first ten days of her new job, and, much in the same way I questioned my desire to work with at-risk youth when I started teaching, Heidi began to dig deep and ask herself the same thing. In her entire life, Heidi had never been spoken to as abusively as she was by the female students at the start of her job. But you either have it in you to teach under those circumstances, or you don't.

Heidi had it in her. She came to understand the abuse these kids had endured, and she knew they were lashing out in pain. And Heidi knew what pain was. So she was able to overcome the initial onslaught of verbal, and at times, physical assaults, and develop meaningful relationships and memories with some of the students that they, nor she, will ever forget.

CHAPTER 17

†

The Measure of A Man

"Be watchful, stand firm in the faith, act like men, be strong.
Let all that you do be done in love."
(1 Corinthians 16:13-14)

"You're awful quiet this morning. Is everything alright?" Heidi asked.

"Ya know, I couldn't sleep last night. After watching *'Beyond Scared Straight*,' I couldn't stop thinking about J.D. and Lucy."

"What were you thinking about?"

"Do you remember when the guy told that kid that his choices affect other people? Obviously I know that the choices we make affect other people, but the truth is, Heidi, I never thought about how my choices affected Lucy. Christina is older than Lucy was when I got arrested. It's nearly thirty years ago, and I'm just realizing how bad my choices hurt her. I never looked at my relationship with her from the eyes of being a father. I really feel like I need to tell her I'm sorry."

"Why don't you try to find her?" Heidi asked.

"She's probably married and has a different name. I don't know how I would find her and besides, maybe she doesn't want to hear from me."

But Heidi encouraged me, "We'll try to find her when we get home tonight."

That night after we got settled in, I sat down at the computer and within an hour I had found Lucy. I began to write her about the TV show I had watched and how it made me think about her and her dad.

"I needed to say I'm sorry, Lucy," I wrote. "I don't want you to feel like you have to respond to this letter, but I just needed to validate what you went through because of the choices I made." I hit send and it was done.

A day went by and then a week, and then another week with no response. Heidi and I wondered if Lucy ever got my message.

Then, one day, her name appeared in my email inbox.

I told Heidi as I opened the message, "I feel nervous," and then I began to read.

"Oh my God," Lucy began, "I've been looking for you for years." It turned out that Lucy was happy to hear from me. She was married, with a family of her own, and seemed to be very happy. When I asked her about J.D., she told me that her dad had had lung cancer, but was in remission. I also learned that J.D. was upset with me, because he felt like I had turned my back on him when I came home from prison. I decided to write J.D. a letter and tell him otherwise.

"*Hello J.D. It's been a long time,*" I wrote. I brought J.D. up to date with everything that had led to me contacting Lucy, and then I told him what I was really writing him about: "*I never turned my back on you.*"

"*I served three years in prison, J.D., but six and seven years later, I was still dealing with this thing about Vinny's murder. I had to finally hire an attorney, who told the cops, 'Either charge my client, or leave him alone.'*"

I informed J.D. about my little visit from the prosecutor the day we were sentenced too. "All you have to do," the prosecutor explained, "is tell me what I want to know about J.D and you can go home today."

"I could have left prison that day but instead I told him, 'Pound salt,' and then told the officer to take me back to my cell."

After all I'd been through, it wasn't like I owed J.D. an explanation, but I didn't like the fact that he was believing something about me that wasn't true. I knew that I had been like a son to him, and I'm sure he was hurt when I never came to see him or his family when I got out of prison.

"I do understand how you could have interpreted my absence the way you have, but I never turned my back on you, not ever!"

I don't know what goes through a man's mind at the end of his life, but I imagined what I might be thinking if I were J.D., and so I told him, *"I've never laughed harder with anyone than I have laughed with you, J.D. If we had it to do again, I am sure that we both would do it differently. I want you to know that I know you never meant any harm to come my way. I was fond of your family, and didn't even realize until recently that I never mourned the loss of our relationship. You were like a father to me, and I remember as if it were yesterday, standing in the cell together. You patted me on the cheek, and affectionately said, 'You've been like a son to me.' I never had a moment like that with my own dad, J.D., and he left this world without validating me. Validate your children. Let them know that you love them and approve of them."*

"I hope you are at a place where you are at peace, J.D." I knew that in my life, experiencing peace was a matter of having a relationship with the Lord. There were a couple of times when I was in jail that I finally got up the nerve to tell J.D. about the changes I was going through spiritually and the peace I had found. He didn't knock me for it, he just responded, "As for religion, some of the guys here are into that, but I'm not really into that stuff."

Though J.D. was a Jewish man, he celebrated the Christian holidays, too, because his wife was Christian. When I asked him one time about how that works he remarked, "I'm covering all my bases."

"I don't know what your spiritual convictions may be these days, but I want to also encourage you if you haven't, to place your hope in God. You know by now you can't place your hope in man. We've been there and

done that! I told my brother Lou the same thing before he passed away. His response was, 'I ain't no hypocrite. I've lived my whole life this way. I ain't gonna ask God for forgiveness now.' I told Lou what I had heard once before, 'I didn't think that asking God for forgiveness was being a hypocrite. I can't think of anything more difficult as a man than to admit at the end of my life, that I wasted my entire gift of life.'

"For me J.D., I wasted a large portion of my life. I have failed at everything I have ever done up until about seven years ago. I had some bright moments here and there, but ultimately, the reality was, I failed. It wasn't until I finally came to a place where I surrendered and said, 'Take it God. I can't do this anymore' that things began to turn around in my life. The Bible tells me that Jesus came that I might have life and have it more abundantly. The life he is referring to is everlasting life, eternity. I found that to be an encouragement in my life and I believe you're at a place in life where you can find hope and encouragement in what Jesus did on the cross."

I closed my letter to J.D. by saying, *"I wrote this letter for two reasons. One, I don't want you to believe that I turned my back on you, and two, I don't want you to believe that God doesn't love you, because he does, J.D."* If J.D. was serious about covering all his bases, I was gonna take this opportunity to tell him that, *"'There is therefore now no condemnation for those who are in Christ Jesus.' (Romans 8:1) We have believed enough lies in our lives, and those lies have cost us great heartache and loss. Let's finish this race strong."*

It wasn't long after I wrote the letter that J.D.'s cancer returned. Unfortunately, I never heard from him before I went to pay my last respects at his funeral. Lucy told me that he had talked about trying to meet up with me, but he didn't want me to see him sick and frail. I may never truly know how J.D. received the letter I sent him, but this I do know: Lucy called me one day shortly after I wrote that letter and said, "My dad's acting weird. He called me up today to tell me he loves me."

Make no mistake about it. For J.D., that was an act of courage. In fact, for many men today that would be an act of courage, that is, to become transparent, to show emotion, to appear vulnerable and to tell someone you love them. It took me forty-eight years to be able to do it myself. It made me happy to know that what I had written to J.D. inspired him to reach out to Lucy and tell her he loved her. I know it meant everything to Lucy to hear it from her dad, because she couldn't recall him ever saying it before. Even now, it means the world to her to have that memory.

There was a time in my life when being a man was measured in terms of being a tough guy. I walked tough, talked tough, and I fought tough, even if I did lose on occasion. Whether I was taking your money, your drugs, or beating you down just for the fun of it, it made me feel like a man – but what made me feel like a man came at the expense of other human beings.

Today, I measure manhood and personal success in terms of how my life positively impacts the lives of those around me. I am no longer a taker, no longer an abuser, no longer a tough guy. There is no amount of money, or power, or fame that can compare to the thrill of knowing that someone out there is better off for having known me.

In this picture of my parents on their wedding day in 1955, it's hard to detect the open wounds inflicted in their childhoods by alcoholism, domestic violence, and in my mother's case, also sexual abuse.

My parents didn't deserve what happened to them as children, nor did I deserve the effects of their unattended trauma on their own parenting. For many years, I was angry with them. I didn't even like being around them, but that's because my emotional injuries never allowed me to stop looking at my parents from the eyes of a child that felt unloved. My time with Eleanor Buscher helped me to deal inwardly with the anger and resentment I felt towards my parents, particularly my father. In time, I healed emotionally, enabling me to look at them with new eyes and forgive their mistakes and break free from the chains that kept me living in the pain of my past.

I was able to enjoy a relationship with both my mother and father before they passed away. It was even an honor for me to deliver the eulogy at my father's funeral in 2009.

Chancellor Academy Graduation Day 1996, Greg Snyder presented me with a plaque that read, "Thank you for saving my life."

Me and Greg in our downtime while working on a home flooded by Sandy

Richard Sheridan and his wife Donna with Heidi and me on our wedding day in 2008

*This is the evidence
of a man who
stopped caring in
2005*

*This picture speaks
for itself in 2013*

*Champ, a man's best friend. Heidi always made sure
I had company while I was writing*

AFTERWORD

†

Trust in the Lord!

Writing this book has been an incredible journey for me, one I never anticipated. Foremost, God's calling required me to reflect upon fifty years of life. In order to do that, I needed to be in a place where I could think deliberately about the story of my life and that specific need forced me to get alone. I had set out to tell a story that would inspire and bring hope to others in a way that honored God, but the deeper I got into the process of writing, the more I became aware of God's primary call for me to write this book. God intended the process of writing to bring healing and restoration to my life.

Many nights, I sat for hours in front of my computer and never wrote a single word. At times, the pain that accompanied a lifetime of failure left me asking God, "Why? Why did my life have to endure so much hardship and pain?" He communicated very clearly the answer to that question when he said, "The experiences of hardship and pain about which you are writing are the trials that brought you into relationship with Me."

This wasn't the first time I had heard that message. I had heard a similar message in November 1983 in Essex County Jail. Twenty-four hours had passed since the confrontation in my cell with Lenny. I had just finished reading *Holes in Time* when I picked up a Bible, randomly opened it, and fixed my eyes upon the words from Isaiah, 48:10: *"Behold, I have refined you but not as silver, I have tried you in the furnace of affliction."*

Now, three decades later, God's answer to my question regarding heartache and pain left me to consider once again the words from Isaiah

48:10. From those reflections came healing and restoration.

Throughout my life, I have reacted to affliction in a multitude of ways. In prison, affliction drew me near to God, but apart from my prison experience, affliction caused bitterness and anger to harden my heart. Ultimately, however, it was the experience of affliction that exposed the depth of my sinful nature and prompted me to pursue God and have a relationship with Him in a way I never had before. It is through fellowship with God that I have grown to understand His purpose for allowing and perhaps even at times appointing the experience of affliction in my life. Ultimately, affliction can build faith, separate man from a lifestyle that opposes God, and raise up believers whose lives will honor and glorify Him.

Making the decision to use your life to bring glory to God can be difficult, particularly when you have lived most of your life absent of that conviction. At the age of fifty-three, it is sad to say that I have spent more of my life glorifying the mentalities and behaviors that destroy this world than I have honoring the God who created it. The good news is this: *"And we know that for those who love God all things work together for good, for those who are called according to his purpose."* (Romans 8:28) It is comforting to know with confidence that God is the refiner of our lives. With spiritual wisdom, I can accurately reason that the experience of affliction in my life has been for the benefit of my salvation and the privilege to honor and glorify God.

That is not to say that there are not times when I experience conflict between what God is saying and what my ability to reason is telling me to do. However, when I experience an internal conflict that challenges the Word of God, I take a stance against even my own ability to think. The reason being, my greatest opponent in life has been my ability to rationalize that what is unreasonable is reasonable. After all, it was my best thinking that landed me in prison. If I want to continue to experience the peace and joy that comes from the knowledge of God, then what I think isn't that important.

The game of football taught me a lot about the importance of taking such a stance in life. In fact, from the age of ten when I first began playing football until the age of twenty, the very first order of business every season was for all of the players to practice our stance. Why do you suppose our coaches paid so much attention to how we positioned ourselves against our opponents? Because the stance you take against your opponent will determine victory or defeat on the field of battle.

The battle on the gridiron, however, is nothing compared to the battle being waged every day of our lives. Many of us are aware of neither the battle being fought nor the opponent waging war against us. In fact, I would encourage you to stop reading and take a minute to observe our opponent in action.

Go to your computer or television and turn on the news. Take an inventory of what is going on at this very moment with mankind. It doesn't matter whether you tune into national, local, world, social, or sports news, you will see evidence of a world that has fallen victim to the bondages of addiction, alcoholism, depression, disease, greed, obesity, pornography, poverty, and violence. You will see the depravity of murder, rape, starvation, war, and torture on a scale unparalleled to any other time in the history of our world. I don't know about you, but when I look at those images, I see the evidence of a fierce battle being waged against all of mankind by an opponent who is a master of deception.

How is this possible? We have access to more technology, more information, more medical resources, and more wealth than ever before. Where access to all of these resources should improve quality of life, the human tragedies we witness across the globe are the proof that even our resources are being misused. Our leaders are considered smarter and more educated than they have ever been and yet, with all of our might, using all of our intellect and ability to reason, we are surrendering our purpose to live a meaningful life and accept a condition of decay.

I am going to give a reliable explanation as to how this is possible. The explanation comes from the Book of Proverbs in the Bible. In the twenty-fifth verse of the sixteenth chapter, in the Book of Wisdom, King Solomon states the following: *"There is a way that seems right to a man, but its end is the way to death."*

This verse contrasts the self-reliant man pursuing what he intuitively believes to be right in exchange for what will surely cause his death. Such a man may possess knowledge, but in the end, he certainly lacks wisdom. Historic examples that document the accuracy of King Solomon's spiritual principle include the likes of Bernard (Bernie) Madoff, a Wall Street executive who pursued a Ponzi scheme that spanned decades and defrauded customers of approximately $20 billion. In exchange, he received a life sentence in prison. Then there is Rod Blagojevich, who intuitively believed political corruption was the way to wealth and perhaps fame. For his corrupt investment, Blagojevich received a fourteen-year prison term. Finally, Solomon's spiritual wisdom was recently documented during the Michael Jackson trial, when Dr. Conrad Murray was found guilty of irresponsibly administering surgical anesthetic to Michael Jackson to help him sleep. What seemed right to him caused him to lose his medical license and receive a four-year prison term for involuntary manslaughter.

These are all highly educated men, and yet their end is like that of a fool. A fool considers only the way that seems right to him, and has no interest in how his way may end until the end comes. The end of the matter for these men is prison. It is a place where they will sit in their cells and ask themselves, "How did this happen to me?" It is where they will realize the injuries of the people they swindled, the public they deceived, the lives that were lost, and the families they betrayed. It is where they will come to grips with the consequences of having been deceived.

Having made similar decisions in my life, I understand humankind's attraction to the things that destroy our lives. In Chapter Six, after much thought I acknowledged, "The only reasonable explanation I can give now for my belief that such behaviors would elevate or position me to succeed can be explained in one word: *Deception*."

Much of my life has been compromised because I have had tendencies to believe in and pursue that which ultimately harmed me. No matter how well intended I may or may not have been in my pursuits, *Deception had been my enemy*. Apart from being deceived, why would anyone give their time and energy to the things that contribute to their own demise?

Deception exists in many forms, operating on many levels, at times simultaneously, and always serving one purpose: to influence us to believe something other than what is true. Deception is the root of every way that seems right, and yet it gives no proof that it is right. Being deceived reliably explains the destruction of marriages, the spread of diseases, the slaughtering of unborn children, murder, rape, and – if its way succeeds – the extermination of lives. The question becomes, however, how does one stand against an opponent whose way ends in death?

In the sport of football, you study your opponent long before you stand against him in battle. You learn as much as you can about your opponent prior to the battle being fought so that you can use that information to develop a strategy to defeat him. You prepare mentally, you prepare physically, and then you put on your armor and go to battle. When finally you step on the field, there are no surprises!

Unlike the sport of football, we cannot see our opponent, for the opponent we battle is not of flesh and blood[1]. Yet there exists a strategy to defeat him. The Bible calls our opponent Satan and the father of lies. He is a master of deception and his very nature is to lie.[2] He comes to steal, kill, and destroy,[3] and he prowls around like a roaring lion looking for someone to devour.[4] Our ignorance of his clever schemes remains his greatest strength.[5]

After attending Christmas Eve service in December of 2004, I made a conscious decision to take a stance to defeat the enemy of Deception responsible for my prideful and self-reliant approach to life. The stance I took opposes everything about the way that seems right to man. In fact, my stance came from the very book that warned me of the consequence of following a way that seems right: the Book of Proverbs. In verses five through eight of the third chapter, in the Book of Wisdom, King Solomon offers the following strategy to defeat Satan:

Trust in the Lord with all your heart, and do not lean on your own understanding. In all your ways acknowledge him, and he will make straight your paths. Be not wise in your own eyes; fear the Lord, and turn away from evil. It will be healing to your flesh and refreshment to your bones."

Abiding by this spiritual wisdom is not just a stance; it is a promise! These words are armor for anyone who has to battle the enemy of Deception.[6] Your choice to engage your opponent is a decision only you can make. And depending upon your situation, this could be your equivalent of my confrontation in the prison cell. For some of you, all of the ways that previously seemed right have brought you to your end. The choice for life and death now stands before you in the form of whatever deception may be destroying your life. No matter how smart you think you are, no matter what your financial resources may be, and no matter who you may think you know, you will fight this battle alone, and you will do it in one of two ways – not because I said so, but because there exists no other option. You will choose for your weapon either Pride or Surrender. And how you choose to fight this battle will define your life moving forward.

The weapon of Pride is not moved by such a stance as this. Pride's position is, *"Why should I render trust to any standard of religious doctrine when I am more than capable of making straight my own paths? Why should I humble myself to fear One whose face I've never seen? It is I, the weapon of Pride, that is worthy of being feared."*

The wisdom of God is but foolishness to Pride[7]. Far better is the condition of decay than for Pride to admit it is the wisdom of the Lord that makes straight his path. Pride's thoughts are the greatest opponents of God's wisdom, and those same thoughts are the root cause of Pride's failure to recognize that the end of his way leads to death.

Surrender has taken a different stance. The weapon of Surrender declares, *"I will abandon my abilities, even unto the ability to understand, in order that the Lord make straight what I have made crooked."* The fear of the Lord is the embodiment of the weapon of Surrender. His reverent fear and awe of the Lord will bear the fruit of healing and refreshment throughout his life.

Moreover, the condition of decay is restored by Surrender, whose very nature will lead you far from the way that leads to death. Foremost, Surrender is the crux of the way that leads to life!

Much of my life, I have earned a living as a carpenter, and during that time my approach to every job has been the same. I begin by reviewing a set of architectural drawings (construction plan), from which I build or renovate a home. If I don't use the plan accurately, there could be significant consequences, particularly where the construction or restoration of a home relates to the foundation that will support the structure above. Everyone gets excited about the kitchen or the master bedroom suite, but time has proven that nothing is more important than the foundation upon which those rooms are built. If the foundation of the home is not constructed using the proper materials and reinforcement, the structure above will collapse under its own weight[8].

Had I approached building my life like I approach building a home, I would have begun by using a plan. After all, there is a plan for building our lives and it is drawn by the Architect who created life. Failure to use His plan caused my life to collapse under the weight of its own sin. Fortunately, the Architect made a provision in His plan for the weight of sin in every person's life.

The provision came by way of a carpenter named Jesus. Jesus, the Son of God who is the Architect of life, came to bear the weight of our sins.[9] Through His life we are saved, and in His death we are redeemed. He came, and like a lamb, surrendered His body to be slaughtered, even His life unto death, that we might have life and have it more abundantly.[10] His one act of surrender was His gift to us.[11] He became the foundation upon which every man and every woman can stand with confidence against the enemy of deception.

I want to end this book the way I began it. I want to remind my readers that without God, I have no story, and there is no miracle, no redemption, no restoration, and no salvation. Without God, my story is like that of any number of people in whose hands I hope this book lands – people who believe the same lies I once believed and whose pride and deceptive beliefs are robbing them of the very life God intended them to live.

I have said that going to prison was a condition of the heart. Repentance too, is a condition of the heart. We can will ourselves to do many things, but true human reform exists only where there has been a sincere change of heart. Surrender is the posture from which hearts are changed, and only from a place of surrender can we humble ourselves in order that we may begin to hear a new voice –a voice of truth! So tough guy, what's it going to be, Pride or Surrender?

"Knowing that you were ransomed from the futile ways inherited from your forefathers, not with perishable things such as silver or gold, but with the precious blood of Christ, like that of a lamb without blemish or spot." (1 Peter 1:18-19)

ENDNOTES

1 For we do not wrestle against flesh and blood, but against the rulers, against the authorities, against the cosmic powers over this present darkness, against the spiritual forces of evil in the heavenly places. (Ephesians 6:12 ESV)

2 You are of your father the devil, and your will is to do your father's desires. He was a murderer from the beginning, and has nothing to do with the truth, because there is no truth in him. When he lies, he speaks out of his own character, for he is a liar and the father of lies. (John 8:44 ESV)

3 The thief comes only to steal and kill and destroy. I came that you may have life and have it abundantly. (John 10:10 ESV)

4 Be sober-minded; be watchful. Your adversary the devil prowls around like a roaring lion, seeking someone to devour. (1 Peter 5:8 ESV)

5 ...so that we would not be outwitted by Satan; for we are not ignorant of his designs. (2 Corinthians 2:11 ESV)

6 Finally, be strong in the Lord and in the strength of his might. Put on the whole armor of God that you may be able to stand against the schemes of the devil. For we do not wrestle against flesh and blood, but against the rulers, against the authorities, against the cosmic powers over this present darkness, against the spiritual forces of evil in the heavenly places. Therefore take up the whole armor of God, that you may be able to withstand in the evil day, and having done all, to stand firm. Stand therefore, having fastened on the belt of truth, and having put on the breastplate of righteousness, and, as shoes for your feet, having put on the readiness given by the gospel of peace. In all circumstances take up the shield of faith, with which you can extinguish all the flaming darts of the evil one; and take the helmet of salvation, and the sword of the Spirit, which is the word of God, praying at all times in the Spirit, with all prayer and supplication. To that end keep alert with all perseverance, making supplication for all the saints, and also for me, that words may be given to me in opening my mouth boldly to proclaim the mystery of the gospel, for which I am an ambassador in chains, that I may declare it boldly, as I ought to speak. (Ephesians 6:10-20 ESV)

7 The fear of the LORD is the beginning of knowledge; fools despise wisdom and instruction. (Proverbs 1:7 ESV)

8 He is like a man building a house, who dug deep and laid the foundation on the rock. And when a flood arose, the stream broke against that house and could not shake it, because it had been well built. (Luke 6:48 ESV)

9 For God so loved the world, that he gave his only Son, that whoever believes in him should not perish but have eternal life. (John 3:16 ESV)

10 The thief comes only to steal and kill and destroy. I came that they may have life and have it abundantly. (John 10:10 ESV)

11 For by grace you have been saved through faith. And this is not your own doing; it is the gift of God, not a result of works, so that no one may boast. (Ephesians 2:8-9 ESV)

TO MY CHILDREN

To Mark, Tony and Christina, my heritage from the Lord,

I have not always been the father that I had hoped I would have been. In many respects, I am flawed, and I want to apologize for the actions and examples in my life that may have left you feeling unloved or abandoned. The Bible says, *"The fear of the Lord is the beginning of knowledge; fools despise wisdom and instruction."* (Proverbs 1:7) I have been the fool to which that scripture refers and it is important for me to publicly acknowledge the pain each of you endured for my disregard of wisdom and instruction.

Today, you see in me a new man, a new example being set. You have witnessed in my life a deep love and respect for the things of the Lord, most particularly, the wisdom and instruction that come from pursuing the knowledge of God. My hope is that my story has revealed to you the wisdom and instruction necessary to live your life well and free from the mistakes I have made; the wisdom and instruction I failed to impart early on in your lives.

I thank each of you for the gift of your genuine forgiveness and for the gift of your enduring love. It is important that you know how deeply I love each one of you, and how proud I am to call you my children.

"Behold, children are a heritage from the Lord..." (Psalm 127:3)

With all of my love,
Dad

ACKNOWLEDGMENTS

In my case, reform took a complete overhaul of my life, emotionally, physically, and spiritually. Along the way, God directed my steps to the care and concern of some amazing people to help accomplish that goal.

More than thirty years ago, Pastor Paul Pedrick, with his father, also a pastor, and many other people of faith, stood on an empty parcel of land in Delmont, N.J. The land was designated for the construction of Southern State Correctional Facility, a medium security prison. Pastor Paul and the others prayed earnestly to God to transform the lives of every man who would one day pass through that prison. To Pastor Paul and all of those who prayed for me, your prayers have been answered, and I could never thank you enough. *"The prayer of a righteous person has great power as it is working."* (James 5:16)

Thankfully, after I had been sent to Southern State Correctional Facility, God put in my path Father Al Hewitt, a Catholic priest at the prison who boldly challenged me to "grow spiritual muscles," as opposed to the physical muscles I was building from lifting weights. If I hadn't changed my focus, he said, "You'll be nothin' but a good lookin corpse." You had a way with words, Father Al, and I will never forget you nor your passion for Jesus Christ, *"For while bodily training is of some value, godliness is of value in every way, as it holds promise for the present life and also for the life to come."* (1 Timothy 4:8)

I want to thank Reverend William Farrow, and his mother Lynn Farrow, for the Wings of Eagles Prison Ministry and for their many years of dedication and commitment to spread the gospel of Jesus Christ to men like me in a place where few care to go. *"How beautiful are the feet of those who preach the good news!"* (Romans 10:15)

Eleanor Buscher, L.C.C., You have been an amazing counselor and I am forever grateful for how you have helped me become an emotionally healthy man. It feels good to be emotionally alive! *"He heals the broken-hearted and binds up their wounds."* (Psalm 147:3)

John Reynolds, C.C.N., Your guidance and support have led me to embrace a healthy physical and nutritional lifestyle whereby I lost sixty pounds to date and no longer rely on the aid of medication to do what my body was created to do naturally. *"Or do you not know that your body is a temple of the Holy Spirit within you, whom you have from God? You are not your own, for you were bought with a price. So glorify God in your body."* (1Corintians 6:19-20)

Dr. Robert Kayal, It is nine years and seven surgeries later, and you are still the man! People think I'm crazy when I tell them the story about my tendon growing during surgery, but you saw that miracle first-hand. I am thankful that God directed my steps to a surgeon, and more importantly, to a man of God with whom I can pray before each surgery. After all, I'm on the other end of the knife! I thank you for your passion for orthopedics, and I thank God for gifting you with the skills necessary to be the extraordinary surgeon you are. *"But they that wait for the LORD shall renew their strength; they shall mount up with wings like eagles; they shall run, and not be weary; they shall walk, and not faint."* (Isaiah 40:31)

I had made a mess of a lot of things in my life, and when that mess required the guidance of a legal counselor to help straighten them out, I called on my attorney and now my good friend, Gary Steele. Thank you, Gary, for all you have done to help me persevere through some of the most difficult times of my life. Heidi and I consider you and Fran a blessing in our life. *"Where there is no guidance, a people falls, but in an abundance of counselors there is safety."* (Proverbs 11:14)

To Anita Colatta of the Morris County Department of Education, I will always remember the way you cheered me on during the process of acquiring my Standard Certification for Teacher of Carpentry. It was more than just a job for you. You took a personal interest in my circumstance and helped me overcome the obstacle of my past. You were just the right person to walk me through that journey and I will always be grateful. *"Therefore encourage one another and build one another up, just as you are doing."* (1 Thessalonians 5:11)

Thank you Pastor Don James of Bethany Church. The words you spoke at a Christmas Eve service in 2004 and your passion for Christ compelled me to rise up from the ashes of my life and restore my broken relationship with Jesus Christ. *"For I am not ashamed of the gospel, for it is the power of God for salvation to everyone who believes."* (Romans 1:16)

To Pastor Ray Tate of Life Chapel Church, thank you for your wisdom and guidance regarding this book but most of all, thank you for your daily example of humility and genuine love for people – qualities uncommon to men in our culture. That example inspires me to be the very best man that I can be. *"The reward for humility and fear of the Lord is riches and honor and life."* (Proverbs 22:4)

To Jen Singer, my editor and literary midwife, thank you for helping me overcome the throes of literary labor and bring to life this living and breathing memoir. It is clear to Heidi and me that you have been a divine appointment, without whom, this amazing story of God's mercy and transforming love was not possible. Certainly, you have given of yourself more heartily than we could have ever expected or hoped for. From the bottom of our hearts, we thank you, Jen. *"Whatever you do, work heartily, as for the Lord and not for men."* (Colossians 3:23)

I want to acknowledge Champ, a man's best friend, for keeping me company on this journey and for making me smile, always!

Finally, to the most excellent woman I have ever known, Heidi. I am honored to be your husband. To know each day when I wake up, that I am loved by a woman as wonderful as you brings joy and comfort to my heart. When readers flip through the pages of this book they will never realize the thousands of hours you spent alone in order that I could pursue the endeavor of writing this book. In the light of your selflessness I have felt selfish to say the least. Your enthusiasm to make such a personal sacrifice on my behalf embodies the fullness of your love for me. Heidi, you are the crown of my life! *"An excellent wife is the crown of her husband."* (Proverbs 12:4)